Six Seasons
and a Movie

Six Seasons and a Movie

How Community Broke Television

Chris Barsanti, Brian Cogan, and Jeff Massey

APPLAUSE
THEATRE & CINEMA BOOKS
Essex, Connecticut

APPLAUSE
THEATRE & CINEMA BOOKS

An imprint of Globe Pequot, the trade division of
The Rowman & Littlefield Publishing Group, Inc.
4501 Forbes Blvd., Ste. 200
Lanham, MD 20706
www.rowman.com

Distributed by NATIONAL BOOK NETWORK

Library of Congress Cataloging-in-Publication Data

Names: Barsanti, Chris, author. | Massey, Jeff, author. | Cogan, Brian, 1967- author.
Title: Six seasons and a movie : how Community broke television / Chris Barsanti, Jeff
   Massey and Brian Cogan.
Description: Essex, Connecticut : Applause, 2023. | Includes bibliographical references
   and index.
Identifiers: LCCN 2023003069 (print) | LCCN 2023003070 (ebook) | ISBN
   9781493066551 (paperback) | ISBN 9781493066568 (ebook)
Subjects: LCSH: Community (Television program) | Situation comedies (Television
   programs)—United States. | LCGFT: Television criticism and reviews.
Classification: LCC PN1992.77.C64 B37 2023 (print) | LCC PN1992.77.C64 (ebook)
   | DDC 791.45/72—dc23/eng/20230424
LC record available at https://lccn.loc.gov/2023003069
LC ebook record available at https://lccn.loc.gov/2023003070

∞™ The paper used in this publication meets the minimum requirements of American
National Standard for Information Sciences—Permanence of Paper for Printed Library
Materials, ANSI/NISO Z39.48-1992.

Contents

Acknowledgments

Many thanks to my parents, who believed that *not* attending college was never an option for me but who would likely have preferred I did join a study group (though not to play Dungeons & Dragons).

Chris Barsanti (Winger!)

Deep thanks to my wife Lisa, who really enjoyed watching and talking about it. And special thanks to Jeff and Chris, members of the *Community* study group!

Brian Cogan (Professor Professorson)

A hearty shout-out to all the many, many collegiate "study" groups that I've been a part of over the years. Heck, I even met my wife in college! No reroll for me, thanks.

Jeff Massey (Annie's Boobs)

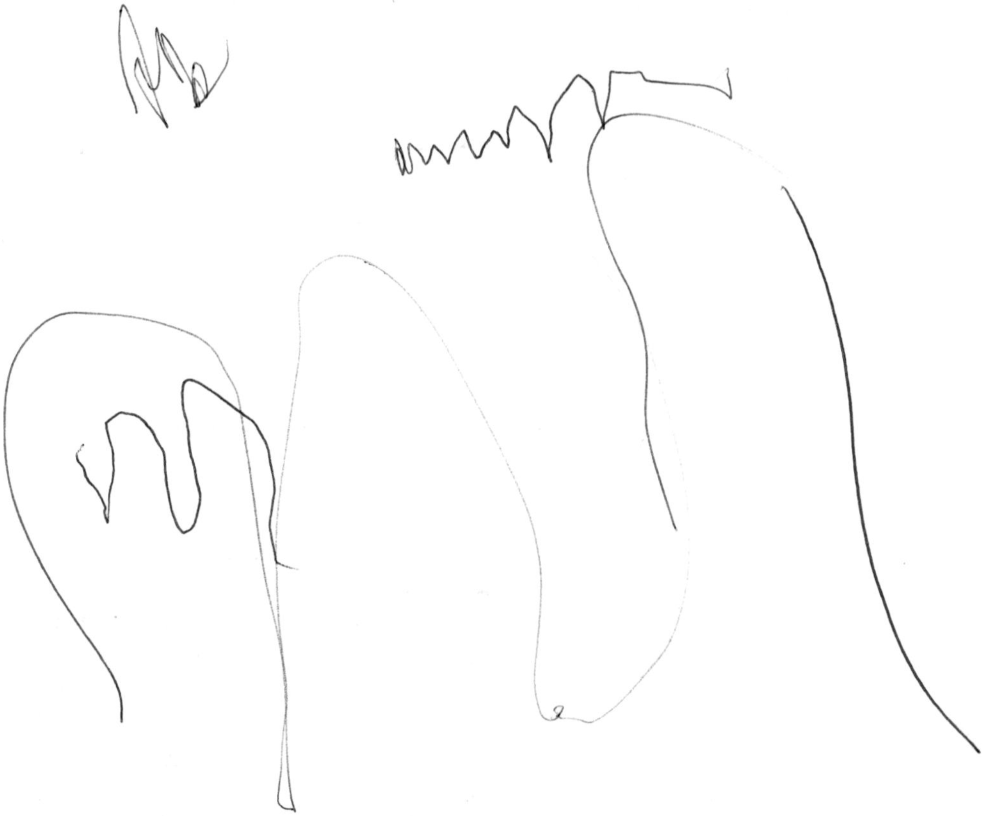

Introduction—A Note from the Dean: "What Is Community (College)?"

> Community was a beautiful, strange bird—beloved by a passionate few, misunderstood by many, and, like all strange birds, eventually chased into another yard.

—JOEL MCHALE, THANKS FOR THE MONEY

FIRST BROADCAST in September 2009 as part of NBC's new fall sitcom lineup, the pilot episode of *Community*—more mini-movie than TV episode, according to creator Dan Harmon and company—introduces the audience to a set of stereotypical characters (high school jock, overachieving nerd, spectrum kid, sweet-natured Christian mom, self-important white dude, self-important and also pervy and old white dude) stuck in a stereotypical setting (college) only to then suddenly upend those stereotypes via *Breakfast Club* parallelisms and meta-homages. It's understatedly impressive in a have-your-cake-and-eat-it-too way.

The episode begins as the stately sounds of clocktower chimes ring out while the camera pans across Greendale Community College's bland concrete-and-glass campus (no *Gilmore Girls* ivy prep here!), only settling on the Dean when the auditory marker of hallowed academia is revealed to be nothing more than a recording of bells on a recalcitrant boombox. Clearly there is disjoint here. After some tech fumbling (a painfully accurate depiction of academia, btw), the Dean greets the milling freshman class with some inspirational words regarding community college. His oration leads to whip pans across campus that bring focus to some of our major characters. Each actor snaps to the camera as they hear their derogatory, self-identification markers called out across the quad (ironically recalling the heyday of must-see-TV opening credit character rolls). And so in short order, we are introduced to:

- "remedial teen" Troy
- "twenty-something drop-out" Britta
- "middle-age divorcee" Shirley
- "old man circling the drain of eternity" Pierce

The Dean's fumbling of his cue cards then leaves these stereotypes dangling. That leaves the audience to fill in the blanks, as it were, regarding the possible three-dimensionality of these characters. Over the following six seasons (and a movie?), Harmon and company stretch the Greendale Seven's initial two-dimensionality to the breaking point . . . even if they have to use two-dimensional cartoons to do it!

But honestly, an attentive audience—even those focusing solely on the "Sam and Diane" central couple in the pilot—would see that the status would definitely not remain quo for long in this series. The main arc of the episode plays with the tension between Britta, an upright advocate of the truth, and Jeff, the surprisingly open liar. Yet by the time the episode is over, Jeff will have told the truth and Britta will have confessed to having lied. Ah, reversal!

And perhaps that's the point from day one: everyone and everything is never quite what they seem at good ol' Greendale.

A *Community* Common Core Curriculum

This book hopes to bring a less-than-stereotypical focus on a show that broke the bounds of television in a wide variety of ways over its sometimes halting run. But despite a few of us being stuffy-pantsed, professor types who think the show should *really* have just focused on the dashing Dr. Ian Duncan and his erudite adventures in red wine and sweater vests, we don't just want to tell you what to think. Really! This isn't a lecture class, er, book. It's a guide, at best, designed to inspire you, to provoke discussion and independent thought, and to get you revved up for *Community* (college or movie, your call!). It is, dare we say, a whole curriculum.

So think of your authors as your academic advisors as you take your first steps into the less-than-hallowed halls of Greendale. (Those of you enrolled in Air Conditioning Repair and HVAC Management, of course, should leave now and enter the gold-plated chariots to your left: the Hogwarts of Colorado awaits!)

As for the rest of you lot, let's take a look at the common core curriculum, shall we?

Remedial Courses (Recommended Freshman Year)

- **History 101:** A survey of sitcoms, comedy, and American standards and practices. Classes will view episodes of *I Love Lucy*, *The Dick Van Dyke Show*, *Cheers*, *Seinfeld*, and *30 Rock*. Readings will include TV tropes, narrative arcs, and "televisual equilibrium." Satisfies major requirements for both Business and Communications majors. May also be taken as pass/fail.
- **Composition 101:** This course introduces students to Dan Harmon in the Beforetimes, from the Dead Alewives' geeky sketch comedy to collaborations with comic-book genius/buddy/faux-antagonist Rob Schrab, *Monster House* Hollywood success, failed Hollywood pilots, and *Acceptable TV* semi-success at Channel 101. The semester ends with a marathon viewing of *The Sarah Silverman Program*. An optional essay on "Intentional Fallacies" and "Story Circles" is available for extra credit. See your instructor for details.
- **Acting 101:** All the world's a stage, and every actor had their start somewhere . . . even the Greendale Seven. This survey course looks at the early careers of *Community* mega-talents Alison Brie, Yvette Nicole Brown, Chevy Chase, Donald Glover, Gillian Jacobs, Joel McHale, and Danny Pudi as well as second bananas Ken Jeong, John Oliver, Jim Rash, and Dino Stamatopolos. The final exam will include trust falls, improv, and small group workshops.

Undergraduate Courses (Students Must Take Courses in Sequence!)

- **Community 101:** Cross-listed as "Season 1: Seven Characters in Search of a Purpose." This course introduces students to key concepts, characters, and running gags in the *Community*-verse. Includes guest lectures by faculty in Spanish, Film Studies, Social Psychology, Criminal Law, Gender Studies, Statistics, Home Economics, Environmental Science, Religious Studies, Journalism, Dance, Communication, PhysEd, Art, and ESL. Please see syllabus for dates and chicken fingers.

xii INTRODUCTION—A NOTE FROM THE DEAN: "WHAT IS COMMUNITY (COLLEGE)?"

- **Community 102:** Cross-listed as "Season 2: Blow It Up, Repeat." This course—arguably the most popular offering at Greendale— provides students numerous opportunities for extracurricular participation, from paintball and wine tasting to D&D club, space simulation, student elections, and blanket forts. Also, a guest lecture from the School of Animation just before the holiday break! Note: Class often meets outside regularly scheduled time.
- **Community 103:** Cross-listed as "Season 3: Physics of the Multiverse." This meta-course surveys a wide range of chaotic meta-timelines, meta-theatrics, meta-anime-tion, meta-video games, meta-musicals, and pillow fights. Of course this semester could all be a meta-delusion, in which case no grades will be granted and this meta-course must be retaken. Meta!
- **Community 104:** Cross-listed as "Season 4: Biology of Zombies." Note: The (previously) tenured teaching faculty for Community 104 is on sabbatical this semester. Regardless, this class remains a required part of the six-course sequence. In unrelated news, if anyone smells a gas leak, please notify custodial immediately. Thank you.
- **Community 105:** Cross-listed as "Season 5: The Science of Syndication." This course—sponsored by Subway!—will test students' ability to accept change and loss as class dynamics may be shifted randomly during the semester. Note: All students must submit to a polygraph during the midterm exam. No exceptions. Go Joe!
- **Community 106:** Cross-listed as "Season 6: Theories of Closure." Virtual coursework this semester supplements traditional, in- class assignments as students learn the practical skills required to survive outside Greendale. Satisfies major requirements for Communications, Film Studies, and Robotics majors. Additional technology fees may be applied.

Graduate Courses (No, Your Credits Will Not transfer to City College)

- **Advanced Acting Seminar:** Cross-listed as "What Can You Do with a BA from Greendale?" This course surveys the post- graduation careers of the Greendale Seven in media ranging from television and animation to off-Broadway and franchise Hollywood.

Students will be required to binge-watch *GLOW* and *Atlanta* during finals week. Perhaps simultaneously.

- **Advanced Composition:** Cross-listed with "Introduction to Blockbusters." This course follows the graduate careers of the writing and directing staff at *Community*, including the Russo Brothers ("Avengers Assemble!"), Justin Lin (*Fast and Furious!*), Seth Gordon (*Marry Me!*), and Rob Schrab (*Rick and Morty!*). The final project for the course requires students to apply "Story Circles" to every post-*Community* project discussed during the semester.

Elective Credit

- **New Media 201:** Podcasting for Accountants and *Harmontown*. All students (21 and over only!) must sign waivers before enrolling. Travel and bar fees apply. Note: This course satisfies no core requirements for any major. May be taken for repeat credit every semester for all eternity.
- **Game Theory 201/202:** Advanced Introduction to D&D: *HarmonQuest*. Led by Professor Crittenden, this course introduces students to the gaming world of dungeons and dragons (although, for copyright reasons, not actual *Dungeons & Dragons*). Highly animated group discussions feature fellow faculty members Harmon, McGathy, and Davis alongside a rotating lecturer/dead-man-walking. Dice are included; snacks (edible) are not.
- **Library Science 201:** Intermediate Wikipedia and *Great Minds with Dan Harmon*. Team-taught by Professors Harmon and Crittenden, this course combines stale, old history with modern pseudo-science and an unhealthy dose of self-psychoanalysis. Unexpected (and brief!) guest lectures by Beethoven, Hemingway, Edison, Mary Wollstonecraft, Shakespeare, Idi Amin, Betsy Ross, Earhart, Freud, Poe, Siddhartha Gautama, John Wilkes Booth, Ada Lovelace, Harry S. Truman, and JFK, among others (?) may occur sporadically; do not be late to class! Satisfies core requirements for both History and Mad Science majors. Laboratory and off-campus fees are required: check with your professors.
- **Animation and Joke-Telling Seminar:** Wubba lubba dub-dub!

As you can see, Greendale has so much to offer beyond air conditioner maintenance. So choose your classes (and study groups) wisely!

Remember: college is more than just a collection of classes. It's a collection of misfits who—if you're lucky—form a community.

But enough of this life-advice nonsense from your academic advisors. Go, get out there and become the Human Beings that you know you already are! Or, to cite the awe-inspiring words of our esteemed Dean: "I wish you luck!"

History 101—"Who Indeed?" 1
TV Sitcoms and Critical
Analysis

TV's rules aren't based on common sense. They're based on the studio wanting to milk their profits dry.

—ABED

22 Minutes and a Little Epiphany

THE HISTORY OF SITUATION comedy starts a little something like this: after World War II, millions of Americans discovered that those radio-with-pictures boxes—the ones that had been so expensive in the 1930s—were suddenly quite a bit more affordable now that all the factories weren't turning out bombers and tanks. By 1956, almost 70 percent of American households had a television. When not mowing their newly acquired suburban lawns or driving massive, fuel-guzzling cars on President Eisenhower's autobahns, the Greatest Generation settled down to watch whatever the new-fangled box would beam at them.

Though technically a new format, television comedy was able to get a running start by drawing on what had worked in the past. "TV desperately needed content," noted comedy historian Kliph Nesteroff, "and even the stalest routines made it to air." From the late 1940s to the early '50s, variety showcases like *Your Show of Shows* and *Texaco Star Theater* resuscitated acts from the vaudeville and nightclub circuits, beaming stage acts into households across the nation. At the same time, televised situation comedies—in which a steady cast of stock characters dealt with slightly different and slightly funny situations week after week—essentially added video to the scripts of existing popular radio shows like *The Life of Riley* and *Amos 'n' Andy*.

It wasn't long before sitcoms' steady reliability and relatability built their audiences to the point where they eclipsed variety shows (which, though often funnier by a minute-by-minute accounting, were more of a high-wire act given that each episode had to produce laughs from scratch rather than rework slight variations on proven formulas every week). Given how the first sitcoms built on what had worked so well for radio comedies, the genre unsurprisingly became something of an assembly-line product in relatively short order. What changes there were came about in incremental fashion, not via great creative leaps.

The first blockbuster sitcom, *I Love Lucy*, which started its run in 1951, used many staples of the genre—a live audience, wacky neighbors, a gently bickering couple, farcical sequences based on misunderstandings—but refined the formula with tighter writing and use of a three-camera setup that remained standard into the next century.

Leave it to Beaver *(1957–1963) was so typical of gentle sitcoms at the time that it only achieved real popularity many years later in reruns.* PAT MCDERMOTT/WIKIMEDIA COMMONS.

The following decades experienced shifts that looked significant only from a distance. Year by year, viewers only noticed minor changes. The adjustments that did happen were primarily more in subject matter than format. The happy, nuclear family sitcoms of the 1950s (*Leave It to Beaver*) shifted in the 1960s to sillier setups (*Gilligan's Island*) before detouring into social commentary in the 1970s (*All in the Family*) and coming right back to the family in the 1980s (*The Cosby Show*).

Though sitcoms remained a broadly white genre, occasional clusters of black-oriented shows broke through in the 1970s (*The Jeffersons*), the 1990s (*Martin*), and the 2010s (*Black-ish*). There were even occasional bursts of inventiveness with the format, such as when the success of *The Office* bred similar mockumentary-style shows (*Parks and Recreation, Modern Family*).

But for all the changes over the years (for a while canned laugh tracks were in vogue, then live studio audiences, then a single camera with no laughter either live or recorded), the sitcom remained remarkably durable. The jokes zinged out by Norman Lear's writers would have caused a national conniption if Desi Arnaz had voiced them. But the format in which those jokes were delivered had not changed much whether it was Lucy whining to Ricky about her latest misadventure or Archie Bunker barking racial epithets for laughs.

Some things remained largely immutable about the sitcom. In a little under a half hour (22 or 23 minutes to leave space for commercials and so *never* an hour, which was and is still today strictly for dramas!), the following will take place:

- A problem is introduced.
- Minor complications ensue. (This pads the running time and also leaves ample side-situations for additional jokes.)
- The problem is solved.
- A character has at least one learning moment or miniature epiphany.
- Everything by the end is reset to zero.

The last step is particularly crucial for sitcoms. That end-of-episode restoration of the status quo ensures that viewers can tune in next week (or next season) and know they won't have missed anything life changing: the dad will still make gruff pronouncements, the kids will keep trying to get away with miniature rebellions, and the mother will be ever-sighing in loving exasperation with her hands on her hips.

Trope Talk

The basic plot structure and emotional payoffs of sitcoms changed so little that even when they are contrasted, the similarities shine out more than the differences. The premise of the 2021 Marvel series *WandaVision* centers on Wanda, a witch who uses her powers to reshape reality so it matches what she remembers from classic family sitcoms. The show's pitch-perfect renderings of everything from *The Dick Van Dyke Show* to *Malcolm in the Middle* and *Modern Family* are notable for the decades-spanning breadth of styles they exhibit. But ultimately each sitcom world is created for the same reason: to impart a sense of familiarity, family, and security. Wanda, and generally the audiences for all these tonally disparate shows, gets the same thing from each of them. Sitcom surfaces might change but the sense of soothing safety and emotional gratification they provide does not.

Saul Austerlitz puts it neatly in his 2014 book *Sitcom*: "The sitcom, in short, is about the preservation of equilibrium."

That truism often remained the case no matter the subgenre of the sitcom or its level of sophistication. Some sitcoms, like the first iteration of *Roseanne* in the late 1980s, began to experiment with narrative continuity by introducing new characters and actual changes to the family's living situation (Roseanne opens a restaurant; Darlene leaves for college). But for the most part, the blockbuster sitcoms like *The Big Bang Theory*, *Two and a Half Men*, *Everybody Loves Raymond*, and even the great *Seinfeld* largely stuck with re-establishing equilibrium week after week, season after season. Sitcom families might suddenly find themselves with a new baby, but really, nothing much changed. Which is how we like it, apparently.

And Then Came Abed

Of course, television had not planned on Dan Harmon, Greendale, or Abed. Who could? When the first episode of *Community* aired on September 17, 2009, it entered a media landscape experiencing a charged, high-stakes reckoning with the future of the format that registers as even more absurd now than it did at the time.

On the surface, *Community* was just another sitcom.

The seemingly unremarkable fish-out-of-water premise crafted by Dan Harmon featured a charming scoundrel stuck in a place he believes is beneath him but who grudgingly agrees to lead an ever-squabbling group of students trying to find their way in life. It had jokes with edge but also heart grounded in a matrix of wildly disparate and often desperate people who become an unintentional family.

Community had its antecedents in classic ensemble sitcoms of yore loved by Harmon. In just about every interview from the period wherein Harmon—who already had a reputation as a brainy smart-ass—discussed his influences, he never played the brainy smart-ass card or denigrated the sitcoms that came before him. Instead he sang the praises of mass-appeal shows like *Cheers* and *Taxi* that he loved as a child. Like those sitcoms, *Community* was about a situational rather than biologically related family, giving it more room to explore and expand than a scenario limited by one mother, one father, and some children; call it a post-detonation nuclear family.

The inaugural episode had already built buzz as something different by the time the pilot episode was broadcast. (NBC, thinking they had a hot show that would appeal to a cool, younger, Internet-savvy, advertiser-appealing demographic, was so confident they premiered it early on Facebook.) The humor was sharp, layered, deeply self-aware, and pop culture–literate. At the same time, it left room between the jokes for a character-centered story about how seven damaged people could begin to knit together some kind of shared purpose.

The fact that NBC was putting so much behind this out-of-the-box sitcom seemed important to those who even casually studied media in the late 2000s.

At the time, though Americans for the most part still watched network TV in numbers that would be hard to imagine a decade and a half later, they did not expect much from it. They definitely did not respect TV, particularly sitcoms.

As a result, when any show seemed to break the mold, it was news.

It may be difficult for younger readers to imagine, but in 2009 before the streaming deluge, broadcast networks ABC, CBS, NBC, and to a lesser extent Fox still had significant cultural cachet. Even as prestige cable threatened on one side and the vast chaotic time-suck of the Internet loomed on the other, the shows occupying the 8–11 pm Eastern Time slots garnered audiences hard to imagine by the 2020s. Reporting, gossip, and speculation about ratings, time shifts, and cancellations littered

Trope Talk

The attitude that many people had toward TV, and TV comedy in particular, was well illustrated in "The Virgin," an episode of *Seinfeld* from 1992. One of the few self-referential sitcoms with some degree of dramatic continuity to predate *Community*, *Seinfeld* had a running subplot about Jerry (Jerry Seinfeld) and George (Jason Alexander) trying to create a very *Seinfeld*-like sitcom for NBC. In the episode, even though he had yet to write a word of dialogue for the show, George started referring to himself as a writer to pick up women. This seems to work well for George until he explains to one woman that he's working on a sitcom. Rather than act impressed, she recoils in disgust: "How can you write that *crap?*" Telling her friend what she just heard, they both erupt in mocking laughter, the first woman shoveling more disbelief and verbal abuse on George's pretend profession: "And he actually tried to use it to hit on me!" Even in the early 1990s when middle-of-the-road sitcoms that nobody remembers today (*Just Shoot Me!?* Anyone?) could still easily garner millions of viewers, little respect was given to the form by the audience.

newspapers' entertainment sections. TV critics pilloried their villains and celebrated their heroes with fiery passion.

And so while not everyone might have watched NBC's Thursday-night lineup each week, people generally knew what was on. It was in the electrified air.

By the late 2000s, TV was no longer the lens through which to understand everything of consequence in American culture (as Chuck Klosterman wrote of the 1990s). But the fragmentation of individualized media streams was far from complete. Broadcast TV was still crucial to understanding the national zeitgeist.

Nevertheless, the people in charge knew change was coming.

Before *Community* was greenlit, writers like Harmon simply did not secure deals for prime-time sitcoms on major networks. He was not a network veteran or hot stand-up comic who had blown away the studio brass at a comedy club industry showcase. Harmon was a comedy insurgent from Milwaukee who had cowritten the most expensive and never-picked-up sitcom pilot episode of all time, had been fired from the last show he worked on, and was best known for making mock sitcom videos that were only known to a few hundred inside-comedy nerds.

Networks preferred familiarity, known names, people with industry track records who already knew how to produce shows that millions of people would reliably tune in for. A more inventive show generally needed to have proven itself elsewhere (preferably on British TV, such as *The Office*) before the network brass would hand any creative types the brass ring. Alt-comedy types like Harmon were supposed to be the ones yelling about what *should* be on network TV, not the ones given a chance to make it.

Risky as it proved to be, *Community* could only have happened on NBC. In September 2009, this last-place network did not have a lot of options. CBS had both strong reality franchises such as *Survivor* and broad sitcoms like *How I Met Your Mother* that played great in Peoria. ABC boasted big reality shows (*Dancing with the Stars*), the rare broadcast drama getting HBO–level critical attention (*Lost*), and even some single-camera sitcoms (*Ugly Betty*) that were not only diverse for the era but intentionally goofier and stranger than the usual fare. Even normally ignored networks like Fox and the CW, though they still could not boast any noteworthy sitcoms, were getting younger audiences and curious adults to tune in for buzzy shows such as *Glee* and *Gossip Girl*.

In contrast, NBC's lineup did not have a lot going for it. The onetime pinnacle of broadcast TV was now weighed down by lumbering dynasties like *Law and Order* and a slew of soon-forgotten hour-long dramas. Thursday, once the network's crown jewel for mass-appeal sitcoms like *Cheers* and *Friends*, was now something of a critic's ghetto. Rebranded "Comedy Night Done Right," the 2009 season's Thursday-night schedule for NBC was filled with innovative, multicamera no-studio-audience shows like *The Office* and *30 Rock*. They eked out mildly unimpressive ratings but stayed on the air due to advertiser-friendly demographics, positive reviews, and a dearth of other options.

In hindsight, *Community* would be seen as setting a new standard for network comedy boundary-pushing. When it first started, though, while the series seemed fresh and forward-looking (at a time when most sitcoms had at most one non-white character, almost half the actors in the core study group were people of color) it also came across as simultaneously more relatable when compared to NBC's more adventurous-seeming shows due to the show's appetite for slapstick.

Harmon did not come out the door with a half-hour version of the go-for-broke shorts he had recently been making, like *Computerman*: no

FBI agents getting Ethernet cables shot up their anuses here! Like a smart nightclub comic who warms up the crowd with milder material to get them on his side before launching into something more challenging, he didn't start out with a *My Dinner with Andre* episode or fill the pilot with Charlie Kaufman references.

This was completely intentional. As Harmon told *Entertainment Weekly* in 2020, "It wasn't my goal to do something crazy; it was my goal to get a pool and a health plan." Nevertheless, he still kicked the show off in a somewhat off-kilter fashion that made critics and viewers sit up a little straighter and wonder, "What's this?" One can imagine a different version of *Community* that tried to undermine every sitcom trope in the pilot episode running on some streaming service in 2020. But this was 2009. Not wanting to be a flash-in-the-pan critical favorite, Harmon spent time building characters with familiar hopes and anxieties whom the audience could invest in.

Once that template was established, though, Harmon and his writers used the apparent relatability of the characters in *Community* as a base from which they could scramble expectations, turn the format on its head, and rewrite what people thought the American sitcom was capable of.

Composition 101–Dan Harmon in the Beforetimes

The thing you have going for you when you start is your naiveté.

—DAN HARMON

Origin Story: Wisconsin

LIKE A LOT OF AMERICAN KIDS, Dan Harmon grew up in a lower-middle-class suburb on the outskirts of a somewhat unexceptional city in middle America. Also like a very specific subset of American youth who came of age in the 1980s and '90s, he was socially withdrawn, plinked around with computers, played Dungeons & Dragons, and inhaled network TV and geek culture with the same level of commitment some contemporaries put into huffing glue; he spent a lot of time in his head, in other words.

Unlike many American kids, though, Harmon found his passion while still in high school and successfully pursued it. Part of this was luck. Growing up in the pre-Internet age (Harmon was born in 1973, right in the median for Generation X), there were not a lot of outlets for a philosophically inclined, intellectually voracious, and comedically loquacious Midwest teen with a penchant for acting out, coming up with imagined worlds, and writing sequels to movies he liked. But just by dint of being raised in Milwaukee, he had opportunities that an alternate self who grew up in Wichita would not have had access to.

Building on the success of improvisational comedy groups like Second City, which started just a little further south down in Chicago in 1959, the improv group ComedySportz opened in Milwaukee in 1984. Harmon found an outlet for comedy in the group's combination of freewheeling "Yes, and?" improvised skits and comic competitiveness (the basic premise of the group was to have two teams of comics face off with a referee there to manage things).

Harmon's time with ComedySportz (and a stint doing stand-up) likely helped him learn how to work a crowd and generate comedic bits at a quick clip, skills that would be crucial in his later roles as showrunner of *Community* and mayor of the live podcast *Harmontown*. But while the rapid-fire pace of instant worldbuilding on a stage in front of easily bored strangers honed Harmon's storytelling skills, the experience really taught him how to write more than anything else.

Unable to balance late nights of stand-up with making it to classes, Harmon dropped out of Marquette University in his freshman year. He joined the Dead Alewives, another Milwaukee improv group, albeit one with a more anarchic and R-rated style than was preferred at ComedySportz. With Dead Alewives, Harmon had his first long-term collaboration with fellow deceased-fish Rob Schrab, a like-minded, nerd-adjacent comic who became Harmon's creative partner and occasional mock-arch-nemesis (more on that later).

By definition, the work of most improv groups, no matter how brilliant, is lost to history. But the Dead Alewives produced an album in 1996 that includes a number of their skits, including their best-known bit, "Dungeons & Dragons" (also known as "Summoner Geeks"). Any skit about a group of awkward teen gamers whose D&D session keeps getting interrupted by demands for Mountain Dew and girls "to do" might seem

Elsewhere in the Multiverse

Harmon's D&D knowledge was put on even fuller display in *Community*'s Season 2 episode "Advanced Dungeons & Dragons" and on many episodes of his podcast *Harmontown* where he and guests played the game live in front of an audience. Heck, the *Harmontown* RPG sessions even spun off into *HarmonQuest* and gave birth to the phenomenon known as Spencer Crittenden! *Community* also paid tribute to the Dead Alewives at the end of Season 5 by having Abed wear a shirt with their logo on it (a fish corpse with a cigarette in its mouth).

Rob Schrab, definitely not wearing an Inspector Spacetime *shirt.* JD LASCIA, CC BY-SA 2.0/
WIKIMEDIA COMMONS.

insulting to modern geeks raised on *Stranger Things*—given the Alewives'
now-stale gags involving *Revenge of the Nerds* snorting and retainer-inspired
speech impediments—but 1990s nerds listening to Dr. Demento memo-
rized the sketch with self-reflexive glee, recognizing that the performers
were clearly a part of their own social circle. The nerds weren't yet in
charge, but they certainly recognized their own.

During this period, Rob Schrab started work on a project that would
take him and Harmon far from Wisconsin. Schrab began writing, drawing, and self-publishing the indie comic *Scud: The Disposable Assassin* in
1994. Set in a future where deadly C-3PO–styled robot assassins can be
purchased at vending machines, the bullet-spattered and bleakly satirical
story follows the existential crisis of one of those robots when he discovers he will self-destruct after completing his mission. *Scud*'s freewheeling,
world-building, blitzkrieg violence and alternately tortured and laissez-
faire attitude to moral quandaries prefigured—by more than a decade—the

Dan Harmon in the Beforetimes. JD LASCIA, CC BY-SA 2.0/WIKIMEDIA COMMONS.

animated series *Rick and Morty*, which Harmon created with Justin Roiland (and which Schrab would also write for). *Scud* was a much-sought-after gem among indie comics geeks throughout its sporadic, pre-2000s run before it stalled (for a decade) after twenty issues.

Schrab imagined *Scud*—whose in-your-face Tarantino- and Raimi-esque comedic violence was very on-point for the decade's indie cinema and comics—as a Hollywood pitch all along. He tried from an early stage to get it in front of industry people and even included "suggested voice talent" ideas in each issue (hinting which characters would be best voiced by, say, Tommy Lee Jones or Joe Pesci). Harmon was an occasional cowriter of the comic, also penning a nine-issue cyber Mafioso spinoff called *La Cosa Nostroid* (1996).

Scud was published through 1998, picking up a significant (by indie-comic standards) and dedicated audience. By then, Harmon and Schrab had already moved to Hollywood after Oliver Stone's production company optioned *Scud*. It was not a lot of money, but as Harmon told the *Hollywood Reporter*, "We were in Milwaukee, and Oliver Stone, Hollywood and $10,000 meant an awful lot to us."

Gone Out West

Unfortunately, Oliver Stone's *Scud* never came to fruition. Which is a shame, since at the time Stone was taking the kind of big creative swings (*Natural Born Killers*, *U-Turn*) that a gonzo, sci-fi, action satire like *Scud* would have needed.

After taking up residence in the dream factory, Harmon and Schrab campaigned to write the *Scud* screenplay. But being comic-book improv guys from Wisconsin without any credits, they failed to get anywhere further with that pitch.

Fortunately, during the late 1990s the entertainment industry was starting to shift out of its previous schematic approach in which every project was slotted into rigidly defined categories. Cable television offerings were expanding, the networks were looking to reinvigorate their tired formulas, and big studios wanted to show they could be just as daring as insurgent indies like Miramax (then in the full bloom of its *Shakespeare in Love* phase).

Also involved in Harmon and Schrab getting their feet in the door: writing high-concept ideas fast. Not to mention luck.

To prove the gatekeepers at Stone's production company wrong, Harmon and Schrab wrote a screenplay called *Big Ant Movie*, about giant insects taking over Los Angeles. Naturally. Though ultimately never produced, the screenplay got the pair into meetings with players like Jim Henson Studios, DreamWorks, and Ben Stiller (not a studio, but still a player). In relatively short order they secured an agent and a two-picture deal with Robert Zemeckis (director and cowriter of *Back to the Future*, one of the main inspirations for *Rick and Morty*). Of the ideas that Harmon and Schrab pitched to Zemeckis (including "Rot Gut," a story about a mummified cowboy, which could well have inaugurated a new genre if it had been greenlit), the pitch that most appealed to Zemeckis was about a group of kids menaced by a haunted house that comes alive.

The script Harmon and Schrab turned in for *Monster House* should have been just what Zemeckis was looking for. A clear homage to the earlier work of executive producer Steven Spielberg, it mined a similar vein of suburban eeriness while mixing sarcastic comedy with earnest emotion. But the project languished for years. It was eventually released in 2006 in stop-motion animated format (the uncannily creepy technique that Zemeckis inexplicably insisted on using for many of his movies at that point) with extra script work from Pamela Pettler (*Corpse Bride*).

The final product was clever, genuinely funny, quite well-reviewed, Oscar-nominated, and for many years the most successful creative endeavor with Harmon's name attached to it. However, Zemeckis and

Monster House *producer Robert Zemeckis, whom Dan Harmon did* not *call a moron.* DAVID SHANKBONE, CC BY-SA 2.0/WIKIMEDIA COMMONS.

Spielberg's *Monster House* was far enough removed from the original vision that Harmon disowned it.

Harmon's blunt response to the film—contained in a thoughtful, compassionate, and sweet-natured letter that he sent to a seven-year-old girl who had been having nightmares after seeing it—typified a few notable aspects of his personality. One was his willingness to get into public feuds with Hollywood people significantly more famous or powerful than himself; in this instance, he called director Gil Kenan a "hack" and Spielberg a "moron." Another was his dead-serious dedication to his work. Lastly, Harmon's response revealed his belief that a story that is inauthentic or pointless ("even a scary story, if it's a good scary story, takes us into strange, dark places that don't make sense at first, and helps us see that they do make sense, and are therefore not so scary") is not just wrong, but borders on offensive.

All of which might make it unsurprising that even after co-authoring a screenplay for one of the biggest players in Hollywood, it took Harmon some time to find secure footing in the industry.

Heat Vision and Jack

Nobody was biting on "Rot Gut" in the late 1990s. But Harmon and Schrab were still able to get meetings with people in suits. However, those meetings kept not turning into movies or television shows. Stuck in an unsatisfying deal with ABC, the pair decided the only way out was to write a show that would only amuse the two of them. Sure enough, the script made its creators delirious with laughter but led to ABC buying them out of their contract.

The unexpected part came when Ben Stiller got hold of the script. He thought it was the funniest thing he had ever read. Stiller being peak Stiller at that moment (right between *There's Something About Mary* and *Meet the Parents*), his personal interest piqued industry interest. Stiller also being an unusual combination of A-list movie star and alt-comedy nerd—his eponymous 1992 sketch show on Fox was a rare and quickly snuffed-out attempt at off-the-wall broadcast TV humor, and featured future *Community* writer Dino Stamatopoulos—he leveraged his star power by trying to turn Harmon and Schrab's dealbreaker script into an actual TV show.

Produced in 1999 as a half-hour pilot directed by Stiller, *Heat Vision and Jack* is an archly goofy mashup of *The Six Million Dollar Man*, *Knight Rider*, and every 1970s and '80s series about a squinty-eyed loner roaming from town to town, solving problems, and finding love. The hero is Jack (Jack Black), an astronaut who develops super-intelligence after flying too close to the sun (sure, why not?). He is now (the pilot claims to be episode 14) on the run with his talking motorcycle, Heat Vision (drolly voiced by Owen Wilson). Together, the two try to evade a NASA assassin on their

The pilot episode for Heat Vision and Jack *might have been responsible for* Community *even though it never aired.* AUTHOR'S COLLECTION.

tail (Ron Silver as himself . . . the idea being he enjoys moonlighting as an actor when not being evil) and not get tied down by the hot blonde sheriff (Stiller's wife and comic actress Christine Taylor—you know her as the hot Marcia Brady).

Both ludicrous and dryly understated, *Heat Vision and Jack* remains just about the funniest half-hour of comedy produced during the 1990s. But since it was also the kind of thing made to send an audience of VHS bootleg-trading pop culture obsessives into gales of knowing laughter, it was also practically designed to evade the happy, middle-American audience most network executives aimed for at the time. As a result—and *possibly* because it was, despite the purposefully grungy effects, reportedly the most expensive pilot episode ever made—nobody seized the opportunity to produce what would have inevitably been the great talking-motorcycle show of all time.

Heat Vision and Jack exists today as a lo-res YouTube artifact and a fascinating what-if point of discussion for people who like to imagine how well its self-aware, bottom-drawer genre humor might have slotted into the lineup between *The Simpsons, Malcolm in the Middle,* and *The X-Files.*

Quite well, it appears in retrospect.

Channel 101

With *Monster House* in development purgatory, no other Zemeckis scripts moving forward, and nothing happening on the TV front, Harmon and

Schrab could have moved back to Wisconsin or tried a different line of work (e.g., disposable assassin). Instead, they started a film festival and TV network.

Kind of.

According to lore, Channel 101 got its start in 2001. (According to unfounded speculation, the name may have been a nod to Channel One, a comedy troupe including future *Community* star Chevy Chase that showed satirical videos in a Greenwich Village theater during the late-1960s and early '70s.) One night, Schrab asked some friends over to watch *Jaws 4: The Revenge* (the Michael Caine one) but with a stipulation: they had to bring something that predicted the movie's plot. Puppets were involved, but most people made short videos. Schrab's semi-legendary contribution featured his penis (with duct-taped fin) as the shark and an orange as Michael Caine. Word spread and more people started coming by Schrab's place with their video predictions. By 2003, Harmon and Schrab were hosting live events at bars or theaters where they dispensed with the original conceit and simply showed the videos.

The format (which Harmon once referred to as "comedic battlebots") harkened back to ComedySportz, mixing DIY moxie and competitive zeal. It also parodied the business of network television by turning a collection of random video geeks into downmarket network executives. Audiences watched ten videos, each of which was no more than five minutes long and acted as a miniature pilot for a full-fledged TV show. The audience voted for their favorites, and the winning videomakers could then bring a new episode back to the next screening.

In the dark times before YouTube was founded in 2005, short videos occasionally went viral after being uploaded to P2P file-sharing services, getting emailed around, or through long-gone websites like JibJab and Icebox. But otherwise, short-form indie weirdness (Winnebago Man outtakes, *Jesus vs. Santa*, even *Heat Vision and Jack*) was just as likely to be seen through exchanges of VHS dubs or at screenings like Channel 101. The festival began hosting the videos and its annual mock-Emmy Awards, the Channys, online but remained largely a live experience.

During the pre-*Community* years, Channel 101 served as both comic clubhouse where Harmon and Schrab could build a community of like-minded weirdos and as a testing ground for up-and-coming talent who had an inside-out understanding of TV conventions . . . as well as a knack for snappy concepts, Gen X snark, and willful amateurishness. It was all a labor of love. Harmon and Schrab were hyped in a *Time* article from 2006 as an "impoverished writing duo" who "hate the executives who run television" and then "took their revenge" by cutting the suits out of the pilot greenlighting process. They did not charge for tickets and had no hopes of making money off Channel 101. But it did turn out to be a well-regarded talent farm, a development that likely had been in its creators' minds all along.

The trial-by-fire screenings and try-anything ethos made Channel 101 resemble a less-algorithm-optimized Funny or Die or jackass kid brother to the Other Network (a floating festival that showed only actual unaired TV pilots and included theme nights dedicated to the likes of Judd Apatow and Bob Odenkirk . . . the latter of whom also hit the Channel 101 circuit).

Like Odenkirk, the comedy trio the Lonely Island (including Andy Samberg) had success at Channel 101 with a long-running mock–*The O.C.* Malibu-set teen soap opera called *The 'Bu*; after graduating to *Saturday Night Live*, their goofily absurd digital short films like *Laser Cats!* drew straight from the Channel 101 playbook. More established comics like Sarah Silverman and Jack Black made appearances as well in bits like *Channel 101: The Musical* (which included Harmon playing a tyrannical riff on himself, singing lines like "I'm Dan Harmon and I shit gold") and the self-explanatory *Laser Fart*, respectively.

Channel 101 was also a proving ground for Harmon's later *Rick and Morty* partner Justin Roiland. His *House of Cosby* (a creepy/funny series about a guy who loves Bill Cosby so much he keeps cloning new Cosbys) ended only after receiving a cease-and-desist letter from Cosby's legal representatives. His *The Real Animated Adventures of Doc and Mharti* (2006) was essentially a dry run for *Rick and Morty* only with an even more explicit *Back to the Future* vibe and significantly higher quotient of testicle jokes.

Trope Talk: Yacht Rock

Did Channel 101 change the world? Absolutely. One of its most popular series was JD Ryznar, Hunter D. Stair, and Lane Farnham's *Yacht Rock* (2005). Running for twelve episodes, it depicted infighting and jealousy between smooth-music practitioners of the 1970s (Michael McDonald, Kenny Loggins, Hall & Oates) who hung around Marina del Rey in loose, mellow, yacht-ready attire. While ultimately funnier in conception than execution, the series launched a thousand streaming service playlists and gave a name to a genre everyone previously knew existed but couldn't put their finger on.

Other Channel 101 players included the exceedingly enthusiastic Abed Gheith (guess which *Community* character he inspired?), Paget Brewster (who joined *Community* over a decade later), the duo Tim & Eric, Jason Lee, Jimmy Kimmel, Kumail Nanjiani (later a custodian on both *Community* and *HarmonQuest*), and future *Harmontown* comptroller Jeff B. Davis. Bigger names like Chevy Chase and Joel McHale popped into Harmon's multi-episode mock-procedural *Water and Power*, but that was something of a cheat given that he had already started *Community* by then.

Acceptable.TV

By the mid-2000s, cable channel VH1 had shifted from being MTV's boomer-rock-video offshoot to a dependably horrific dumping ground for the worst reality TV the decade had to offer. The lineup included everything from celebrity trainwrecks like *Flavor of Love* to shows with all the hallmarks of Channel 101 parodies (*Ice-T's Rap School*, *Celebrity Paranormal Project*, *America's Most Smartest Model*) that were somehow made in earnest.

So it made a perfect kind of sense that in a flailing, sure-why-not? attempt to fill the airwaves with *something* that seemed of the moment— and to compete with other channels that had started shows that mimicked Channel 101's premise—VH1 contacted Channel 101 for the real thing. In response, Harmon and Schrab put together a version of their festival to annoy viewers looking for the next episode of *Rock of Love with Bret Michaels*.

Called *Acceptable.TV*, the 2007 series was structured as a half-hour show comprised of five shorts (including one created by viewers). Viewers voted online (or by phone!) for which two would come back the following week. In a commercial for the show, whose tagline was "The unavoidable future of entertainment," executive producer Jack Black announced that the show was so exciting, "TV just got a little less [bleep]."

Channel 101 fans who might have been concerned about VH1 demanding higher-quality visuals, less-juvenile humor, or a more limited devotion to mocking television had nothing to worry about. *Operation Kitten Calendar* smooshed together an *Apprentice* parody (complete with stereotypical reality TV character types) with a dash of kitty meme-ing. *My Black Friend* imagined a bottom-tier reality show in which a white guy upset about not having any black friends auditions several strangers for the role. Justin Roiland's *Mr. Sprinkles* reimagined *The Cat in the Hat* in the modern era (the kids call 911 when a strange creature bursts into their home, and said creature develops an identity crisis) with his trademark mix of gallows humor and despair.

There was, on the whole, less testicle humor than Channel 101.

VH1's desire to bring *American Idol*–style audience interaction together with Internet comedy virality was apparently unfulfilled. *Acceptable. TV* lasted for only eight episodes. But before the first one even aired in March 2007, Harmon and Schrab already had another show going on a different cable channel.

The Sarah Silverman Program

Based largely on their guerrilla comedy reputation from Channel 101 and the cult shadow still cast by *Heat Vision and Jack*, Harmon and Schrab were brought on to cocreate *The Sarah Silverman Program* with its namesake star for Comedy Central.

After a very brief stint on *Saturday Night Live* in the late-1990s, Silverman bounced around the comedy world, doing bit parts in movies and trying to find her voice before turning to stand-up. She vaulted onto the comedy A-list after her 2005 special *Jesus Is Magic* became a surprise hit on its theatrical release. Her coy way of dancing right up to the line of offensiveness by playing an obnoxiously entitled character while simultaneously sowing doubt about how tongue-in-cheek she was being made her the new face of shock comedy (sample line: "I don't care if you think I'm racist, I just want you to think I'm thin").

Like many other striving comics with more ideas than outlets, Silverman had also fallen into the Channel 101 orbit. Besides *Channel 101: The Musical*, she also appeared in *The Most Extraordinary Space Investigations*, whose stoner humor is so chintzy and cheap it made the rest of Channel 101 look like Jerry Bruckheimer productions.

Silverman's willingness to provoke with a smile and a song meshed well with Harmon and Schrab's tendency to push the boundaries of acceptability. Her screen persona also complemented their dark wit with a somewhat sunnier disposition. The combination worked well for a series that was for a time one of the funniest and freshest (though also most divisive and controversial) things on television.

The Sarah Silverman Program had a short inaugural season of six episodes in the spring of 2007. A cracked-mirror kind of sitcom, it starred Silverman as a manipulative, selfish, and unemployed waster who sponges off her upstanding sister (played by real-life sibling Laura Silverman). She spends most of the show getting away with murder through sheer brazenness, a twinkly smile, and the occasional part-whimsical, part-cynical musical number.

The show has a certain *Pee-Wee's Playhouse* for grown-ups vibe to it, like a kids' show that discovered day-drinking and went looking for somebody to offend ("Her vagina looked like Cat Stevens' face"). Going against then-current typecasting, the show gave Silverman two gay friends (Brian Posehn and Steve Agee) but made them fairly deadpan and prone to saying "dude" rather than snapping their fingers and making catty remarks (sorry: no *Will and Grace* "Just Jack!" here).

The show also seemed to hunt for taboos to bust: Sarah has a sexual relationship with God, looks back fondly on her several abortions while Green Day's "Time of Your Life" plays, and puts on blackface for a day to back up her claim that being black is easier than being Jewish. This gained the show both notoriety and committed fans but also led to some episodes being taken out of later circulation (e.g., blackface). The show's go-for-broke attitude could have been at least partly a reflection of Harmon's desire to finally make a mark and get something notable on the air after so many years of Hollywood-adjacent toil.

Dan Harmon and Rob Schrab's Emmy-winning music number for Hugh Jackman at the 2009 Academy Awards used cardboard, glitter, and snark. AUTHOR'S COLLECTION.

Awards, Awards, Awards

In 2009, Harmon and Schrab reunited to write (with Ben Schwartz of *Robot Chicken*, *Parks and Recreation*, and Upright Citizens Brigade) one of their more inexplicable, falling-backasswards-into-luck projects: the opening musical number for the 2009 Academy Awards, starring Hugh Jackman. Somehow, possibly because one of Jackman's producers was a big fan of *The Sarah Silverman Program*, Harmon and Schrab were brought on board. They quickly threw together a riotous, in-jokey, and nerd-ish singing-dancing medley about all the Best Picture nominees . . . as well as a pointed complaint about *The Dark Knight* getting snubbed. With the excuse that the economic crisis had led to budgetary cutbacks, Jackman performed the snarky yet still bubbly numbers with his usual giddy gusto in front of hot-glue-and-cardboard sets built by Schrab that came straight out of the Channel 101 garage-comic aesthetic. The whole thing ended up bringing the house down and won the three an Emmy

But before the first season was even over, Harmon was gone. Neither he nor Silverman went fully public about how things broke down between them at the time; that sort of complete public dissection of inner-Hollywood conflict was not yet common. Still, rumors floated around for years about Harmon being difficult.

Silverman herself confirmed that when she appeared in the 2014 documentary *Harmontown*. She explained how, in short order, Harmon became not just no fun to work with but also highly controlling. It quickly became too much for her. "I'm his biggest fan," she says in the Harmon-produced documentary, "and *I* fired him." Schrab stayed on the show.

In a 2011 interview on Marc Maron's podcast *WTF*, Harmon sardonically describes himself at the time as thinking he was the show's Larry David to Silverman's Jerry Seinfeld (meaning he would be head writer and she primarily the talent). He imagines Silverman must have been thinking at the time, "Why is this asshole who I pulled out of the gutter thinking he's Larry David?" Harmon said that when they parted ways, Silverman told him, "I need to be the only crazy person in the room."

With *Community*, Harmon was able to be the Larry David. He was also able to be the only crazy person in the room—which worked for that show.

Until, somewhat famously, it didn't.

Acting 101–The Cast and Crew before Harmontime   3

> *Casting is probably the most important thing in television production. A well-written show will accomplish nothing in a medium where you need them to fall in love with these heads in a box, and you need them to do it fast and for a long time.*
>
> —DAN HARMON

ONCE UPON A TIME, before Childish Gambino, before *Rick and Morty*, before John Oliver wittily dissected the news in the most charming British accent in the former colonies, before Ken Jeong was *Fresh Off the Boat*, before *Avengers: Endgame*, and before Chevy Chase did whatever he does in the privacy of his own home, the relatively young and relatively untested cast and crew of *Community* were struggling young actors, comedians, and (in one instance) a doctor.

Let's take a look at where they were before Spanish study group back in the days when even Señor Chang was learning Spanish 101 (which, admittedly, he continued doing at the same time as his students).

The Actors: The Greendale Seven

The actors who heeded the class bell to assemble in Spanish study group ranged from relatively new blood to TV vets to grizzled comedy veterans. Here's a look at what one of the finest casts ever brought together for NBC's "Thursday Really, Could You Please Watch Some TV?" was doing before they enrolled at Greendale.

Alison Brie

One of Alison Brie's many jobs before she became an in-demand actress was as a clown at children's parties. This seems to be the ultimate boot camp for working in televisual drama and comedy. She graduated with a degree in theater from the California Institute of the Arts and studied at the Royal Scottish Academy of Music and Drama in Glasgow. This was, of course, perfect training for her first television role as a budding hairstylist on *Hannah Montana* (2006). She later showed up as a high school student in the ABC Family series *My Alibi* (2008) and a cleavage-forward cocktail waitress in the tongue-in-cheek exploitation series *Hot Sluts* (2009).

Brie's versatility and training led to her breakout role on *Mad Men* as Trudy Campbell, the long-suffering wife of Pete Campbell. In the hands of most performers, Trudy could have easily been a little-noticed background character. But Brie's nuanced performance highlighted the character's quiet conflict as she negotiated whether it was worth staying with a husband who she knew was not right for her in order to get the things she yearned for (the suburbs, children, and the constructed world of consumer choice that Pete and the other ad men sold as a manufactured reality).

Even though the world of *Mad Men*—being a deeply researched, period-specific, historical drama—was significantly different than that of *Community*, there were some similarities in how Trudy and Annie Edison (Brie's *Community* character) navigated their internal tensions. Like Trudy, "Little Annie Adderall" was a buttoned-up striver who had an image of the perfect life in her head and was willing to do whatever it took to achieve it.

At the same time, Trudy did not have some of the same challenges as Annie such as having a monkey named after her breasts (Season 1: "Contemporary American Poultry").

Yvette Nicole Brown

A little bit older than most of the cast and well suited to her *Community* character of the bubbly-but-experienced Shirley Bennett, Yvette Nicole Brown was born in Cleveland. An accomplished singer, she had a contract with Motown Records while still a teenager and showed up on the East Coast Family's 1992 New Jack Swing single "1-4-All-4-1." After her musical career seemed to stall, she moved to Los Angeles to try out acting. She spent a few months performing in a gospel play before doing the struggling-actor circuit and picking up commercial work. (Hamburger Helper? Check! Pine-Sol? Check! DiGiorno Pizza? Check!)

In addition to selling cleaner and frozen pizzas, Brown also found steady TV work booking guest roles in *That's So Raven*, *Entourage*, *That '70s Show*, the NBC version of *The Office* (a brief appearance that prefigured the nice-then-tough turn she perfected on *Community*), *Girlfriends*, and *Malcolm in the Middle*.

Movie work was harder to get. But Brown built up a decent resume of small-but-memorable roles in movies as varied as *Dreamgirls*, *500 Days of Summer*, and *Tropic Thunder*. The old cliché (so old, we're not even going to look up how old) has it that there are "no small parts, only small actors." It is true that some actors can steal scenes even in the tiniest roles. But there are also actors whose years of laboring for just a few minutes of screen time helps them grow as performers (and not just to sell Hamburger Helper). Because Brown paid her dues as a working actor for so many years, by the time she was cast as Shirley Bennett on *Community*, her success as the moral center of the study group seemed to come from her innate understanding of the character's struggles.

Chevy Chase

Underground comedy went mainstream in America when *Saturday Night Live* premiered on NBC on October 11, 1975. Created by Lorne Michaels

Chevy Chase on Saturday Night Live*'s "Weekend Update," c. 1975.* NBC/PHOTOFEST.

(among others), during its early years the show was populated by numerous stars who became Hollywood mainstays or went on to notable but
lesser fame (look them up, we don't have all day here!). *Saturday Night Live*
also featured John Belushi (*not* Jim, whose very name became a slur and
metaphor of mediocrity for *Community* writers) and Gilda Radner, both
of whom died before reaching their true potential. But despite the strong
bench (Laraine Newman, Jane Curtain, Garrett Morris) during the show's
first season, the only cast member the press wanted to talk about was the
break-out star and "Weekend Update" segment anchor, Chevy Chase.

The actor born Cornelius Crane Chase in 1943 was a naturally gifted
comedian whose self-appraisal was apparent in his delivery of the opening
line of "Weekend Update": "Hi. I'm Chevy Chase. And you're not."

Despite his ever-present air of smugness, there was something unmis-
takably charismatic about Chase. He could command a stage with ease, had
impeccable comedic timing, and employed his improvisational training to
devastating effect. He started out as a writer, contributing to *Mad* magazine
and the *National Lampoon Radio Hour* (a spin-off of the revered satire magazine which also included future *Saturday Night Live* colleagues Belushi,
Radner, and Bill Murray) before turning to acting. He gained notice from
his early- and mid-1970s work in the off-Broadway hit *Lemmings* and the
comedy-skit flick *The Groove Tube*.

After two seasons on *Saturday Night Live*, Chase went out on his own.
He had his share of misses (an eponymous variety show that quickly failed
and the 1980 classic *Oh! Heavenly Dog* in which Chase is reincarnated in
the form of Benji the dog). But for roughly the next ten years, Chase
starred in more hit comedies than most actors would dare to dream of:
Fletch, Caddyshack, Three Amigos!, Vacation, Spies Like Us.

Given that record, it is ironic that in the years immediately preceding
Community, Chase was sometimes best remembered as a failed talk show
host.

By the early 1990s, Chase's film career was in a bit of a slump. Meanwhile, the late-night talk show landscape was undergoing some shake-ups.
The undisputed late-night king, Johnny Carson, retired from NBC's *The
Tonight Show* in 1992. Although David Letterman was seen as the heir
apparent, some stations began to wonder if Carson's four-decade reign
had been a fluke. Maybe *anyone* with charisma and a quick wit could do
the job?

Upstart network Fox, always more willing to fling things at the wall,
decided to give it a shot even though they had already tried a rival late-
night talk show back in 1986 starring frequent Carson guest-host Joan

Rivers. That late-night experiment crashed, burned, rolled off a cliff, and exploded, after which the wreckage apparently drifted into the upper atmosphere where it froze into a cluster of failure that then hovered above Fox's broadcast facilities waiting for the right opportunity to try it all over again.

That moment came on September 7, 1993 when *The Chevy Chase Show*, filmed at the (newly renamed) Chevy Chase Theater and featuring host (wait for it . . .) Chevy Chase debuted. Fox, with high confidence that their host would grab all the eyeballs not dedicated to Leno or Letterman, had given the show a generous budget and Chase himself a few U-Hauls filled with cash. The show lined up Hollywood heavy hitters. Old comrades like Aykroyd, Martin Short, Garrett Morris, and Al Franken showed up in the first few weeks along with show business royalty such as Robert DeNiro, Dennis Hopper, and Don Rickles.

Even so, the result was not so much a train wreck as a metaphorical re-enactment of the *Hindenburg* disaster.

The primary issue was that the host could not, well, host. Chase mumbled, lost his cues, sweated profusely, tried one-liners that brought more confusion than actual laughs, and in desperation even brought back his classic *Saturday Night Live* pratfalls; obviously, if there was anything that audiences in 1993 wanted, it was impressions of Gerald Ford.

Nothing worked. It was the proverbial party where the host can't wait for you to leave so he can be alone again. The show was put out of its misery after just five weeks. Chase spent the next decade and a half slogging through undistinguished and largely under-the-radar roles.

Nevertheless, Sony (the production company behind *Community*) decided that the weird little show needed a big name star. Harmon (who had wanted a more deadpan performer in the role of Pierce Hawthorne like Fred Willard or Patrick Stewart) eventually came on board. Neither Harmon nor Chase knew that in a relatively short amount of time, Chase would be playing a caricature of himself that proved increasingly accurate as the show progressed.

Donald Glover

Before he was Childish Gambino(!), before he made *Atlanta*(!!!), and before he was Lando Calrissian(!!!!!), Donald Glover was a high school student voted "most likely to write for *The Simpsons*." A hyper-talented polymath who could write, act, sing, dance, play music, perform stand-up, and generally ace whatever skill he tried to learn, Glover graduated from

New York University with a degree in dramatic writing in 2006. While still a student, he pursued multiple creative pathways. Starting in 2008, he began releasing music under the stage name Childish Gambino (which he reportedly took on after it was spit out by a Wu-Tang Clan name generator; for what it's worth, the author of this particular chapter goes by the *Wu de plume* Gentlemen Genius). He joined the NYU sketch group Derrick Comedy, which racked up enormous YouTube popularity with edgy sketches (a boy arranges a hit on his parents for failing to buy him a bicycle; a *To Catch a Predator* spoof about "bro-rape"; and Thomas Jefferson inexplicably still being alive in 2010). Unusually for a college senior, Glover was also hired as a writer for *30 Rock*, whose buzzy and meta-referential style would be a similar hallmark of *Community*.

Derrick Comedy released the very low budget but very clever movie *Mystery Team* (starring and with music by Glover) in 2009. The same year, Glover quit *30 Rock* to try his hand at stand-up comedy. But Harmon, impressed by Glover's work in *Mystery Team*, asked him to audition for the character of Troy Barnes on *Community*, sending Glover right back to NBC sitcom land.

Unlike most of the other cast members not named Chase, Glover was not a striving actor who had been looking for the right role. He was a relatively inexperienced up-and-comer whose stage name might as well have

Donald Glover on 30 Rock. NBC/PHOTOFEST.

been Bound for Stardom. Though Troy is typically portrayed as the least intelligent of the show's study group, Glover's easy, gliding confidence turned the character from a simple punchline into a kind of transcendent savant.

Gillian Jacobs

Gillian Jacobs grew up a lonely, isolated child whose mother enrolled her in acting classes when she was seen talking to herself at school instead of interacting with the other students. So perhaps it's not surprising that Jacobs nailed the role of a character who once described herself as having "peed alone my whole life."

Growing up in Pittsburgh, Jacobs moved to New York City and studied acting at Juilliard. She then did the usual round of roles in off- and off-off-Broadway shows (including work with respected directors like Adam Rapp and Philip Seymour Hoffman) and on the *Law and Order* franchise (so many people have acted on one of those shows, there is a good chance that you, dear reader, did as well at some point). After getting good reviews for her theater work, she started booking Hollywood jobs in the mid-2000s. Jacobs picked up roles on NBC's Christian-ish drama series *The Book of Daniel* and dark films like *Choke* and *The Box*, none of which showcased the vulnerable kind of looniness she brought to her unhinged role on *Community* as Britta Perry, apparent love interest. Showing up for her audition nauseated from the flu and without makeup, she impressed Harmon as capable of bringing a grounded reality to a character that he admitted to having initially written as a kind of fantasy figure.

Joel McHale

The smarm! The warmth! The Swa-warmth? No matter how you define the presentation style of Joel McHale, the longtime host of the preternaturally cynical gossip-snark show *The Soup*, it made a perfect kind of sense for him to play the alternately amoral/nurturing lead on *Community*.

Born on Mercer Island, Washington, McHale showed little aptitude for acting in high school or at college. He played on the football team but only in a theoretical sense, never seeing a second of game time on the field. If pressed, we might argue this is much like how Jeff Winger initially enrolled to be student at Greendale . . . but only in a theoretical sense.

Frustrated with his career prospects and with being regarded as a dumb jock, McHale spent the 1990s trying to locate a different path in comedy. He joined the improv group Unexpected Productions (kind of like the

Joel McHale paid his comedic dues on E!'s The Soup *before* Community. AUTHOR'S COLLECTION.

Second City of Seattle, which if we are being honest, is more like the Fifteenth City). He interned on *Almost Live*, akin to a Seattle-based *Saturday Night Live*, and worked his way up to full-time cast member.

McHale left the show to get a master's in theater arts while also working on corporate videos for Microsoft, Ford, and even Jack LaLanne (for those blessedly too young to remember, LaLanne was Schwarzenegger before Schwarzenegger, having essentially introduced America to physical fitness and one-size-fits-all leotards). After graduating in 2000 with an MFA in acting from the University of Washington, McHale moved to Los Angeles and spent a few years working various angles at getting into the business.

He ended up with a speaking role on an episode of *Will and Grace* (first iteration) and promptly gained and lost agents. After the usual series of disheartening commercial gigs, he found out in 2004 that the E! network was looking for "a smarmy dick" to comment on all the new reality shows flooding the airwaves. *The Soup* (a continuation of the old snark-fest *Talk Soup*, whose host Greg Kinnear had gone on to bigger things). McHale's years in sketch comedy made him well suited for his plum gig on *The Soup*, which consisted of running clips of celebrities and cracking wise (the Kardashians were a frequent target).

According to McHale's autobiography *Thanks for the Money: How to Use My Life Story to Become the Best Joel McHale You Can Be*, Harmon was looking for an actor who could play a "sarcastic, arrogant, self-obsessed character." These were all characteristics that McHale—whose comedic persona expertly entwines self-deprecation with self-regard—happily understood quite well.

Danny Pudi

Like Harmon, Danny Pudi attended Marquette University in Milwaukee. Unlike Harmon, Pudi graduated, thus marking him as an altogether different kind of nerd than the one he would play on *Community*. Born and raised in Chicago with a mother who put him in dance classes from the age of five, Pudi has the distinction of being the first student at Marquette to win the Chris Farley Scholarship (which is a thing!) and one of the few working comic actors who can tap dance . . . just in case a role calls for it (which it did in Season 1's episode "Interpretive Dance").

After graduation, Pudi moved right into improv comedy both at Chicago's Second City and also with the Asian-American comedy group Stir Friday Night. Since improv has not, will not, and never could pay the bills, Pudi relocated to Hollywood like every other funny kid who does not want to end up in a temporary office job for the rest of their life. He kept the lights on by doing phone recruiting work and snagging commercial gigs (e.g., the immortal T-Mobile butt-dialer ad). He also put together a solid if short reel of appearances from a one-shot on *The West Wing* to recurring roles on *Greek* and *Gilmore Girls*.

Even though Pudi only had a few years of experience under his belt when he was cast for *Community* (and none of it with very much actual

---

Cool Cool Cool

Television being television, many of the shows Danny Pudi worked on before (as well as during and after) *Community* could only see one aspect of his background, and often not even that correctly. Although part Indian and part Polish (he is, in fact, fluent in Polish), Pudi has typically been cast as characters with South Asian or Arab identities. Thus he has been known on screen as Raj (*Gilmore Girls*), Mahir (*ER*), Sanjay (*Greek*), and Abed (*Community*) but not once as Jakub or Stanislaw.

screentime), coming out the gate with his first Abed Nadir monologue, it felt as though he had been commanding attention in sitcoms most of his life.

The Actors: Study Group Auxiliary

Ken Jeong

Born in Detroit to Korean immigrant parents and mostly raised in the American South, Ken Jeong did what delights every immigrant parent: he started working as a stand-up comic. Since, curiously enough, telling jokes to drunk strangers does not usually pay the bills, after Jeong graduated from Duke University, he decided to actually make his parents proud and obtained an MD in internal medicine from the University of North Carolina. However, he never lost the itch to hone his stand-up career so the good doctor started taking theater classes and continued telling jokes to drunk strangers.

Figuring he could keep both careers working simultaneously, Jeong relocated to Los Angeles to work as a doctor and a comedian. His routines were continually groundbreaking, indulging in physical comedy but also diving headlong into the truly weird. He soon got walk-ons in episodes of *Curb Your Enthusiasm*, *The Office*, and *Entourage*. By the time he was cast on *Community* as a Spanish teacher who knows *muy poco Español*—and eventual study group auxiliary member and all-around wild card—Jeong was already starting to break.

The same year that *Community* premiered, he also appeared in two movies, *Knocked Up* and *The Hangover*, which even your aunt who really really does not like "the kind of movies they make these days" has heard of. Given that, it is little wonder that Jeong's supporting role bloomed into something *muy especial*.

John Oliver

Like half of his favorite comedy troupe, Monty Python, the English-born John Oliver attended Cambridge University, making him altogether quite a bit fancier than the rest of the cast of *Community*. He joined the legendary Cambridge Footlights, which spawned the career of many a British comedian. Oliver's first major acting gig once out of college was performing at the prestigious Edinburgh Fringe festival in 2001, where he played the role of a comedic journalist, a role that would help him prepare for the rest of his career. Before coming to America, Oliver also joined several improv comedy troupes, built up a successful and increasingly political stand-up show, and before long was appearing as a guest on the satirical British television show *Mock the Week*.

All of this was precursor to being hired by Jon Stewart and *The Daily Show* as their "senior British correspondent" in 2006. While working on *The Daily Show* (as both writer and writerly on-screen personality known for his drolly absurdist delivery), Oliver received three Emmy Awards for outstanding comedic writing. In fact, Oliver was so committed to *The Daily Show* that he turned down an offer as full cast member on *Community*, preferring to keep his day job.

Jim Rash

Featuring the look and demeanor of a one-time mathlete who never quite got the hang of adult life (making for a nervy and potentially volcanic vulnerability), Jim Rash put in his years at the Los Angeles improv training camp the Groundlings during the 1990s. While learning and performing there alongside the likes of Melissa McCarthy and Maya Rudolph, Rash became friends with fellow Groundling Nat Faxon, whose surfer-dude looseness is like a photo negative of Rash's buttoned-up-yet-manic style. As Rash was notching brief appearances in a range of media that were subpar (*According to Jim*), at par (*That '70s Show*, *Reno 911*), and potentially above par (*Sky High* and *Minority Report*, though his role in the latter was cut), he and Faxon became writing partners. Their pilot *Adopted* (2005) was not picked up, but on the strength of their touching family comedy *The Way Way Back*—one of the better-known long-unproduced screenplays around Hollywood—Alexander Payne hired them to write his George Clooney drama *The Descendants* (2011), a job that won Rash and Faxon an Oscar.

Rash was one of the last major characters to be cast for *Community*, which had already begun shooting by the time he came on board as Dean Pelton. The range he had built up during his years at the Groundlings and in sitcom work gave him the tools necessary to pop off the screen as Pelton, fully inhabiting the character's increasingly manic enthusiasms.

Dino Stamatopoulos

Years before playing the aggressively one-note character of Star-Burns on *Community*, Dino Stamatopoulos had knocked around the Chicago comedy scene, performing with friends like Andy Dick and Scott Adsit. After relocating to Los Angeles like everyone else looking to have a career in this thing called show, Stamatopoulos spent a few years orbiting Hollywood. Eventually Dick urged him to submit his writing (including a previously rejected spec script for *The Simpsons*) to *The Ben Stiller Show*. He joined the staff in 1992. Although that forward-looking show was unjustifiably short-lived, Stamatopoulos's time there opened a lot of doors. His impressive writing career subsequently ranged from gone-too-soon series like *The Dana Carvey Show* to critical darlings like Cross and Odenkirk's *Mr. Show* and late-night warhorses like the *Late Show with David Letterman*, *Late Night with Conan O'Brien*, and *Saturday Night Live*.

Despite having written for just about every eponymous comedy show of the 1990s and 2000s, Stamatopoulos ultimately became better known for a generally maligned subset of comedy: animation. His stock-in-trade was the kind of subversive animation he worked on for Robert Smigel's *Saturday Night Live* "TV Funhouse" shorts. Stamatopoulos came on board relatively early at Comedy Central's nighttime alter ego, Adult Swim, starting his own stop-motion animated series, *Moral Orel* (a satire of religious morality shows like *Davey and Goliath*), in 2005.

Unlike the rest of the auxiliary cast, Stamatopolos was originally brought on to *Community* as part of the writing staff. But after being given the part of Star-Burns, a seemingly throwaway gag character, he found himself returning episode after episode to portray the man with the most significant sideburns in television history (hey, it's a kind of immortality).

Community 101–Season 1: 4
Seven Characters in
Search of Purpose

I just wanted to get to L.A. and make one of those shows that make people happy.

—DAN HARMON

N 2003 WHEN HARMON was still finding his way in Hollywood—this was after Fox declined to pick up *Heat Vision and Jack* and before he helped create *The Sarah Silverman Program*—he started taking classes at Glendale Community College. He later said his impulse to take Spanish with his then-girlfriend was something he came up with at the time as a way of doing something together to reconnect.

The relationship didn't last.

But in his year and a half at Glendale, Harmon fell into a biology study group with two younger Armenian-American students whose success or failure he found himself oddly invested in. He discovered he really wanted to just goof off with the study group even when they were actually trying to study. Tucking away that experience, he pulled it out later as a more emotionally grounded story (meaning no talking motorcycles) he could pitch once he found himself in a room again with network executives looking for a new idea.

Harmon later recalled for *Entertainment Weekly* that moment of realizing he could produce a show about an older "jackass" like himself who finds togetherness with a random assortment of strangers.

> I don't have to pitch them the robot show or the show about people who produce your dreams, or the conceptual medieval fantasy thing. I can finally satisfy myself and them by saying, "This is a show about a fish out

---

Extra Credit

In late August 2009 about a month before *Community*'s premiere, a series of web shorts appeared on the NBC website. Called "The 5 A's of Greendale," they are a string of purposefully cheap-looking fake ads that seem meant to run in between *Judge Judy* episodes. Possibly due to the late casting of Jim Rash as Dean Pelton, Harmon himself plays Dean of Admissions Pat Isakson, a stiff bureaucrat in polo and khakis doing his best to tout Greendale's best attributes ("air conditioning!") and repeat the school's mantra, "You're already accepted!" before having an on-camera mental breakdown. Oddly enough, one of the students who proclaims the greatness of Greendale is Randall Park. Six years later, Park would cameo in the episode "Intro to Recycled Cinema."

---

of water, because that fish out of water is me, and it's an asshole, but one you'll learn to like because you'll cast a handsome guy in the role." It's about the kinds of things that people care about.

In order to avoid any embarrassment with his semi-alma mater (who may not have appreciated story lines about fake classes, black mold, collapsing roofs, zombie pandemics, or a dark conspiracy operated by an air conditioning repair school), Harmon relocated the school from California to Colorado and barely tweaked the name from *Glendale* to *Greendale*.

By doing so, Harmon not only changed television comedy for the better but also showed that post–high school education always pays off. Always!

Episode 1: "Pilot"

Based solely on this first episode, viewers could easily have thought that a better name for *Community* might have been *Winger!* At first glance, this looks to be a sitcom whose success or failure will hinge on the likeability of Jeff Winger (Joel McHale). A once high-flying attorney brought low by the state bar's discovery of his lack of a college degree, Jeff arrives at Greendale with little intention of actually studying and every intention of grifting the system, slacking off, and being the center of attention. By the end of the episode, Jeff has been humbled (but only somewhat), the ensemble has started to take form, a will-they-won't-they sexual tension is established,

The Study Group Assembles. NBC/PHOTOFEST.

and characters are introduced with quirky defining characteristics that can later be mined for comedic effect.

But appearances—tropes, even—are seldom that easy at Greendale, and the heart of the show shifts quickly from Jeff to Abed Nadir (Danny Pudi). His personality would undergo a few adjustments during the first season, pivoting from a somewhat stereotypical motormouthed OCD personality toward a wiser figure who frequently understands more than the rest of the study group put together.

Abed first appears here in a blaze of verbosity, drowning Jeff in dialogue after being asked the time. Initially annoyed, Jeff is happy to discover Abed's no-boundaries habit of questioning everyone (like a brilliant-but-off-his-meds TV detective) has its benefits. After Abed delivers a tranche of personal details about "the hot girl from Spanish class," Britta Perry (Gillian Jacobs), Jeff tells him bluntly, "I see your value now." This causes Abed to say, with the unadorned honesty (direct and somewhat toneless but not flat) that Pudi invested in the character from the start, "That's the nicest thing anyone's ever said to me." This is an early example of people around Jeff finding unintended returns from his selfish, lazy behavior.

Jeff's self-serving con game runs on two tracks through the episode. In the first, he tries to wheedle and then muscle a year's worth of test results out of Professor Ian Duncan (John Oliver), a former client whom Jeff impressed with his courtroom verbal jiujitsu ("I still cannot figure out how you got a jury to connect September the 11th with my DUI"). In the second, he creates a fake Spanish study group as an excuse to meet up with Britta. He fails miserably on both accounts, stuck with taking tests and accidentally creating a real study group after Britta sees what he is up to and invites other students to join them: Abed; washed-up jock Troy Barnes (Donald Glover); Jesus-loving divorced mother of two and budding brownie entrepreneur Shirley Bennett (Yvette Nicole Brown); perky Tracy Flick-ish perfectionist Annie Edison (Alison Brie); and unctuous, silver-spoon, boomer millionaire Pierce Hawthorne (Chevy Chase).

Despite failing in his first of many shortcut scams, Jeff also introduces the theme of relativism that will be played with throughout the series. This is highlighted in two scenes, the first of which is a line Jeff delivers to Duncan: "I discovered at a very early age that if I talked long enough, I could make anything right or wrong. So either I'm God or truth is relative." The joke is an insight into Jeff's not-funny-if-you-think-about-it-too-much cynicism as well as Harmon's interest in toying with the limits of morality and truth (which he would take to extremes later in *Rick and Morty*). In any case, the soliloquy delivers a significantly darker and yet simultaneously more human style of humor than normally seen on Comedy Night Done Right. The second scene that zooms in on relativistic moralism is where Jeff delivers the first of his many rousing speeches—a series trope that the show would later dissect for self-satirical purposes—by explaining to the study group the true randomness of human connection.

> I can pick up this pencil, tell you its name is Steve, and go like this [snaps the pencil in half] and part of you dies just a little bit on the inside. Because people can connect with anything. We can sympathize with a pencil, we can forgive a shark, and we can give Ben Affleck an Academy Award for screenwriting.

Jeff's courtroom-trained emotional puppeteering is exposed by Britta, leading Abed to say in disappointment, "I thought you were like Bill Murray in his films, but you're more like Michael Douglas." This neatly establishes Abed's habit of viewing the world through media, heightened a few scenes later when he busts out Bender's "Know What I Got for Christmas?!" speech from *The Breakfast Club*. Of course, after Jeff testily counters with a less-than-composed retort—"You have Asperger's"—Troy and Pierce share a juvenile moment as they both chuckle, "Ass burger." There's a lot of character reveal in this scene, really.

Even though the episode ends with the group accepting Jeff as their de facto leader despite his exposed manipulation, their deep need to belong to anything that provides purpose, structure, and companionship essentially proves his point.

Jeff is their Ben Affleck.

Cool Cool Cool

Part of the pilot episode was shot on the former campus of Washington Mutual Bank (aka WaMu), which went bust in the 2008 financial crisis. It was then the largest bank failure in American history. This backdrop of greed, poor planning, and societal collateral damage seems fitting. Harmon's vision for *Community* was to focus on a less-prosperous segment of society than is usually seen in sitcoms, people for whom Greendale—junky and subpar and featuring frighteningly low standards for teachers as well as a disturbing number of riots—is the best of all the bad options.

Episode 2: "Spanish 101"

It takes most successful sitcoms several episodes at least to lock into the right tone, story, and banter that will carry them confidently through ratings' valleys and peaks and into syndication. The pilots are usually uncertain, flinging a lot of things at the studio audience to see what gets a guffaw. Then it takes a little time to work out the kinks, find out which studio boss's notes can safely be ignored, and discover what about the show is actually unique.

Community achieved that in the second episode. That is not to say "Spanish 101" will make anybody's list of the series' best. But it efficiently sets the scene for what follows without wasting time figuring out who the characters are, establishing most of the bonds and intramural conflict that will sustain the show for most of its run.

One episode in and the study group has already decided Jeff is their unelected boss, cool buddy, idol, and father figure. Abed's presentation is slightly tweaked from the pilot; he is quieter and less intrusive, making his off-the-cuff life-as-media commentary that is already tiptoeing into a mode of self-awareness that is more meta and moody than snarky. After noting that the frequent PA announcements are like the start of a new scene in a TV show, he points out that "the illusion lasts until someone says something they never say on TV, like how much life is like TV. There. It's gone."

In the A story, Britta's off-handed reference to a murdered Guatemalan journalist inspires the normally apolitical Annie and Shirley to hold a protest whose style (brownies, general perkiness, Annie's desire to "have a candlelight vigil like lesbians do on the news") offends Britta's sense of cool. The resulting confrontation pushes Britta from the smart and ironically distanced beauty of the pilot episode to a frazzled, judgy poseur always tripping over herself while firming up Annie and Shirley as the study group's goody-two-shoes.

The B story, where Pierce pushily tries to befriend Jeff when they are paired up for a Spanish assignment, begins Pierce's seasons-long quest to be seen as a worthy peer. This does not cover much ground beyond showing the depth of Pierce's queasy neediness. But it leads to the show's first truly memorable sequence: a dialogue-free montage in which Pierce's class presentation turns into an epic, baffling series of set pieces (robots, a canoe, and parts Jeff describes as "a little homophobic . . . and gratuitously critical of Israel") set to Aimee Mann's "Wise Up," a cinematic flourish that would feel like overkill for most sitcoms but here points to the makers' media literacy and grandiose intentions.

Pierce proves his Spanish is muy bueno. NBC/PHOTOFEST.

"Spanish 101" hints at the level of educational attainment possible at Greendale by introducing the group's Spanish teacher, Ben Chang (Ken Jeong), whose free-associative rant ("They call me 'El Tigre Chino' because my Spanish knowledge will bite your face off!") suggests his language skills are as strong as his grasp of reality. If early fans at this point had to guess which character would at some point later in the show's run be greasing themselves up to slither through the school's air vents while hunting down a monkey, the smart money would already be on Chang.

But the most rewarding part of the episode—even more than the first appearance of the ever-put-upon drug dealer Star-Burns (Dino Stamato-poulos)—comes in during the last few seconds of the closing credits when Troy and Abed, half-studying on a couch, beatbox and deliver a quick rap layering textbook Spanish ("*Donde, está, la biblioteca*") with gibberish ("*Bigote de la cabra as Cameron Diaz*"). Besides cementing the Troy-Abed bond, the scene points toward the show's commitment to nonsensical gags and complex wordplay.

Episode 3: "Introduction to Film"

An episode that deftly mixes humor with heart—exactly the combination that so many wrong-headed critics tried to claim (as some do with any brainy comedy) was missing from the supposedly too-snarky series—"Introduction to Film" provides an early encapsulation of everything that made *Community* special before it started diving into more outré topics.

Harmon leads with another '80s movie reference but doesn't leave it at that. Jeff is thrilled to be in a class taught by Professor Whitman (John Michael Higgins, one of the episode's two stellar guest players), a giddy free-spirit in the *Dead Poets' Society* mold who proclaims, "No tests! No papers!" Jeff excitedly thinks he found the ultimate blowoff class (a born scammer, he sees the guileless Whitman as a mark), thinking he can get an easy A by staging fake, seize-the-day spontaneity and goofy, rainbow, *Mork and Mindy* suspenders. When Whitman sees through the ruse, Jeff is baffled and frustrated by the teacher's inexplicable joy, shouting, "This is no way to teach accounting!" (the first and last time the class's actual content is mentioned).

Just two episodes past the pilot, the show establishes Abed's family background with such clarity that it needs little further illumination, leaving the character free to plot his own mysterious course without the continual parental drama of Pierce, Jeff, and Britta. Raised by his divorced father Gobi (Iqbal Theba, the principal from *Glee*), Abed is pressured to

---

Inspector Spacetime

"Introduction to Film" featured some spectacular background gags, from a "Racism Does Not Compute" study room poster with three otherwise identical but differently colored robots on it to barely glimpsed stands at the school fair (particularly those of the Disco Club and Karate Kid Club, either of which deserved their own episodes or spin-off series).

---

take only classes that will help him run the family restaurant, which has been struggling for a few years: "9/11 was pretty much the 9/11 of the falafel business." After Britta pushes Gobi to let Abed take the film classes he loves, his father storms off in a rage: "You want to raise him? You raise him!"

Britta's frustrations mount as her busybody good deed turns out to be more than she bargained for, with Abed throwing her money around and filming everything like it was a documentary (because documentaries, he explains, are "like real movies, but with ugly people"). Editing his footage into a goofy, touching film, Abed shows Gobi, Britta, and Jeff the world through his eyes: a confusing place filled with emotions that don't quite register and people who turn their confusion about his spectrum disorder into angry attacks. Though Jeff admits the film is "not exactly *Citizen Kane*," it has a surprising impact, communicating Abed's life of isolation and forced self-sufficiency without veering into mawkishness. It also finally gives Gobi a window into his hard-to-understand son, whose film classes he agrees to pay for, freeing Abed to pursue his media mania for the remainder of the series.

While this development allows Abed to follow his passion, it also leaves Britta and Jeff saddled with being the study group's mother and father figures. They are now in charge of raising this ersatz family, like it or not.

Episode 4: "Social Psychology"

The study group continues to feel each other out, and a surprising amount of humor is mined from a supporting character's rather tiny nipples in this solid character-builder of an episode.

The centrality of Jeff to some of the first season's plots becomes apparent here though not in a necessarily good way. Moving abruptly on from the Jeff-Britta kiss that concluded "Introduction to Film," this episode has Jeff mooning around in a funk because Britta has picked up a boyfriend. Vaughn (Erik Christian Olsen) is a dirty-blonde hacky-sacker with a no-worries-VW-bus-bodhisattva vibe and comically tiny nipples, the latter of which provides grist for the gossip mill being churned by Jeff and Shirley, who have discovered their only way to bond is by talking smack about people.

Pierce remains primarily off to the side, starting to show his potential for spreading chaos through nosiness and Sharper Image, boomer-gadget acquisition as he will the next season in "Aerodynamics of Gender" (this time with a pair of "earnoculars" that help him hear conversations from a distance and thus sow dissension).

A better sign of things to come is Duncan's psychology class experiment. His vaunted "Duncan Principle" boils down to putting volunteers in a room, telling them the experiment will start in five minutes, never starting it, and watching through a closed-circuit camera as each boils over in frustration. Annie, eager to juice her transcript and wash off the disrepute of her pill addiction (which led her to "lose my scholarship and virginity"), recruits Troy and Abed. Troy eventually breaks like the other volunteers, crying, collapsing, and dragging himself out of the room like a wounded animal in a genius bit of improv. But Abed hangs on and breaks the Duncan Principle by never folding, which reduces Duncan himself to a weeping frazzle. This presages Abed's often-relied-upon superpower of intense focus, dedication, and loyalty, which the study group usually misses because of his deadpan demeanor. Asked by Annie why he didn't leave, Abed simply says, "Because you asked me to stay and you said we were friends."

In a different show, this might have registered as the cringeworthy sentimentalizing of a person on the spectrum. But Abed's staunchness and clarity of thought make clear he is no figure of pity. The pitiable figures are Duncan and Annie, who thought an exercise in filmed sadism could pass as a research paper–worthy experiment only to be brought down by one subject who just did not mind . . . waiting.

Episode 5: "Advanced Criminal Law"

The difficulties of making Pierce anything but an annoyance to the rest of the study group become apparent in this more standard-issue episode that nevertheless features some smart writing. After claiming musical genius and insisting on writing the new Greendale school song, Pierce implodes—isolating, procrastinating, and snarling at whoever interrupts his lack of progress—in a self-deprecating take by Harmon on his own writing habits. Like much of the episode's boilerplate plotting, the story works not for what happens (Pierce ends up tossing out a not-even-disguised rip-off of Bruce Hornsby's "The Way It Is") but what is revealed along the way.

In this instance, Annie delivers a sharp, cutting speech that's ostensibly about motivating Pierce but is really a glimpse into her own compulsiveness and harsh upbringing not to mention the show's dedication to telling the stories of characters who never fit in.

> I'm gonna tell you what my mother told me when I wanted to quit cheerleading: "You're not pretty, you have no boobs, and you can't do a basket toss to save your life, but you made a commitment. So pick up your pompoms, Pierce, stuff your bra, and get ready for the team bus to forget you at a Taco Bell, because life is tough."

Similarly, the story where Britta is sent before a school tribunal—Chang, Duncan, and the Dean, all holding court at the Greendale pool for no reason other than the Dean wanting to show off school facilities—for allegedly cheating in Spanish class is just a means for Jeff (as Britta's counsel) to show his courtroom chops and make the first of many impassioned pleas to maintain Greendale as an island of last resort for misfit toys: "If crazy people can't be at Greendale, where are we supposed to go?"

A minor thread in which Abed tries to get past his gullibility by faking out Troy is not in itself funny or eventful but it gives Abed the layers needed to further free him from autistic character cliché. It also starts laying the foundation for the transition of Troy from the pilot's clueless jock to the sweeter, weirder, wonder-struck character who became for many viewers the show's true lodestar.

Unlike earlier episodes, the pop culture references here strayed further from the obvious.

The event for which Pierce composes the song is the unveiling of a statue of Greendale alum Luis Guzman, a real-life character actor who only film buffs (meaning a tiny, tiny fraction of NBC's Thursday night audience) would be very familiar with.

"Señor Chang" briefly takes time off from teaching horrible Spanish to pin televisual nicknames on the class, choosing "Ja-KAY" (as in Jackée Harry, the gossipy neighbor from 227) for Shirley. This first prompts her annoyance at being relegated to "some black female caricature" before tripling down on that caricature by saying, "If the Good Lord hadn't been watching, I'd have slapped him upside the head." Whereas some

> ### Inspector Spacetime
>
> "Advanced Criminal Law" introduced several recurring characters
> and bits: rule-breaking adult scholar Leonard (Richard Erdman), first
> seen here swimming in the nude; the first time Star-Burns tries to
> assert an individuality beyond his signature follicle sculpting ("my
> name is Alex!"); the premiere of Troy and Abed's trademark hand-
> slap; and the first full usage of the Dean, who gets a big entrance,
> his first pun ("Dean you later"), and the chance to drop a heavy hint
> about his sexuality in the tribunal ("I go both ways. Oh, let's strike
> that").

shows aim for edginess with jokes that simply recycle plain old-fashioned
offensiveness, this gag used one worn-out racial trope (all black female
TV characters must conform to some stereotypical idea of sassiness)
to highlight a particularly tone-deaf way minority characters are often
written.

In other words, a level of commentary NBC probably did not sign up
for.

When Abed passes Duncan in the hallway, he says, "*Cheers, M*A*S*H,*"
only for Duncan to crack back, "*Fawlty Towers,* game over," constituting a
lightning-fast round of "Whose Country Has Better Television?"

Were the writers making a blatant pitch to include themselves in that
pantheon of televisual greats? More likely it's a signpost for the television-
as-television meta-analysis to come.

Which NBC really did not sign up for.

Episode 6: "Football, Feminism, and You"

There were many points throughout *Community*'s run where people could
point and say *that* was when the show found itself. For many, it's when
the corridors of Greendale are first redecorated by paintballs. For some,
it's more esoteric moments like when in "Physical Education" (Season 1,
Episode 17) Jeff throws his ego and underwear to the side while rocking
to Warren Zevon, or the *Goodfellas* homage in "Contemporary American Poultry" (Season 1, Episode 21) when the show declared just how
far down the rabbit hole it was willing to go. Dedicated students of the
show's arcana may feel it only finally fully flowered in the last season when

Frankie Dart and Elroy Patashnik took their well-deserved places at the study group table.

But the sixth episode is a less obvious but still strong contender for When Everything Came Together. It is the one you would show a neophyte who wanted a good feel for what the rest of the run would be like. One could say the episode has it all: Troy rapping, Britta flailing, Annie fuming, Abed exploring his interior hall of televisual mirrors, a limited amount of Pierce, and concluding music by the Violent Femmes. Although the episode is still following a somewhat templated approach to conflict and resolution, the writing (largely by Hilary Winston, in her first *Community* credit) is more engaged with the comedic filigree around the action.

Discovering that his photogenic face is plastered all over Greendale's promotional materials and desperate to keep his attendance secret, Jeff agrees to the Dean's scheme (a "Deame," if you will): if Jeff convinces Troy to be quarterback for the school's losing team, the Dean will take down the posters. This upsets Annie, who thinks she's finally found her angle as Troy's tutor—which she hopes will lead him to appreciate her romantically in a way he never did in high school—and worries he'll go back to ignoring her if he returns to his jock roots.

Meanwhile, Britta confronts just how awkward she is at connecting with other women when Shirley has to tutor her in female bathroom etiquette (treat it as a place to "share, listen, support each other, and discretely eliminate waste" and *not* say things like "I'm willing to try some more mainstream feminine stuff"). It's a storyline that only barely connects to the rest of the episode but stands well enough on its own particularly for chipping off the last scrap of Britta's standoff cool from the pilot.

Where the episode shines are the bits that have nothing to do with the plot—it would take some time for the writers to fully invest in complex storylines. They start one of the show's eeriest running gags: Greendale's mascot, the Human Being, a deeply creepy and deliberately racially and sexually anonymous person in a white body suit with a black scrawl of smeared facial features on its mouthless and eyeless mask that is more suitable for Arkham Asylum than a college campus.

To signal Troy's return to athletic swagger, he delivers a deeply '80s hippity-hop-style rap in the cafeteria. It's a signature scene not just for its blatant self-awareness (Annie asks in confusion, "Why are you doing our politically conservative high school's shamefully outdated fight rap?") and the micro-specificity of its pop-political references ("Your team's

---

Meanwhile, Off Campus . . .

"Football, Feminism, and You" echoes the off–NBC career of Donald Glover, who had started performing hip-hop as Childish Gambino the year before. In September 2009, Glover released a mixtape titled *Poindexter*. In the episode, which aired that October, Glover's character Troy, embodying his jock persona, slaps the books out of the hands of a student he calls "Poindexter."

Al Gore / Because your views are wrong") but as a standalone sketch-comedic moment that makes no sense in the broader sitcom idiom.

Meanwhile, Abed's life-as-TV and TV-as-life lens comes into sharper focus in this episode. He briefly appears in the beginning punctuating a back-and-forth of charged Sam-and-Diane bickering between Britta and Jeff with an eyebrow-raised, "Will they or won't they?" After Jeff tells Abed the group is creeped out by his discussing them like TV characters, Abed responds, mostly to himself, "I can lay low for an episode." And then he actually does disappear, only appearing again as he waves to Shirley from across the cafeteria. Imagine *The Big Bang Theory* building a joke like this around one of its awkward characters and then actually sending them off screen for the rest of the episode without a punch line.

This action is possible because unlike the rest of the characters on *Community*, and indeed on just about every other show on at the time, Abed knows who he is: a character on a sitcom.

Episode 7: "Introduction to Statistics"

The college rager is enough of a played-out stereotype that *Community* toyed with it by waiting several episodes to have a blow-out and then—after Shirley pre-gamed by getting some tequila and renting *Van Wilder II: The Rise of Taj*—making it a humdrum Día de los Muertos party where the closest things get to *Animal House* is Pierce taking the wrong pill.

Later on the frequency of parties, dances, and other events at Greendale became a series standby. Those moments provided the show with an easy excuse to jam all the characters together in a chaotic mess where the Dean was generally done up in a Lady Gaga–worthy outfit. Serving as a trial run for that kind of format, this episode had a relatively small chaos quotient but delivered some top-notch character-defining outfits (but not for the

Dean, still at this point in the series primarily viewed as an antsy, insecure bureaucrat). Troy's Eddie Murphy *Delirious*–era tight red leather suit is memorable and Britta's squirrel costume defiant ("I hate when women use Halloween as an excuse to dress up like sluts," she tells Annie just before Annie reveals her skin-tight skeleton body suit). But the evening goes to Abed's Batman costume, complete with Christian Bale growl and moodily meandering patter (which in addition to nicely aping Christopher Nolan's portentousness also comprises the most recent pop reference at this point in the series). While everyone else is playing a part, Abed is the one who seems to feel completely at home.

The stories are all variations on insecurity. Jeff keeps flinging himself at Michelle Slater (Lauren Stamile), his sultry statistics professor who shoots him down but with just enough flirty insults to keep him coming to prove he's worthy of a grown-up relationship rather than being relegated to the study group's kiddie table. Meanwhile Annie is petrified nobody will come to her party without Jeff there, Britta is vexed by discovering Jeff's tight cowboy outfit gets her a little hot and bothered, Shirley takes out her anger over her ex-husband on Slater's car (even though Britta never admitted to liking Jeff), and Pierce strains for coolness by taking some acid from Star-Burns and nearly dies under a collapsing desk fort.

The slightly slicker look of this episode, with moodier night-time scenes and a mock-epic shot of Batman Abed hauling Jeff and Pierce to safety, comes courtesy of debut *Community* director Justin Lin, at the time in between shooting *Fast and Furious* movies. Not particularly known for comedy, Lin still proved a dab hand at knitting together the episode's fun cosplay and trope shuffling with the first dark blooming of the study group's deeply unhealthy Jeff dependency.

Episode 8: "Home Economics"

This episode is a bit of a backward step despite the halfway decent music numbers and deftly delivered '80s movie analogies (perhaps the only time Goldie Hawn's character from *Overboard* has been used to explain an existential crisis). This is another episode where whenever a story rears its head, nothing good follows. An entire B plot hinges on Annie pouring her unadmitted love for Troy into helping him out on his first date with another girl. At best this serves as a way for the show to finally cut the cord on that dramatically fallow non-relationship. But for the most part it results in Annie using her anime eyes to register deep sadness and Shirley looking frustrated at what Annie is putting herself through.

> ### Visiting Faculty
>
> "Home Economics" features the first guest appearance by Patton
> Oswalt, an alt-comedian whose nerd-centric material places him
> dead center in the *Community* fan base. Playing a nurse who treats
> Annie's supposed appendicitis (she faked it to ruin Troy's date),
> Oswalt jokes about her actually having herpes before explaining
> himself, "I'm kind of the Hawkeye around here." Unlike many of
> Harmon and the writing staff's other Gen-X TV references, this one
> is left unexplained, meaning millennial fans were stuck Googling
> "hawkeye joke." Nope, not Renner—keep scrolling.

The A story shows how Jeff has been knocked down one more peg
in life: sleeping in his car and dreaming of the luxurious condo his former
lawyer self could afford. This detours into an extended bout of delayed
freshman–itis when Jeff moves into Abed's dorm room. There he settles
into a life of cereal eating and sitcom watching. This is one of the first
instances of the show presenting TV as a kind of Zen ideal. Of course what
Abed appreciates as unfiltered serenity ("You can do whatever you want
. . . For me, it's Lucky Charms and TV") turns out to be a therapeutic
hideout for Jeff ("TV never abused and insulted me. Unless you count *Cop
Rock*") before morphing into sloth.

More might have been worth exploring with what Britta terms Jeff
"dorming it up" but instead the show brings back Britta's ex-boyfriend
Vaughn. He first uses his oddly '90s ska-ish band to deliver a breakup
song, "Getting Rid of Britta," before then repurposing it to get back at his
erstwhile band member Pierce, again over-staying his welcome. There's
some easy hippie humor here (Vaughn calling Britta "the exact opposite
of an antioxidant") along with just about the entire cast getting cut down
to size.

Episode 9: "Debate 109"
The episode that launched a thousand giddy fanfic videos, "Debate 109"
was a big leap forward for certain viewers by dodging around the already
backburnered Jeff-Britta romantic question mark and generating a new
possibility for intra-group hanky-panky with a spark being lit between
Jeff and Annie. The impetus for this is what would become a reliable

stakes-generator for the show: the Dean needs help showing that Greendale isn't just a school for losers and it turns out Jeff is the only one who can help.

This time Greendale is facing off in a debate contest with the snobs from rival school City College (Boo! Hiss!) and Annie needs a debate partner. Professor Whitman backs the Dean up, pleading with Jeff to give to the common good rather than spending the night "romancing your nether regions in front of the E! channel" (a pointed dig at the home network of McHale's show *Talk Soup*). Annie and Jeff's study session, where Jeff discovers Annie's sexuality after she pointedly lets her hair down and puts her décolletage at his eye level, is somewhat hackneyed but given an extra charge by the inappropriate age difference (Annie being nineteen and Jeff thirty-something). The debate itself—Jeff and Annie take the pro side on "Man is good"—is an early example of the show's knack for high-low comedic scenarios, mixing references to *Lord of the Flies* and the Stanford prison experiment with Jeff singing ELO's "Evil Woman" and a high-concept pratfall in which Jeremy (Aaron Himmelstein), City College's snooty, soul-patched debater, launches himself out of his wheelchair into Jeff's arms to make a point about humanity's inherent decency. Jeremy's gambit fails, because Annie pulls Jeff in for a kiss and causes Jeff to drop Jeremy; she then closes the debate with "He was horny, so he dropped him: Man is evil!"

But while that storyline motivated viewers who had been waiting for a new boundary-crossing sitcom romance ever since Jim and Pam finally got together on *The Office*, there were as usual richer and weirder possibilities in Abed's B story. Troy discovers Abed has been posting short videos for his film class that were not just barely fictionalized versions of the study group's real interactions but eerily prescient, filming dialogue scenes that would be unknowingly repeated by the real people weeks later. Though this panics the deeply Christian Shirley ("He's a witch!"), Abed explains that because he's simply a student of human behavior, he can generally predict what people will do or say. It's a relatively short sequence overall but one of the first season's most fascinating (particularly as setup for the inside-out end tag where Troy and Abed film the people who played them in Abed's films, only this time they're recreating the "Biblioteca" rap from the second episode, and failing miserably per Troy's diva director tantrum). Abed shows again that his spectrum-ish behavior does not make him blind to how people interact and also that his media mania—specifically the ways that his beloved sitcoms sort and explain behavior and character—does not distance him from humanity but in some ways makes him closer to it than other supposedly more normative people.

Episode 10: "Environmental Science"

As cross-network promotions went, NBC's 2009 Green Week (the network's long-running environmental promotion campaign) could have been worse. On *30 Rock*, Al Gore played himself. *The Office* had Dwight channel his inner cosplayer to create a PSA monster named Recyclops. On *Community*, the Dean stepped in it not once but twice: temporarily changing the school's name to "Enviro-Dale" and printing up thousands of likely unrecyclable posters—even though (as Star-Burns points out) the school's name already has *green* in it—and announcing a free concert by Green Day only to discover the band he booked turns out to be the septuagenarian Celtic rockers Greene Daeye.

Jeff's selfishness is again center stage as the study group enlists his dark powers to stop an increasingly punitive Chang from assigning extra work but Jeff ends up just getting himself a pass. That story is primarily an introduction to the inner world of Chang, presented here in its early stages of mental collapse. Talking with Jeff in his office—whose dark-wood, overwrought Mexican-ness looks like the den of a hacienda as decorated for a studio film from the 1950s—Chang reveals that his harshness is due to marital problems. Though Jeff solves those with the deft manipulation skills of a born liar, Chang's progression toward deeper volatility is set.

We are also given a glimpse of the Dean's future when he is shown watching Alex Kovas's briefly Internet-infamous YouTube video of him dancing suggestively in a skintight Dalmatian suit. The Dean murmurs to himself, "This better not awaken anything in me" even though he will end up succumbing to that fetish in just three more episodes.

The depth of forward planning in these scenes suggests the writers had in mind a longer arc for these characters than just getting to the next week's Very Special Episode.

The same cannot be said of the other subplots, both self-contained stories about facing fears. Shirley, who hates public speaking, gets advice from Pierce on her class presentation (basically Napster for brownies). Troy confronts his paralyzing fear of rats when he has to help Abed hunt down one of the creatures for their biology class experiment. The comedy is limited but it does underscore Troy and Abed's winsome adorability through their duet of "Somewhere Out There" (because of course Abed named the rat Fievel in homage to *An American Tail*).

Though none of the stories by themselves are especially engaging, director Seth Gordon (mostly known then for the 2007 arcade game documentary *The King of Kong: A Fistful of Quarters*) brings them all together in the kind of cross-cutting concluding montage that shows like *Modern Family* were already making something of a cliché.

Episode 11: "The Politics of Human Sexuality"

People start realizing some of their limits in one of the show's first episodes to feature honest-to-goodness sitcom hijinks.

Troy's competitiveness is triggered by discovering that Abed is not just a geek but also preternaturally athletic ("stick to quoting movie lines!" Troy shouts in frustration). This starts a series of contests in which Abed beats Troy without breaking a sweat—including a slo-mo arm wrestling homage to *Over the Top* that Abed nods to by putting on a backward baseball cap and adopting a Stallone-ish lip curl. Troy concedes defeat, letting Abed save the day by racing to the Dean's office to tell everyone not to use the school-issued free condoms because they have holes in them, though the punch line is he ends up just announcing that people should avoid condoms.

Annie starts the episode in her sweet spot: organizing an event (with all the perkiness of a sorority girl shopping for kittens) and overlooking its name: STD Fest '09. She's thrown off, though, by the Dean's request that she be the one to demonstrate putting a condom on an anatomically correct penis. To help Annie get over her anxiety about doing it right (her one sexual experience being with a guy who turned out to be gay), Britta and Shirley help her try and break into the Dean's office where the model is kept. While inexcusably manufactured, the escapade does lead to the episode's best line, courtesy of security guard Cackowski (Craig Cackowski, one of the many WorkJuice Players from *Thrilling Adventure Hour* like Paget Brewster and Paul F. Tompkins who ended up at Greendale), who discovers the women peeking through a keyhole at the penis and shouts, "What in the reverse *Porky's* is going on here?"

While these hijinks are unfolding, Pierce has shamed Jeff into double dating at the STD Fest after implying Jeff couldn't get a date on short notice. Mirroring Troy's desperation to stay on top, Jeff wrangles a date with the Dean's bubble-headed assistant Sabrina (Sara Erikson), only to be shamed by Pierce's date who's actually an escort named Doreen (Sharon Lawrence): "Sabrina's cute, but she thinks Monty Python is the evil snake from *Harry Potter*." Though Jeff insists he prefers simple over complicated, he will spend many of the episodes that follow proving what a transparent lie that is.

Episode 12: "Comparative Religion"

Sweet but also lightly subversive, this feels like the episode where Harmon and crew finally figured out how to truly bring the characters together. All the writers had to do was follow the same principle that autocratic rulers have used throughout the ages: create an external threat and watch the study group rally against it.

Before that unifying showdown can happen, though, internal strife ripples through the group as Shirley (whose hyper-religiosity grows increasingly obvious this episode) tries to guilt them all into coming to her Christmas party. A quick once-around-the-table reveals not just each character's faith or lack thereof but also a willingness on the part of the show itself to joke lightly through some fraught territory.

When Abed, a Muslim, says "Assalamu alaikum" to Troy, a Jehovah's Witness, he hears back the kind of nonsense phrase a teenager whose closest experience of Arabic was *Aladdin* would respond: "Shama lama ding dong." Declaring that he's a "Level 5 Laser Lotus" in a "Buddhist community," Pierce is informed he's probably not a Buddhist but almost definitely in a cult. Annie, who tells a disappointed Shirley that she's Jewish, holds a baby Jesus doll and says *sotto voce*, "We know you were one of us."

The only real group criticism, though, is directed at Jeff, who—after Britta identifies as an atheist—says he's an agnostic, leading to boos and Pierce calling that being a "lazy man's atheist." (Later, Jeff is given the chance to explain himself and does so quite astutely: "To me, religion is like Paul Rudd: I see the appeal and would never take it away from anyone, but I would also never stand in line for it.") Jeff's refusal to pick a stance is an echo of the episode's opener where the Dean—dressed in a vaguely wizard-ish wintry costume, the first of many increasingly baroque outfits he will sport during the show's run—pretzels himself into absurd contortions to avoid potentially endorsing a religion (calling himself "non-denominational Mr. Winter").

Meanwhile, the primary plot conflict hinges on Jeff having agreed to fight Mike (Anthony Michael Hall), a flagrantly mustached bully who's been picking on Abed. The resulting cross-genre dramatic confrontation couldn't excite Abed more: "It was like *My Bodyguard*, but I was the kid from *Meatballs*, Jeff was from *Full Metal Jacket*, and the mustache guy was the brother of the guy from *Entourage*." Troy and Pierce pitch in to help

Jeff train while Britta snipes from the sidelines about all the repressed homoerotic tension. Hall's performance as a vein-popping, overcompensating mental case seemingly always on his way to or from a gym where sleeves are not allowed and who staples cookies to his forehead to make a point, helps bring elements of dangerous crazy to a show in which psychological ailments have not yet become quite as ubiquitous.

Episode 13: "Investigative Journalism"

One of the first season's imaginative peaks, "Investigative Journalism" is packed with enough comedy and commentary over its twenty-one minutes that a moment of beautiful insanity that otherwise would have been the episode highlight—Chang fakes his own death only to storm back into Spanish 102, announce, "I am a man who can never die," pretend to eat Annie's brains, and leave again while playing his personal battle rap: "I am Señor Chang / And I'm so ill / This is a warning / I can't be killed"—doesn't even rate a mention in some summaries though the second iteration in the long-payoff, sub rosa, furry subplot in which the Dean opens his package with a full-size Dalmatian outfit generally does.

Breaking the sitcom rule about the passage of time—which states that special events (holidays, weddings, a bottle episode where the gang gets snowed in at a cabin) can be acknowledged but otherwise time only moves forward with never a glance back—the episode starts with the study group joyfully reuniting after winter break. The reveal, that the group has been infiltrated by an irritatingly eager new aspirant Buddy (Jack Black), is a complex development, reflecting their newfound giddiness at having created this family. But the flipside is immediately apparent in their discomfort with expanding membership, the price of pride and cohesion being exclusion and elitism.

While Buddy desperately ingratiates himself with the group through songs and jokes, as well as illustrations of his gymnastic prowess ("Your group needs a chubby, agile guy") that leave Jeff with a bloody nose, the group's putative leader strains to maintain his fragile cool. Having accepted his status as a community college student, Jeff happily accepts the Dean's offer to run the school newspaper and declares his new job to be "hanging out, having fun, and cracking wise." Spotting Jeff as the school's Hawkeye figure and figuring he needs a Radar O'Reilly, Abed jumps into *M*A*S*H* mode, even building Jeff a distillery for martini manufacturing in his new office.

Though the running *M*A*S*H* gag is spectacularly well-executed on its own—even giving Abed a beautifully crafted and fully sincere soliloquy

("Hawkeye didn't just bed nurses and drink martinis. He also had blood sprayed on his face and barked orders when the choppers came in . . . He was a leader")—the parallel commentary on how sitcoms reboot and recast based on audience feedback (then coming in more fast and furious due to the show's heat on Twitter) and network notes crackles as well. Bringing in a star like Black and using flashbacks to make it look like he was present in previous episodes plays with the notion of stunt casting as well as clip montage episodes. The concluding gag, where Buddy runs off after discovering that the real "cool group" (which includes Star-Burns, a way-too-stylish-for-Greendale club girl, and Owen Wilson) has accepted him, serves both as precursor to the many episodes where the study group's unity turns to arrogance and a joke about the levels of celebrity and popularity.

This is the first episode where *Community* widens its meta-narrative of TV about TV beyond Abed's imagination. The whole school is now part of the show within a show. When Annie says, "This is Greendale, Jeff, we can do whatever we want," it's the sign of a show starting to discover how potentially boundless the possibilities are.

Episode 14: "Interpretive Dance"

A bundle of romantic misdirects maintains this lightly plotted episode in which the biggest dramatic moment is Troy ripping off his trousers to help Britta through a rough patch in her modern dance recital. Her freezing up has nothing to do with stage fright but rather her spotting Jeff in the audience holding hands with Professor Slater, his now openly acknowledged girlfriend whom Britta insists she does not care about.

This wrinkle in which Troy recognizes the downsides of keeping his dancing skills secret in order to protect his straight dudeness ("I *am* spending a lot of money on breakaway clothing") does not lead to much; the show quickly discards his supposed continuing career as community college quarterback. The development mostly serves to signal that Shirley has actually been right all along about Britta's deeply buried feelings for Jeff. It also establishes the scene where Britta, responding to Shirley's frustration "as a divorced black housewife" about jaded white slackers she calls "you people," says, "What do you mean, *you people*?" and adds in happy wonderment, "I *cannot believe* I got to say that." Which might be one of the sharper barbs ever aimed at some people's deep desire to feel part of an excluded minority.

Inspector Spacetime

"Interpretive Dance" inaugurated *Community*'s love of using Jim Belushi as the standard of all things "meh." In a tête-à-tête with Slater, Jeff argues that truth (as in the truth of his getting claustrophobic in relationships) doesn't have to be original: "Truth is ketchup. It's Jim Belushi. Its job isn't to blow our minds. It's to be within reach." To which Slater (who in an earlier episode noted she had graded enough of Jeff's papers not to be intellectually cowed by him) retorts that just acknowledging a relationship is utterly unremarkable: "It's the Jim Belushi of sexual commitments. It barely means anything and it grows on what's there over time." In case the point is missed, Jeff then mutters, "Boy, that guy's really taking a pounding in this conversation." Though using the Other Belushi this way predated this episode (Conan O'Brien earlier referred to Raul Castro as "the Jim Belushi of Central America"), *Community* helped cement it as an evergreen stand-in for the inexplicable success of monumental mediocrity.

Episode 15: "Romantic Expressionism"

Just over halfway through the first season and already *Community* is highlighting the potential for incestuous claustrophobia in the group. After Annie shows an interest in Britta's ex, Vaughn—the shirtless, shoeless, guitar-strumming quad-lurker Jeff calls "micro-nipples"—Jeff and Britta try to sabotage the flirtation, claiming pure motives. Jeff declares the two of them are Annie's "Greendale parents" and argues they are keeping her safe from other campus dirtbags like Star-Burns. After the two try to romantically redirect Annie toward Troy, the scheme blows up and a round of accusations ripples across the study group table. Annie and Jeff burst each other's bubble by claiming the debate kiss was just for show, Pierce discovers his (likely filthy and at least slightly racist) emails to Shirley are marked as spam, and Shirley deflects the claim she leers at Jeff when he wears tight jeans by pointing to "Abed and Troy's weird little relationship" (to which the pair responds by reaching out to each other and saying simultaneously, "They're just jealous"). In an extended montage following Jeff pointing out that since they are not an actual family, technically everyone is a potential sexual prospect, each study group member looks at the other silently, pondering the possibilities.

While the A story ends sweetly after Vaughn performs a romantic song that surprisingly does *not* sound like "Getting Rid of Britta," the B story feels like a dispatch straight from a late-night session in the writers' room after a Troma movie marathon and too many war stories about bad improv partners. Troy and Abed have people over to watch *Kickpuncher*, a post-apocalyptic cyborg action flick (glimpses of which are made to look like something straight out of the late 1980s–early '90s straight-to-video bin). They grudgingly include Pierce, who doesn't understand the *Mystery Science Theater 3000*–type jokes everyone is making. Pierce hires Greendale's improv comedy troupe—actually Derrick Comedy, the troupe Donald Glover was in while at NYU just a few years earlier—to write gags for *Kickpuncher 2* at the next movie night so he can win a contest nobody wants to have.

The stories knit together in the end tag when Troy and Abed shoot their own version of *Kickpuncher* while wearing tinfoil cyborg suits. In the last shot, Abed is wearing a wig and skirt. Troy steps out of character to ask, "You're sure Britta couldn't do your part?" He then sighs and resignedly agrees. "Let's go film the sex scene."

Cool Cool Cool

One of the more momentous quips in "Romantic Expressionism" comes when Jeff reacts overly aggressively to a complaint by a certain adult scholar: "Shut up, Leonard! Nobody even knows what you're talking about." This becomes a running gag throughout the series. So much so that the writers regularly come up with alternate jokes to play with. Andy Bobrow later posted some great unused "Shut up, Leonard!" tags, including:

- "No one cares what you think ducks are thinking."
- "Methinks you overuse the word 'methinks.'"
- "You're not even that good at yo-yo."
- "Your movie reviews are pointless; we all know *Gone With the Wind* was good."
- "Filming your neighbor rolling through stop signs is not interesting."

Episode 16: "Communication Studies"

The continued existence of an interloping romantic interest becomes more of a nuisance to the study group's dynamic in this Valentine's Day episode where Jeff and Professor Slater's suspiciously easygoing relationship hits a snag. After Britta paints the town red when an old friend from her "anarchist days" stops by, she drunk-dials Jeff, leaving her mortally embarrassed. Abed instantly identifies a sitcom trope, telling Jeff, "You shifted the balance of power, like in a sitcom where one character sees another character naked." By Abed's TV logic, this necessitates Jeff calling Britta to make an ass of himself and so restoring the study group's delicate balance of emotions and status—a quest that Harmon and company would spend the remainder of the show's run tweaking.

Since Jeff can't do the drunk dial on command with Abed eagerly watching ("I can't feel things with you studying me like a beige praying mantis!"), Abed, ever the good director ("Scorsese drank with De Niro"), gets the two of them rip-roaring drunk. They ultimately succeed, and in the process boogie the night away in a dance montage set to "We Are Not Alone" (the season's second *The Breakfast Club* reference).

The B plot follows Troy and Pierce being punished by Chang for a prank actually pulled by Annie and Shirley. Though this is primarily an excuse to put the two men in women's clothing at the Valentine's Day dance, the setup is worth it: Chang killing it on the dance floor in his *El Tigre Chino* jacket and Troy crying while twerking in a Hillary Clinton–esque pant suit makes for a brand of humor that is already far more confident about the unique strangeness of its characters than anything most sitcoms would dare in their inaugural season.

Inspector Spacetime

In "Communication Studies," an off-handedly catty comment about Britta's name by Professor Slater ("What's the blonde's name? Bitter . . . butter . . . Beetlejuice?") sets up the first of the *Beetlejuice* call-outs that will finally get a payoff . . . two seasons later.

Episode 17: "Physical Education"

The study group hierarchy tacitly in place through most of the season up to this point gets overturned in this convulsive episode. Jeff and Britta's putative coolness is knocked down several dozen pegs. Also, in a fairly remarkable turnaround that upends the pitying condescension of so many fictional representations of neurologically diverse characters, everybody figures out they really should not be seeing Abed as some charity case.

Somewhat unusually for the first season, the B story is not a throwaway comedy subplot. Its existence here is certainly primarily meant as a setup for the visual gag. Jeff takes a billiards class looking for an easy grade and an excuse to strut around a pool table in tight black hipster togs. But he is shamed into wearing the regulation phys-ed shirt and skimpy shorts by gravel-voiced Coach Bogner (Blake Clark), who seems designed to maximize any PTSD flashbacks viewers may have due to gym class memories. The two men face off in a billiards showdown set to Warren Zevon's "Werewolves of London," which along with Jeff's show pony moves is meant to evoke *The Color of Money*—at least until the moment underwear-clad Jeff and Bogner rip off their skivvies and embrace, Jeff claiming now to know that appearance does not matter.

Cool Cool Cool

One of the denser cultural references to unpack in "Physical Education" comes when Abed realizes the group is trying to *"Can't Buy Me Love me,"* meaning a "geek to chic" makeover à la the 1987 Patrick Dempsey teen classic. Initially confused, Troy realizes, *"Oh,* he wants us to *Love Don't Cost a Thing* him," referring to the 2003 Nick Cannon version aimed at black moviegoers, but he explains it backward to Shirley: *"Can't Buy Me Love* was the remake for white audiences." Not only is this a circuitously complex back-and-forth that depends on a rare depth of cinematic rom-com knowledge—Pierce speaks for some of the audience when he says in another attempt at face-saving, "Sure glad they are no old people here, this conversation would probably be total gibberish to them"—but it represents what a rarity *Community* was in network TV at the time by having two black cast members when the unwritten rule had always been There Can Be Only One.

In fact, Jeff already knew that. In the A story, the study group had been obsessing over finding Abed a girlfriend. After identifying a student they think was drawing romantic doodles of Abed in one of their Spanish textbooks, the group tries to convince Abed to ask her out, the very loud subtext being they think he is so limited he should jump at the first woman to look his direction. Fileting their condescension without rancor, Abed lets the group know he's fine in that department—"Lots of girls like me because, let's face it, I'm pretty adorable . . . I'm more used to them approaching me"—and explains he was okay with everyone trying to help him because he had enough self-esteem not to really care.

But while Abed and Jeff are coming to terms with things, Britta inaugurates the start of her being the group's punch line when she tries to defend pronouncing *bagel* as *bah-gul*, looking confused, hurt, and lost every time they erupt in laughter or when Chang groans, "You're the worst." Though Jeff maintains a certain degree of stature even after the underwear scene, what was left of Britta's cool remove has evaporated.

Episode 18: "Basic Genealogy"

A feel-good entry that misses more opportunities than it picks up though it does lean into the creepy: a brief spotting of the Greendale Human Being with another smaller and even more bloodcurdling Human Being seems certain to have inspired a few nightmares as does Chang's non sequitur revelation that he devoured his twin "in utero."

Just as "Romantic Expressionism" established the *Community* special event fallback (when in doubt, have the Dean throw a bash in the cafeteria so the characters can organically mingle somewhere outside the library), "Basic Genealogy" cements the "Pierce is a jackass, but he's *our* jackass" trope that would become somewhat repetitive later on. After being unceremoniously dumped by Slater, Jeff rebounds by sleeping with Pierce's stepdaughter Amber (*American Idol* star Katharine McPhee) but has a pang of conscience when he discovers she's grifting the stepfather she despises for ditching her mother. Much like a person who fears commitment, *Community* continually tests the audience by making Pierce increasingly despicable (here an involved Pictionary routine hinges on his drawing a swastika as a clue for windmill) to push viewers away only to then insist on their seeing his humanity no matter how deeply buried underneath racism, sexism, homophobia, and boomer ignorance.

The B story, wherein Abed's father and his burqa-wearing cousin Abra (Emily Ghamrawi) visit for Family Day along with Shirley's two sons, is gentle if unmemorable. Better is the subplot where Troy and Britta play a more extreme version of the dependable sitcom "How far do you want to take this?" arc. Refusing to believe Troy that his sour old Nana (Fran Bennett) is a mean disciplinarian, Britta lectures him about her "old school" charm only to end up letting Nana beat her with a switch to prove her point. "My mom told me there'd be white people that did this," Troy mutters in disbelief, "with pocket watches and coffee grinders and pretending to be into steamboats"—neatly skewering the early 2000s artisanal throwback craze that an aspirational hipster like Britta would very much have wanted to be a part of.

Episode 19: "Beginner Pottery"

Throughout *Community*, Jeff's insecurity in his position as Greendale's Alpha Dude is an evergreen trope that the writers cannot help themselves from falling back on. This is true even when coming just two episodes after Jeff supposedly found a new serenity in not caring what people thought of him ("Physical Education"). That confidence gets shredded the second Jeff, thinking he has found the ultimate blowoff class in beginner pottery ("This class is like a redhead who likes to drink scotch and watch *Die Hard*. I suggest you all get her number") lays his eyes on fellow pottery student Rich (Greg Cromer). Up to this point, Jeff has powered through life with an innate belief in his effortless awesomeness. But after spotting Rich not only mastering pottery on his first try but setting many female students a-flutter with his gentle aw-shucks-did-I-mention-I'm-a-doctor demeanor, Jeff decides the man is a phony who must be destroyed. This sends Jeff on a full-blown, red-thread, conspiracy jaunt, his frantic determination to reveal Rich as a ringer ultimately revealing nothing more than the porcelain fragility of his own ego.

Although Jeff's storyline is a sincere piece of character development, the episode is still riddled with media commentary: Lee Majors's cameo as the teacher of the B story's absurd sailing class (given Greendale's Colorado location, it's held on a sailboat in the parking lot); Abed being admonished by Jeff for doing a voiceover, which Abed admits "is kind of a crutch," which feels like a jab at a sitcom convention; and the pottery class professor (Tony Hale, whose *Arrested Development* frequently relied on voiceover) declaring his "zero tolerance policy" for anybody recreating the pottery scene from the movie *Ghost*.

The episode's cultural commentary capstone, though, is the final scene. The camera closes up on Rich making a pot while the voice of his mother

> ### Cool Cool Cool
>
> Jeff taking beginner pottery was somewhat preordained. Earlier in the "Football, Feminism, and You" episode, Troy suggests to Jeff that he should be more accepting of just being himself: "Take a pottery class or something."

echoes in his mind, her cutting denunciations of his dead brother ("It was supposed to be *you*, Richard!") mirroring the slow transformation of his face into a smirk of mad villainy that echoes the end of *Psycho*. It's an eerie kind of Easter egg that hints at the dark secrets the writers were seeding throughout Greendale, just waiting for them to bloom.

Episode 20: "The Science of Illusion"

By this point in *Community*, Jeff's position as the pivotal lead, Abed's as the key sidekick and wisenheimer, and Pierce's as the irritant are well fixed but the parameters of other ensemble members are less defined. "The Science of Illusion" solidifies the role that many of the others will hold to one degree or another through the rest of the series.

Upset that the study group thinks her a "buzzkill," Britta tries to pull an April Fool's prank but ends up killing a frog, dumping a cadaver out the biology room window onto the quad, and putting the whole Spanish class under suspicion. After she confesses and tearfully admits to her fundamental Britta-ness (what Troy calls her being a "fun-vampire" and Abed in an earlier episode referred to as "her Jodie Foster severity"), even Jeff's attempt at consolation nods at the uncomfortable position she will hold in the group: "You're like the dark cloud that unites us."

Instead of using the April Fool's hook for a hijinks-laden B story, we are instead given Annie and Shirley in a self-consciously gimmicky scenario in which they are deputized for forty-eight hours as campus security to solve the Britta case. Tired of being overlooked (Annie as the goody two-shoes and Shirley as the Christian housewife) and manipulated by Abed's desire to turn the whole escapade into a cop buddy movie, they both vie for the role of "bad ass." Following a disastrous, low-speed chase in which Annie and Shirley roll through campus on their security golf cart while an eager-eyed Abed sits in the back eating chocolate-covered raisins like he's at a movie (later, annoyed that the Dean is not playing enough to type, Abed shows his ability to move from critic to director by yelling at the women in the style of a clichéd black police chief, "Agitatin' my sciatica . . . I'm too old for this!"), they end up realizing that they are likely meant to be decent, quasi-wallflower characters after all.

Elsewhere, Pierce's delusional cult membership is mocked; Leonard's future as senior delinquent (expanded on in Season 2's "Messianic Myths and Ancient People") is foreshadowed when he scrawls graffiti in the school office: "Dean Pelton Sucks"; and in the end tag, Troy and Abed inaugurate their imaginary morning talk show with the catchy jingle *Troy and Abed in the Morning!*, digging further into their role as the show's meta-goofballs who are often so deep inside their imaginary universes that they can barely see the real world.

From this point forward, *Community* shows not just a similarly limited view of the non-Greendale world but even less interest in acknowledging its existence.

Episode 21: "Contemporary American Poultry"

A sign of a great homage is not its fidelity to the source material or ability to make the audience impressed with itself for noticing callouts but instead whether it can evoke a similar mood or effect as the original even when using the source in a wholly different way. That is mostly why this episode succeeds so beautifully. Yes, the reinvention of numerous moments from Scorsese and Coppola films are spot-on not just in cinematic but comedic terms. But they work because they recreate those films' fascination with a secret subculture, power dynamics, the mechanics and delicate ecosystem of corruption, and the rise and fall of an outlaw band that also functions as a kind of family.

Of course, the episode is also fundamentally about the appeal of chicken fingers.

Like most students and prisoners, the study group is obsessed with what's offered in the cafeteria, where the only thing worth eating is the chicken fingers. Problem is, everyone thinks that and so the cafeteria always runs out. Discovering that Star-Burns is running the deep fryer and skimming fingers to give to his friends, the group cooks up a scheme to get Star-Burns fired and install Abed (with his falafel restaurant expertise) as fry cook, after which they can control the supply. After a freeze-frame on Abed accompanied by his Henry Hill–style voiceover ("As far back as I can remember, I always wanted to be in a Mafia movie"), the episode becomes a mishmash of *Goodfellas* and *Casino* that throws in nods to *The*

Godfather and *Heat*. The study group is reframed as a criminal cartel almost instantly drunk with the power given by their chicken-finger access and soon fall prey to their own success.

The Scorsese stylistic imitation is well-crafted and buzzy with long Steadicam takes over a Golden Oldies soundtrack and Abed's narrative explaining the give-and-take system of chicken fingers for favors and friendship: "It was a beautiful time . . . to us, lines were for suckers." Soon the library is filled with hangers-on, from Troy's pet monkey (which he's named Annie's Boobs) to what Jeff refers to in annoyance as Pierce's "hackneyed entourage" of new buddies ("Hackneyed?" Pierce asks, "You see the turban guy?"). When the fall comes, it is scored as it should be, to Derek and the Dominos' "Layla" only without mafioso corpses turning up all over Greendale.

But while the Scorseseian montages hit all the right notes, the episode stands out for a wholly different film reference. Two heart-to-hearts between Jeff and Abed clarify both their bond (possibly the closest in the group) and their tendency to manipulate the group. Jeff does this out of habit and ego (a running gag in this episode is the waning and waxing effectiveness of his shushing hand gesture, first seen in "Investigative Journalism," where he used it to cut off conversation mid-sentence with

Streets Ahead

In "Contemporary American Poultry," Pierce is admonished by Jeff for "trying to coin the phrase 'streets ahead'" by awkwardly jamming the nonsense phrase into the study group's conversations. Similarly to how Harmon's pet peeves made it into the show (e.g., his animus toward *Glee*, a frequent target of out-of-nowhere gags and even one whole storyline), this joke started with a fight: after a Twitter user mocked Harmon for *Community* having placed behind two higher-rated shows in a March Madness–style bracket on Hulu ("both *Modern Family* and *Glee* are streets ahead of your meta bullshit"), Harmon spent months mocking the usage of "streets ahead" and vowed to work it into an episode. It must be noted, though, that since "streets ahead" is actual British slang (meaning "greatly superior," per *The Oxford Dictionary of English Idioms*), it feels less like a Pierce-ism than like something Britta would use incorrectly in a showoff move only to then be embarrassingly corrected by Professor Duncan.

an eerie power). Abed manipulates more as a director since that is his way to understand and connect with people: through the common language of media. Jeff offers a deal: if Abed shuts down the chicken finger ring, Jeff will help Abed connect with people and Abed can also help Jeff be a better person.

Abed just has two requests. The first is one of his only frank admissions of vulnerability (albeit still filtered through a TV screen): "Please don't do a Special Episode about me." The second is more on-point: he and Jeff eat a last plate of chicken fingers while sitting at a candlelit table à la *Sixteen Candles*. Like the original, the moment is sweet, unexpected, and does not overstay its welcome.

Episode 22: "The Art of Discourse"

On the surface there's a lot going on in this joke-packed episode (Chang stealing cookies from Girl Scouts, Britta knitting a tiny eye patch for a new rescue cat) that gets most of its humor from purposefully sophomoric gags that both indulge in and comment on their childishness. In the B story, three high school kids taking college credit classes at Greendale start mocking Jeff and Britta as thirtysomething losers. This sends the pair into an insecurity spiral that leads to Jeff trying to sleep with one of the kids' mothers in revenge and ends with all five in an epic cafeteria standoff trying to see who can shout "Duh!" longest and loudest. The simplicity of its concept—trying to win a contest of wits with adolescents is an exercise in futility—is why it succeeds.

But really, the episode is a referendum on Pierce.

The setup is provided by Abed, already back to parsing reality via TV and movies despite Jeff's agreement from the previous episode to stop him from doing just that . . . which may have to do with this episode being shot out of order. Having decided that a successful first year of college requires notching off college movie tropes ("Bond with a group of loveable misfits? Check"), Abed smashes Pierce's guitar; notes he's already made out with the "hottest girl" on campus (causing Annie and Britta to exchange confused looks as neither has kissed Abed and both clearly imagine themselves the hottest); and pantses Troy. Eager to join in, Pierce pantses Shirley. After an enraged Shirley says it's him or her, Pierce is booted from the group. Even after further proving his racist bona fides (mistaking another black woman for Shirley when he grudgingly tries to apologize), he is eventually allowed back in.

Although by this point the study group have only been acquainted for a few months through school, their family dynamic is well enough established that the desire to keep Pierce ultimately outweighs any of his transgressions. He is essentially the racist, homophobic uncle or grandfather who people do their best to work around but do not feel they can cut out of their lives. This need of the group to keep banding together against threats (real or perceived) feels like another nod to the limited relationships each has in the non-Greendale world. It is also presented as a survival decision: Pierce's departure removes an easy target for everyone's complaints, causing them to turn on each other. It's only Abed's realization that "it's only a matter of time before one of us becomes the new Pierce" that convinces them to welcome the pathological grump back into their midst.

Fortunately the episode ends on a higher note with Abed's college-movie-trope quest leading to hijinks that include a car wash, a robot they call Boob-a-Tron 4000, and a cafeteria cream pie fight that ends in an *Animal House* freeze-frame montage promising Troy and Abed's return in a fake sequel (*College Cut-Ups 2: Panty Raid Academy*) and scored to a purposefully generic theme song ("Party Where Your Heart Is") that feels like it deserves inclusion on a *National Lampoon Presents: Rockin' Party Tracks!* CD.

Episode 23: "Modern Warfare"

The art of the concept episode is a delicate one. Veer too far from the show's roots and fans will be alienated. Step out with a big idea but fail to make it worth people's time, and fans will be disappointed. "Modern Warfare" navigates those risks adroitly, putting the study group into a strange new environment that bends the sitcom genre's structural parameters while still incorporating a running subplot that threads it into the rest of the season without marooning the episode.

What makes "Modern Warfare" stand out from other frequently cited concept episodes—*The Simpsons*' arthouse "22 Short Films about Springfield"; *Seinfeld*'s backward "The Betrayal"; *Buffy the Vampire Slayer*'s musical "Once More, with Feeling"—is that Harmon and crew didn't wait until they were comfortably into syndication territory to take a conceptual flyer; they shot the moon in their first season. Ironically, the potentially riskiest episode was also the one that truly cemented *Community*'s status as the Sitcom to Watch and set off a brushfire of thrilled social media commentary.

This was the episode *Community* and its fans had been waiting for even if they did not know it.

The setup is part of a multi-pronged joke that draws most of its energy from a densely packed homage to zombie, action, and war films. Much as a disaster film has to engineer a specific catastrophe to meet its dramatic requirements, for "Modern Warfare," writer Emily Cutler has the Dean propose a game of paintball assassin. Once the campus realizes the prize is priority registration—a fantastical dream for any viewer who remembers days of one class at 8 a.m. and no other until early afternoon—that is all the excuse needed for the school to descend into anarchy. Jeff takes a nap in his car and wakes up to find the entire Greendale campus a post-apocalyptic, paint-spattered battleground prowled by students who have already formed feral gangs.

Unlike many high-concept TV episodes, "Modern Warfare" does not wall itself off from the rest of the show's narrative as a standalone odd-ity. The splintering of the student body into role-specific gangs expands the show's universe into broader Greendale while also leaving room for jokes at the expense of *Glee* and the chess club. Jeff and Britta's bickering, shown at the episode's start as finally getting on everyone's nerves (Abed has to inform them that despite their attractiveness, they are "no Ross and Rachel"), first feeds their over-the-top competitiveness before leading to them finally sleeping together.

Most of the episode's comedy comes not just from the absurdity of community college students instantly becoming action-flick avatars but the depth of their commitment to the very serious play they are engaged in (not to mention the extent of the Dean's laughable incompetence which afterward becomes a go-to for the show). Showing again his knack for balancing action and comedy, director Justin Lin gives the episode a high-gloss look that amplifies the pretend drama in exceedingly satisfying ways. Cutler's script stacks the references many layers deep. These range from the highly specific (*The Warriors*, *28 Days Later*, *Rambo II*, *Terminator 2*, *The Road Warrior*, *Die Hard*, *A Better Tomorrow*) to the broader (war film tropes).

Unsurprisingly, Abed takes to the pretend action like a pretend fish to pretend water, strapping on a bandolier and goggles (where did everyone get all this gear so quickly?) and leaping off a wall to plug Leonard before he can shoot a still-confused Jeff. The rest of the group, save the ever clue-less and untrustworthy Pierce, adjusts rapidly as well with Shirley showing unexpected levels of double handgun badassery.

"Modern Warfare" is a dangerous episode to watch if one does not have an extra week to catch up on all the movies it reminds you of. It

Ben Chang's "Modern Warfare" outfit, and his "El Tigre Chino" striped paintball assault rifle, achieved legendary status. AUTHOR'S COLLECTION.

rewards multiple viewings just as much as many of its inspirations. Also, it signals that from this time on, everything will be different. Not for nothing did Saul Austerlitz use this episode as the concluding chapter of his book *Sitcom: A History in 24 Episodes from* I Love Lucy *to* Community.

Cool Cool Cool

Chang's role as the reliably unreliable wild card is used to great effect in "Modern Warfare." As Greendale's resident paintball veteran ("I'm one of those douchebags that brings his own equipment"), he puts himself at the Dean's service to end the fighting. His scene—which starts with him in full slo-mo Chow Yun-Fat mode (à la John Woo's *A Better Tomorrow* films) blasting away with a paintball assault rifle and ends with him loudly cackling while setting off a suicide vest that floods the study group room with green paint—is one of the most unexpected, manic moments in modern sitcom history.

Episode 24: "English as a Second Language"

A lighthearted follow-up to the previous week's paintball gunplay, "English as a Second Language" puts forward a fairly ho-hum conundrum as a means to generate tension around the study group's longevity.

Chang confides in Jeff that his degree is also fake. If the school finds out it will invalidate everyone's work and imperil Jeff's four-year graduation schedule. Jeff's fixation on getting out of Greendale by not taking any nonessential classes also sparks controversy with Annie, who wants the group to take Spanish 103. Annie rats out Chang after her digital recorder picks up his confession, leading to a blow-up with the group when they realize this will hold them back (for once, Annie's fluttery Disney doe eyes don't get her out of trouble). Meanwhile Jeff and Britta are awkward around each other now as they try to act as though nothing happened between them.

While the A story resolves vividly but simply in an over-the-top Chang-Jeff confrontation involving a keytar and Tasers, the B story is subtler. A mock *Good Will Hunting* scenario reveals Troy's childlike demeanor as hiding unknown depths. But rather than turning out to be a genius mathematician, Troy is shown to be a natural-born plumber. Despite the insistence of a janitor (Jerry Minor) who tries to make Troy understand what a gift he has, Troy re-commits to Greendale in what appears to be one of his first clear steps into adulthood: "So I can think. And get a student loan. And grind my own coffee. And understand HBO."

Like "Modern Warfare" with its web of homages, this episode manages to mine cultural references for absurd humor while still playing it mostly straight. It also lays the foundation quite far in advance for the air conditioning repair school annex storyline in Season 3 and the forthcoming plumbing versus AC battle for Troy's soul.

Episode 25: "Pascal's Triangle Revisited"

Having already knocked out two episodes that each could have worked as finales (the action-packed blowout and the "Do we have to repeat Spanish?" nail-biter), Harmon and crew went for the trifecta with a kitchen-sink closer that combined prom night melodrama with "Who's he gonna pick?" romantic suspense. Also, the Dean is finally allowed to live out his the-less-everyone-knows-the-better Dalmatian fantasy, making him probably the only character who ends the season fully satisfied.

An opening walk-and-talk with Jeff and Annie provides a quick checklist of minor characters (Leonard, Professor Whitman, Vaughn). Abed throws an end-of-year kegger, which initially seems out of character for him but given the season's repeated emphasis on his not fitting some autistic stereotype makes sense. (Of course, Abed would know from movies that pre-summer term keggers are definitely a thing.)

Jeff runs into Professor Slater, who suggests that she might be reconsidering their breakup. In a fairly transparent move by the writers to ensure things end with a prom, the Dean announces there will be a formal dance for all the departing transfer students . . . so, obviously, they'll go ahead and call it the Tranny Dance. The build to the dance is a gut-check moment for Britta, who realizes after seeing Slater making a move on Jeff that she wants to make a play for him as well.

Both women hot themselves up at the dance in a sequence that verges disappointingly close to a catfight but takes an interesting turn when Britta drops all pretense at coolness and announces, "I love you!" to Jeff in front of the crowd. Awkward silence follows, punctuated by shouts of "Team Britta!" and "Team Slater!" which are possibly meant to mimic the more rabid aspects of the show's online fan behavior. In the chaos that erupts after Chang socks Duncan in the face with a roll of quarters (because,

---

Trope Talk

"Pascal's Triangle Revisited" features a few examples of deeply insider-y TV dialogue. In one, Troy gets angry at Abed, who doesn't want them to live together over the summer because he worries it will ruin their friendship. "If you and I move in, we jump the shark," he explains, using the then-common Internet shorthand for when a TV show loses its way. Troy's response is a deft interweaving of his adolescent taste and the writers' meme savviness: "For the record, there was an episode of *Happy Days* where a guy literally jumped over a shark." True. "And it was *the best one!*" Not true.

Later, in the Tranny Dance scene, when people are screaming out whom Jeff should pick, Star-Burns tosses in a "Bring Conan back!" shout. 2010 seems like a lifetime ago but when the episode aired, NBC was in the middle of a ludicrously high-drama fight between late-night hosts Conan O'Brien and Jay Leno. This led to O'Brien being kept off the air, fan protests, and sides being taken in the comedy community, sometimes quite visibly (Dino Stamatopolos had been a Conan writer for years).

well, *Chang*), Jeff slips outside without making a decision between Slater and Britta. In an honestly surprising wrinkle, after Jeff runs into Annie, who had earlier announced she was following Vaughn to Delaware but has apparently changed her mind; they pick up where the debate episode left off only this time with an uninterrupted make out session. While a more dramatic cliffhanger than seen in sitcoms at the time, it didn't exactly resolve the question Jeff asked Annie just before they kissed, "Do you try to evolve? Or do you try to know what you are?"

It's a question that *Community* would keep asking in one way or another for five more seasons.

Community 102–Season 2: 5
Blow It Up, Repeat

God forbid we ever make a normal episode.

—DAN HARMON

WHY DID NBC BRING *Community* back for another go in the 2010–2011 season? The inaugural season was not exactly a ratings bonanza. Sure, the critics were agog. But they often went bananas for any show that broke network television's rules, which almost never saved those shows from cancellation. Reviews don't deliver revenue. Perhaps the network suits believed that this time, instead of being a cult one-seasoner like *Freaks and Geeks*, *Firefly*, or *Police Squad! Community* would be a slow burner like *Seinfeld* and become one of the more off-kilter mainstays of their Thursday night Comedy Night Done Right lineup like *The Office* or *30 Rock*.

That did not happen.

Whenever a show like *Community* went up against tough mainstream competition—*Grey's Anatomy*, *The Big Bang Theory*, *American Idol*—to deliver big numbers, it generally needed to build a fanbase on recognizable components. (As rule-breaking as it frequently was, even *Seinfeld* stuck with a live studio audience, kept its main cast small, and delivered comic beats that were clear and tightly focused.) But when *Community* started its second season with Betty White drinking her own urine, it seemed clear that the network was going to have to settle for a limited, if rabid, audience.

There is some reason to believe that NBC thought sheer virality could carry the day. If Season 1 showed anything, it was that *Community* (through the power of "Modern Warfare" alone) could grab the attention of certain corners of Internet fandom with all the inexorable power of the Death Star's tractor beam.

Having escaped execution, *Community* launched into a never-expected Season 2 as though it too could be the show's final trench run. But in addition to their zeal for deconstructing the format, Harmon and his writers also wanted to serve the kind of devoted fans who had come to the show's first Comic-Con panel just a couple of months after the first season concluded (thus Season 2 would feature not one but *two* paintball episodes).

The result was tonally messy. That will happen with any 26-episode sitcom season with numerous main characters, an ever-growing roster of vivid supporting players, an expanding universe of pop-culture riffs, and increasingly complex running gags. Thus we have a space-themed bottle episode most memorable for its Colonel Sanders gags ("Basic Rocket Science") alongside two Abed-centric episodes—a multi-layered cineaste smorgasbord ("Critical Film Studies") and a holiday animation homage ("Abed's Uncontrollable Christmas")—that together constitute some of the more tragic character explorations ever seen on a sitcom.

With Season 2, *Community* was burrowing into its particular style of strange rather than digging its way out into the mainstream.

Episode 26: "Anthropology 101"

The season begins with a certain "Let's clean that mess up, shall we?" vibe. Having dropped a lot of unresolved Jeff-Britta-Annie mess into viewers' laps just before the summer break, *Community* brings its characters back for the fall semester with a clarifying montage showing each of the study group in their own bedroom waking up and getting ready for class.

First off is Abed, responding to the buzzing alarm by saying, "And we're back" with that mix of excitement and contentment he exhibits whenever in full TV recreation mode. We are then given a brief, illuminating glimpse into the other characters' lives via their bedrooms: Pierce has a smarmy self-portrait that looks very *Fletch*-era Chevy Chase; Annie sleeps in a cocoon of pink cuteness (possibly to hide the fact that she clearly lives in a crummy neighborhood); Shirley's bedroom wall is dominated by a massive cross; Britta's room is a chaotic mess adorned with a Pixies poster; and Troy's wall-mounted football jersey suggests that his ex-high-school-jock storyline is now a thing of the past.

What follows is a plot-packed episode that barely wastes a second. The gang re-convenes for another semester, tracking passed time in a way most sitcoms (where the characters tend to remain in a seasonless limbo until Halloween, Thanksgiving, or Christmas come around) would abjure. Having moved on from Señor (now student) Chang's Spanish class, they settle in to a semester of Anthropology 101. The writers had initially thought putting the group in this class would serve as a jumping-off point for multiple story angles though that never panned out.

This episode's classroom scenes do, however, let the show both undermine and celebrate a key sitcom convention. After Betty White arrives in class as the embodiment of the special guest star, the writers then use her to deliver gross-out humor ("More urine for me!") and unhinged violence (choking Jeff after one of his patented Winger speeches doesn't land and shooting a tranquilizer dart into one of Star-Burns's . . . starburns).

The gang is initially awkward together because of last semester's uncomfortable ending when Jeff ducked out of the Team Britta–Team Slater conflict. When Britta arrives on campus, she notices other female students gawking at her and assumes that she is again the butt of the joke. Meanwhile Dean Pelton handles exposition catch-up duty with his oversharing PA announcements. But when Britta discovers that her very big, very public, and very, very unrequited declaration of love for Jeff in the last episode actually inspired her female classmates, it doesn't take long for her to get high on her own surprise supply of fame.

The episode's conclusion is theoretically built around the reveal that Jeff and Annie kissed and the subsequent threat of group censure due to the couple's cringey age difference (which Annie catches herself playing into by almost referencing Seventeen when telling Jeff, "We didn't just kiss, we technically Frenched. I checked the make-out meter in this month's issue of . . . National Review").

But the real action is with Abed, who goes beyond just delivering a running commentary on their lives as a living TV show ("I'm just excited about the new year, hoping we can move away from the soapy relationship-y stuff and into bigger, faster, self-contained escapades"). Operating as a stand-in for both the "More Paintball!" fans and Harmon's drive to explore, dissect, and demolish the format, Abed buzzes around like a hyperactive media studies major looking for new directions the study group can take. Bored by the "I dare you" subplot in which Jeff and Britta play at being publicly in love, Abed asks Shirley if she would "spin off" with him: "We could open a hair salon together." His life-as-television references are further layered by winking commentary like Jeff asking, "Why are you mining my life for classic sitcom scenarios?" and Shirley's tentative "Abed, are you being . . . meta?"

After the group is grossed out by the revelation not just that Jeff and Annie kissed but that he and Britta had sex on the study room table, Jeff lashes out at Abed in a failed attempt at distraction. Following all the mudslinging, Abed again turns out to be wisest of the group. He explains to Jeff that he does know the difference between TV and real life: "TV makes sense. It has structure . . . and likeable leading men. In life we have this. We have you." It's a chilly turn of phrase that indicates the show's willingness to show the characters in a negative light.

Another precursor of future developments is a running social media gag that foreshadows the commentary of Season 5's "App Development and Condiments" episode (in which a new ratings app, MeowMeowBeenz, takes over Greendale). Troy secretly uses a Twitter account, @oldwhite-mansays, to post all the offensive things Pierce says. In a neat encapsulation of how social media warps perceptions, when Pierce makes a joke about his own penis, the whole table groans in disgust. Seconds later, after Troy posts the joke and they check their phones, they erupt in laughter after reading *the exact same joke* on Twitter.

The episode ends with a foreshadowing of Chang's insanity. Though Harmon apparently wanted the last scene to just be a zoom in on Chang's disturbed face when a baby's cry is heard (recalling the first season reveal that Chang ate his twin in utero), the network preferred the version we see with Chang doing a schizophrenic Gollum routine ("But they're my friends." "*I'm* your friend!").

In this case, the suits may have been right.

Meanwhile, Off Campus . . .

After Donald Glover's profile exploded due to his popularity in *Community*'s first season, a Twitter campaign kicked up to have him cast as Peter Parker. (An inspired choice, for what it's worth, and years before the Marvel machine would truly embrace its films' comic potential.) "Anthropology 101" nods to that by showing Troy wearing Spider-man pajamas during the opening sequence. Andrew Garfield ultimately starred in *The Amazing Spider-Man* (2012). Glover later cameoed in *Spider-Man: Homecoming* (2017). Also, Glover inspired Brian Michael Bendis to write the character of Miles Morales who took center stage in *Spider-Man: Into the Spider-Verse* (2018) in which Troy's pajamas scene appears briefly on a television screen.

> ### Cool Cool Cool
>
> Troy's Twitter account @oldwhitemansays ("If the Mexicans had their way, we'd be using fireworks for currency") was a direct jab at @shitmydadsays. This was likely the first, though probably not the last, Twitter account to spawn multiple books and a sitcom. In the 2010–2011 season, *$#*! My Dad Says* was a half-hour CBS sitcom (also on Thursday nights, like *Community*) that plugged the yawning "What do we watch now?" gap between *The Big Bang Theory* and *CSI*. For those who missed the *$#*!* blip, it was pretty much just William Shatner saying $#*! in front of a live studio audience.

Episode 27: "Accounting for Lawyers"

In this episode, Jeff is reaching his breaking point. The writers were still using his slumming at Greendale as the group's most dynamic character arc. What entices about Jeff's teeth-gnashing over being at community college is that he is the only member of the group who isn't happy to be there. The rest of them see it as a step up—or in Pierce's case, at least a place to hang out and pretend to be young again. But for Jeff, it's a daily reminder of how far he has fallen.

That longing for past glory is driven home when Jeff spies Alan (Rob Corddry), a friend from his old law firm, whom Abed excitedly identifies as a character from Jeff's "origin story," a sleazebag trust-fund kid who calls himself "Sundance" to Jeff's "Tango"—nicknames, as Jeff explains to Abed, picked up because "we worked with different partners" and that make perfect sense to him but will baffle any viewer who doesn't immediately think of *Tango and Cash* and *Butch Cassidy and the Sundance Kid*. Alan then gets Jeff fondly remembering everything he loved about his old life.

Worried that Jeff is high on Alan's amorality and upset that he calls their relationship "dysfunctional," the group does the only possible thing: prove their dysfunctionality by chasing Jeff down to his old firm's Christmas party. The study group's first off-campus outing is done ostensibly so they can prove that Alan was the one who cost Jeff his job. But really, they just want to ensure Jeff does not leave Greendale. Or them.

The party itself is, on one level, a predictable scenario with Jeff initially embarrassed by his goofball friends before being charmed by their clumsy enthusiasm. But it takes a couple of intensely odd turns. One is when Jeff's old boss Ted (Drew Carey) thanks his employees for not gawking at the "big, weird hole in my hand" before showing his appreciation to them by dropping an olive through his stigmata. The other occurs when Troy, Annie, and Abed (positively giddy when showing the others that he "brought stuff people use for capers") repeatedly chloroform a janitor who discovers them breaking into Alan's office in order to find an incriminating email. Weird stuff even for an office Christmas party.

Before Jeff follows the group back to Greendale (where Chang is desperately trying to solo win a group dance-off which they promised to team up with him on but have long forgotten about; it's a busy episode), the show pulls off one of its most revealing Jeff moments. Explaining to Ted why he got into the law, Jeff describes the Mercedes-driving lawyer who handled his parents' divorce as his platonic ideal of a man so cool and detached that the muck and mire of everyday life could not affect him.

But confronted with the truth of Alan's betrayal, rather than follow the example of cool detachment, Jeff goes right back to the muck and mire, returning to Greendale and doing the worm with Troy at the dance-off. For the old Jeff, this wouldn't be as good as a Mercedes, Gucci suits, and racks of single-malt Scotch, but for new-ish Jeff it seems perfectly adequate.

Fade-out on Chang once again laughing maniacally to himself, suggesting a far more dramatic build to villainy than actually transpires.

Episode 28: "The Psychology of Letting Go"

Two steps forward and a step-and-one-half back here. This episode feels a little closer to something that rounds out a sitcom in its fifth season when everybody is really starting to coast rather than a momentum builder in Season 2. At first, it makes sense they pushed this episode back one week to run the superior "Accounting for Lawyers" first—that is, until you look in the background.

The key story starts with a seeming tragedy: Troy, still living at Pierce's mansion, is traumatized after discovering his roommate's mother dead in the garage. But it quickly kicks into absurdity: Pierce, a committed "Reform Neo-Buddhist," serenely refuses to accept her death, believing her soul is residing in an "Energon pod" (clearly just a lava lamp). Jeff tries to rub mortality in Pierce's uncomprehending face. He does this ostensibly to help the old guy face reality. But the truth is that a high cholesterol reading has sent the health-obsessed Jeff into a mortality spiral. Jeff eventually relents and goes to get ice cream with Pierce and Troy, seen here taking what looks like his first step into adulthood.

> ### Visiting Faculty
>
> Jeff's fateful cholesterol reading is delivered by Nurse Jackie (Patton Oswalt, reprising his role from last season's "Home Economics"), who responds to Jeff's indignant "My body is a temple!" declaration with a philosophical aside that starts on the inevitability of bodily decay—"It's made of hamburger; this is a Temple of Doom!"—before weaving in a fate-haunted strand of pop culture commentary: "All good things, be they people or movie franchises, eventually collapse into sagging, sloppy, rotten piles of hard-to-follow nonsense."

Unnecessarily calling back to the Britta-Annie rivalry from the end of Season 1, the episode has them engaged in a contrived fight over who can raise the most money for an oil spill. Britta calls out Annie for her "sexy schoolgirl routine" and in a very having-Harmon's-cake-and-eating-it-too moment, they wrestle covered in oil.

Despite that brief slide into hackiness, the episode redeems itself with the sub-sub-plot in the background. All throughout, sharp-eyed nerds can see what looks like a soap-y melodrama in which Abed coos over a woman's pregnant belly, fights with her jealous boyfriend or husband, and ultimately helps deliver the baby in the back seat of a car, all without a line of dialogue or single shot in focus. Between that, Duncan taking time out from teaching Anthropology 101 ("And I thought psychology was a racket") to enforce his restraining order against Chang, and the end tag—Betty White's now-suspended anthropology professor explaining the plot of *Inception* to a couple of tribesmen—the episode feels more notable for its sideline moments than those placed front and center. If it failed to bolster the ratings, the episode certainly rewarded obsessive fans.

Episode 29: "Basic Rocket Science"

We've got to send them to outer space.

DAN HARMON AT COMIC-CON 2010

The only thing is, they really didn't. The show's first attempt at a bottle episode has ambitions, for sure. Pitched as *Community* does an *Apollo 13* homage or spoof, the episode's somewhat negative reaction may have been due to some fans wanting another paintball blowout and getting instead the study group trying to escape from a Kentucky Fried Chicken–branded space simulator.

The low-stakes, nostalgia-riffing nature of the episode recalls the previous season's "Investigative Journalism" only replacing $M*A*S*H$ callouts with nods to crummy 1980s video-game graphics and overt merchandising tie-ins. In a re-creation of an iconic scene from *The Right Stuff*, the Dean explains how Greendale and rival City College are competing to be the first to have a space simulator. The study group is accidentally trapped inside the old Kentucky Fried Chicken Eleven Herbs and Space Experience (the instruments register Original Recipe or Extra Crispy), which gets towed for being parked in a handicapped spot. Abed plays Mission Control back in the library, helping them figure out how to complete the simulation so they can escape.

Although little happens here character-wise, foreshadowing looms. Britta accidentally falls on Troy, leading to a mildly flirtatious look. Pierce's claustrophobia-induced "space madness" leads him to think that a computer-animated Colonel Sanders is his father, Cornelius (also white-haired but far less interested in fried chicken), who makes his first appearance several episodes later in "Celebrity Pharmacology." The Greendale "E Pluribus Anus" flag is premiered. Most memorable, though, is the introduction of City College's Dean Spreck (Jordan Black), whose fey affect mirrors Dean Pelton's but at a more sinister pitch.

While the day is not saved by a Winger speech, Jeff does sum up the group's hard-to-explain attachment to their terrible, terrible school by calling it a toilet . . . but *their* toilet: "Nobody craps in it but us."

Visiting Faculty

The character of Dean Spreck was originally written with John Hodgman in mind. Though Jordan Black nevertheless steals the day (and literally takes Dean Pelton's breath away in a curiously erotic and threatening whisper), Hodgman—clearly a good sort, given that he once name-checked two authors of this book during a John Cleese panel—later brought his sweater-vest deadpan to Season 3's "Curriculum Unavailable," where he played Abed's psychiatrist.

Episode 30: "Messianic Myths and Ancient Peoples"

The complaints forever thrown at TV series that take a different path to comedy—too much head, not enough heart, *weird* hijinks—were hurled in abundance at *Community*. In what looks like an inspired rejoinder to all the talk that the show was just too insider-y, too much TV-about-TV, too . . . *meta*, the first real doozy of the season took all that carping and made a feast of it.

The episode is awash in media and belief, whether in God, a boundary-breaking filmmaker, or YouTube's ability to stand in for Duncan, who has just given up on educating. Shirley asks Abed if he'll make a viral religious video to help promote her church. Fascinated by the assignment, Abed dives right in, devouring the New Testament and discovering that this Jesus guy is "like E.T., Edward Scissorhands, and Marty McFly combined." He plans an allegorical film in which a director shooting a story about Jesus realizes he himself is Jesus and God's camera is filming him. Abed calls his ambitious project "Abed." Shirley calls it blasphemy.

Abed takes over Greendale for his lavishly self-indulgent experiment, which transfixes the students, who can be heard repeating rumors ("I heard it's the same movie backward and forward") in the way that film geeks once enthused in the innocent days before streaming swallowed the world. Abed's transformation into a cinematic cult leader is inspired, from his gloriously long wig to his leather pants and ability to turn all questions into fortune cookies ("Every minute is a world premiere").

Even though Shirley ends up smashing Abed's film equipment like a furious Pharisee—or Jesus chasing the moneylenders from the temple,

Cool Cool Cool

Abed's meta-movie can be viewed as a satire on self-aware and self-referencing artists like Charlie Kaufman (*Adaptation*), leading to Shirley's frustration over "movies about making movies about making movies. Come on, Charlie Kaufman, some of us have work in the morning." Five years after "Messianic Myths and Ancient Peoples" aired, Dan Harmon and Dino "Star-Burns" Stamatopoulos's company Starburns Industries produced Kaufman's eerie stop-motion animated movie *Anomalisa* in which not a single character is a filmmaker.

take your pick—she only does it as a favor after overhearing Abed, worried about his "self-indulgent, adolescent mess" of a film, pray for delivery like Jesus on the cross: "Please take this project away from me." Pivoting sharply from the religio-cinematic meta-narrative, Shirley and Abed's story ends quite sweetly with them quietly holding hands, having accepted each other's blind faith in something that seems insane to the other.

In the B plot, Pierce starts acting out like a teenager, hanging out with a gang of delinquent seniors known as the Hipsters (because they've each got fake hips). Primarily there to illustrate how the study group is an ersatz family with Jeff as the grumpy dad, Annie as tattletale daughter, and so on, it contains at least one decent sight gag in which a car load of panicked Hipsters crashes into a pole at approximately 0.5 mph.

Episode 31: "Epidemiology"

The Greendale student body is zombified in this horror-flick homage of a Halloween episode that focuses more on the laughs and referentiality but makes it count when finally zooming in on character development.

Greendale's perennial penury shifts from recurring joke to potential, life-threatening, biohazard incident when Dean Pelton serves budget-priced army surplus rations at a Halloween party and the rations turn out to be a top-secret military rabies-spreading delivery system. Before the tainted taco meat turns the student body into a horde of moaning and biting undead, a string of bits shows how each character's costume (much like last season's "Introduction to Statistics") highlights their personality: Jeff's lazy-cool David Beckham; Chang's Peggy Fleming (an excuse to troll everyone who guesses he's Michelle Kwan as racist); Britta's impractical dinosaur costume; and the Dean's overkill baroque Lady Gaga. Over the course of the night, Abed and Troy—as respectively the xenomorph and Ripley from *Aliens*—wrestle and come to terms with their nerdhood.

A highlight of the episode, besides its more cinematic look and the stream of ABBA songs from Pelton's playlist popping off behind the undead mayhem, is that Pierce has almost no dialogue since he is Zombie Zero.

As the study group fights for survival and is steadily whittled down, the episode maintains its genre mood with an impressive lack of wackiness. This is likely due to the direction from Anthony Hemingway, a vet of *The Wire* who threads the humor in a way that is still funny but sharper and more on point (Abed urging Troy to "make me proud. Be the first black man to make it to the end").

The conspiratorial denouement in which the military gasses the student body and wipes their collective memory (of chewing people or being chewed on) feels partly a nod to earlier *X-Files* episodes as well as a precursor to the kind of trick that a Marvel movie would have S.H.I.E.L.D. pull a decade or so later. It also reflects Harmon's basic understanding that a network sitcom cannot have scads of characters die.

Almost as an afterthought, Shirley and Chang—trading in the overt psychosis of the season's earlier episodes for a more mundane brand of mental illness—barricade themselves from the horde in a bathroom and have sex. This not-at-all-foreseen development ends up being a somewhat forced setup for a late-season crisis when a pregnant Shirley worries her baby's father is Chang.

The crux of the episode comes courtesy of another film reference that would have seemed excessive (and non-zombie-themed) if it had not felt so right. When Troy escapes a basement full of zombies after Abed gives him a boost through a window, Troy looks down and says, "I love you." As though practicing for his Han Solo character in the season's last episode, Abed quotes *The Empire Strikes Back*: "I know." Even though Troy had been embarrassed earlier by Abed's nerdy ways, this declaration makes clear that for the remainder of the series, no matter what happens, their love is here to stay.

Episode 32: "Aerodynamics of Gender"

Here's an episode that should be ruined once you learn the secret behind its central mystery and yet retains its appeal perhaps if only because we see Jeff truly relax and appreciate Pierce unfiltered without any attempt to humanize his awfulness.

Shirley, Annie, and Britta are bullied by the campus mean girls, led by Hilary Duff. Abed invites himself to their Women's Studies class only to discover a latent ability for sniping bitchy comments that cut the mean girls down to size. Before you can say "with great power comes great responsibility," the study group women declare Greendale a "Bitch-Free Zone" only to become the very thing they despise. Abed's arc as a kind of insult RoboCop (complete with grainy computer screen POV shots) makes sense for the character but feels like a waste of a seminal movie reference even with the comedic perfection of Chang's peanut gallery "Oh snap!" interjections following Abed's zingers.

The B plot overshadows everything else, though, with Troy and Jeff discovering a hidden garden paradise at Greendale (with trampoline!)

offering the key to happiness, and a gardener named Joshua (Matt Walsh) who dispenses wisdom along with requests to keep the spot secret. The sublime joy Troy and Jeff discover on the trampoline, signaled by Jeff's willingness to wear Uggs and not care when he is insulted about them, infuriates Pierce, who crashes into the garden and exposes the secret.

This segment could have been just a funny if oblique nod to the fuzzy, mystical wish-fulfillment of *Lost*. But it goes further, presenting another of the show's hidden storylines: after Joshua nonchalantly says, "Non-whites ruin everything," a quick montage replays his earlier statements ("Some are just natural jumpers") in an entirely new light while including a new, recovered memory (Joshua showing off a swastika tattoo) that should have clued in Troy and Jeff about Joshua being a not-so-secret racist.

By presenting the garden as a peaceful refuge where immaturity has no shame, the segment also emphasizes the chaos, uncertainty, and tension awaiting the study group in the outer world—making it a kind of miniature Greendale within Greendale. Capping the episode off with the series' second "Troy and Abed in the Morning!" end tag—the two cajole a baffled Star-Burns into being interviewed for their pretend morning show—only reinforces the sense of Greendale as a low-tuition playground where the students just need to keep their eyes peeled for the occasional neo-Nazi.

Episode 33: "Cooperative Calligraphy"

"Cooperative Calligraphy" could have easily been a reference-a-thon as the study group spends the entire episode barricaded in the library trying to solve a mystery Agatha Christie–style. But it neatly sidesteps that issue by getting the meta commentary out of the way with an Abed complaint about being stuck in a "bottle episode." Even that gag has a meaning and emotional resonance that goes beyond TV-trope-cleverness as Abed explains how for a person on the spectrum like himself, a lack of plot (on TV or in real life) and emphasis on dialogue and social cues exacerbates his difficulty with reading people's facial expressions: "I might as well just sit in a corner with a bucket on my head."

The instigating incident—Annie believes somebody stole her purple gel pen—quickly escalates into open conflict. In a development that becomes increasingly common as *Community* goes on, this episode uses a trivial problem like the pen (in other episodes it's seating arrangements and dioramas) to illustrate the deeply dysfunctional aspects of the group dynamic. Characters' vanities are dragged out for examination: Jeff's impatient arrogance; Shirley's belief that her faith puts her above suspicion; and Britta's deflection of personal conflict into poorly reasoned political performance (equating showing the contents of her purse to "cowardly groupthink," "martial law," and being "Guantanamoed"). Even before everyone strips to their underwear and Jeff rips up the carpet, the madness of their self-imprisonment is clarified by Dean Pelton's PA announcements about the puppy parade they are missing ("Better come quick! Every moment, these puppies grow older and less deserving of our attention").

Like some of the other Megan Ganz–scripted episodes, it's tightly constructed with a high conceptual confidence borne out in the execution. The episode does not fall back on its most reliable gags (no Chang!) and (unrealistically?) keeps Abed from going to his pilot episode *Breakfast Club* references. The one clear pop-culture reference, Britta mocking Jeff's underwear ("Don't you usually wear the stripey Beetlejuice numbers?"), is not there for a 1980s callout but to set up a Beetlejuice cameo in Season 3's "Horror Fiction in Seven Spooky Steps" and also to hint that Britta and Jeff have been hooking up the whole season.

As usual, only Abed notices.

Episode 34: "Conspiracy Theories and Interior Design"

An elaborate puzzler that weaves together the show's innocent and cynical strands, this episode brings the show back to widening the world of Greendale. Plots are explored, obsessions followed, and except for Annie's diabolically complicated diorama, no classwork is completed.

Instead, Dean Pelton's stalking of Jeff inadvertently reveals that his target has been getting credit for a fake class: Conspiracy Theories in U.S. History, supposedly taught by a Professor Professorson. When a man claiming to be Professorson (Kevin Corrigan) shows up, Jeff is confused because he thought he'd invented the name. Annie, of course, digs into the conspiracy. Discovering Pelton hired Professorson to teach Jeff a lesson, Jeff and Annie plot an elaborate sting with scripted dialogue and fake guns from the theater department. However, the moment goes south fast as in a rapidly escalating series of fake-out shootings with prop guns. It's a fun, Mamet-esque climax of infinitely layered subplots as well as a satire of both "Wait, *what?*" scripting shenanigans and theater department pretensions.

Jeff and Annie's conspiracy thriller story breaks into the B story when their chase of Professorson leads them into a school-spanning blanket fort that Troy and Abed spend the entire episode building. Primarily a goofy

Cool Cool Cool

A couple of the episode's callouts were tied to its November 18 broadcast date. The Latvian Independence Parade that delays the pillow fort chase is there because Latvian Independence Day is actually November 18. It also seems not a coincidence that Annie's diorama is environmentally themed given that this was the middle of NBC's annual Green Week.

take on Troy and Abed's Peter Pan existence (when Britta sniffs that she'll be doing "grown-up" things, Troy replies, "Enjoy eating fiber and watching *The Mentalist*"), this storyline shows the depths to which the show's easily obsessed characters allow their imaginations to take them. Though just hours-old, the pillow fort already sports a civil rights museum and a "Turkish quarter," the latter of which works as a momentary backdrop for the chase scene, which even though the participants are crawling on hands and knees still spoofs the movie cliché in which chase scenes include characters charging through ethnic neighborhoods.

Perhaps most importantly, though, this episode is the first to mention Abed's love of the sitcom *Cougar Town*, an obsession that will bloom darkly at the start of Season 3.

Episode 35: "Mixology Certification"

While the setup (everyone goes for drinks) has hints of a potential Abed-gratifying escapade, this moody episode shows several characters deepening and growing while Jeff and Britta dig further into their mutually reinforcing neurotic insecurities.

The study group takes Troy out to celebrate his twenty-first birthday after he discovers that he had thought he was just twenty because his mom told him everybody was ten for two years "because fifth grade is really hard." Once operating in a non-Greendale setting like a bar (actually the set of the sitcom *Happy Endings*, which frequent *Community* directors Joe and Anthony Russo were also working on around this time), the group takes on different dynamics. The charge from Jeff and Britta's hook-ups—kept clandestine back at Greendale—becomes apparent the more they bicker and try to one-up each other in a yuppie vs. hipster fight to the death.

Abed appears unusually despondent after initially bonding with Robert (Paul F. Tompkins) over their shared love of *The Last Starfighter* and *Farscape* and getting a drink thrown in his face after turning down Robert's pick-up line. Shirley is crushingly embarrassed when her pre-church-lady past as a bar fly is exposed. After deciding to try on an accent because her fake ID is from Texas, Annie delves into a long soliloquy about her invented life which is as boring to the bartender who mistakenly agrees to listen (Tig Notaro) as it is to the audience.

Just about the only one of the group still noticing people outside their own manias and pretenses is now Troy. Though just one episode away from the blanket fort, he already appears more mature if only because he tells Britta and Jeff off and seems even dad-like for driving all the drunks home and reminding Abed that "nobody likes a tattletale." Also, Troy's prognosis that "alcohol makes people sad. It's like the Lifetime movie of beverages" feels like the wisdom of a man who learned something during those two years in fifth grade.

Episode 36: "Abed's Uncontrollable Christmas"

Like many great television holiday specials, this one holds out the promise of endless possibilities. This is appropriate for an episode with such an unlikely origin story: NBC Universal's chairman told Harmon that *Community* reminded him of *Family Guy* and that they should do an animated episode, proving that even TV executives get things right every now and again. With a green light from the network, a production studio at their fingertips—as luck would have it, Harmon and Stamatopolos had just started their production studio Starburns Industries—and a show that already melded whimsey and melancholy, making a stop-motion animation episode was the next likely step. The risk not only paid off artistically and emotionally but won the show its sole Emmy (for Outstanding Individual Achievement in Animation).

Community was often at its best when starting in a place of deep nostalgia and then unfurling into something entirely different. Crafted in the big-head, herky-jerky style of the old Rankin-Bass Christmas specials, "Abed's Uncontrollable Christmas" looks at first like another dive into Abed's self-referential pop culture hall of mirrors. It's a classic special holiday episode plot: the show's innocent goes looking for the meaning of Christmas. But in this rendering, the premise that Abed believes everyone is animated (the audience only sees what is in his mind) is less charming than it is concerning. As part of the group's intervention with Abed (using

Professor Duncan, the closest they have to a therapist), they follow him on a Tim Burton–style Winter Wonderland journey filled with song, morality lessons, a train chase scene through a howling blizzard, a "remote-control Christmas pterodactyl," and an increasingly bleak tone.

In Abed's mind, all of this is great, just another hero's journey: "When I say test, I mean Wonka-style. I'm talking dark. My advice: Stay honest, stay alert, and for the love of God, stay between the gumdrops." With each of the group rendered in punning holiday cartoon style (Ballerannie, Troy Soldier, Jeff-in-the-Box), they are really just walk-ons in Abed's story. But though Abed tries to hide his underlying pain with this cinnamon-scented Christmas-palooza—using television again as a diversion—the truth of the matter is that for the first time since his parents' divorce, his mother won't be coming to visit him for Christmas.

Having seeded nods to Abed's depressed emptiness throughout the story, the episode has no need to belabor the point by the time his root issue is revealed. In any case, the episode already inoculated itself from closure (finding a *Lost* DVD, Abed says, "It's a metaphor. It represents lack of payoff"). Rallying again around their chosen family, the group bundle themselves around Abed to watch holiday cartoons while still existing in one themselves, suggesting that sticking around inside Abed's mind for a little longer might be a good decision.

Episode 37: "Asian Population Studies"

In this palette-cleanser of character development after the Abed-isode, Chang (introduced here lurking Gollum-like on top of a library bookshelf) is again used as a random element of chaos, threat, and annoyance that helps both bind together and pull the study group apart. Happily reuniting at the start of a new semester, the group again breaks sitcom tradition by acknowledging the time of year (usually only deemed appropriate during special holiday episodes).

Shirley, who continually has the most real-world problems off-campus, introduces the group to her ex-husband Andre (Malcolm-Jamal Warner, here to play the role straight and not as a gag cameo except for one *Cosby Show* sweater joke) with whom she is trying to patch things up. Though nobody enjoys this idea given Andre's cheating ways, once it's revealed that Shirley is pregnant (and potentially with Chang's child from their Halloween hook-up), Andre quickly seems the better choice.

Following a lengthy riff on students whose names the group doesn't know ("Fat Neil?" "Jean Claude Overbite?") that ends with Jeff calling

> ### Streets Ahead
>
> "Asian Population Studies" contains some of the more glorious itera-
> tions of Chang's punny use of his own name: "Chang the subject";
> "Chang your point of view." "Changuage" is essentially used in this
> episode as another way to crank up Jeff's irritation: "It makes me so
> Chang-ry. Oh God! It's happening to *me*."

Abed "brown Jamie Lee Curtis," Annie's new boyfriend is revealed as
Rich (Greg Cromer), the too-perfect-to-be-true doctor from Season 1's
"Beginner Pottery." Jeff's desire to break up Rich and Annie leads him
to a convoluted scheme in which the group will again hold auditions for
a new member as they did in "Investigative Journalism." At the pinnacle
of this campaign, Jeff makes an impassioned speech for the group to select
Chang over Rich because Chang's awfulness ("He smells like Band-Aids";
"He over- and under-emphasizes words at random") is more obvious and
knowable than Rich, the "human question mark." The irony in Jeff's call
for openness is that it's all a smokescreen. After a climactic last-act-of-a-
romantic comedy run through the rain, Jeff shows that his true problem
is less his desire to control Annie than his desire to control Rich's hold
on people. "Give me that power," he pleads to Rich. "So I can abuse it."

Episode 38: "Celebrity Pharmacology"

Another interstitial entry that adds a few glimpses into some of the characters' backgrounds, this episode uses a grade school drug awareness play (put
on by Annie) as an excuse to dress the group in bee costumes.

This is a slightly schizophrenic Pierce episode. In the B story, he is
appalled and confused by discovering Annie lives in a rattrap over the
sex-toy store Dildopolis ("Aren't everyone's parents rich?") so he gives
her a check to help out with rent. While a typical money-as-manipulation
move, this is greater generosity than generally seen from Pierce. He then
squanders the good will by sabotaging Annie's play in a bid for attention
(upset with his dialogue, he turns the character Drugs into a scene-stealer
whom the kids love). Pierce's tantrum potentially feels like both a therapy-
for-the-writers meta–Chevy Chase commentary and a visualization of the
intergenerational trauma nodded at in the old Hawthorne Wipes ad we
see, which includes the first imperious appearance of Cornelius Hawthorne

(Larry Cedar), who has hired an actor to play his son after Pierce ruins a shot.

Elsewhere, Britta reaches near-peak Britta-ness. Trying to flirt via text with her boyfriend, she realizes she's been texting her 14-year-old nephew who now thinks they are going to hook up ("It wasn't a mistake," he assures her. "Don't be afraid"). Chang tries to warm Shirley up to the possibility of having his child by making her a mixtape she can't listen to because who still has a cassette player? Though failing on that front, Chang still fulfills his role as chaos agent by taking over the role of Drugs in the play from Pierce—again, the show layers ideas of performance and identity all throughout the episode in a continual commentary on artificial personas—and insulting the school kids until they assault him en masse.

In a neat end tag that doubles down on Annie's deplorable living conditions and wrings a few more laughs out of the store name *Dildopolis*, she is awakened by its 2 a.m. announcements: "We will be closed for Presidents' Day. Just kidding. Dildopolis never closes."

Episode 39: "Advanced Dungeons & Dragons"

Given what a large role the roleplaying game Dungeons & Dragons played in Harmon's early comedy career—especially the "Summoner" sketch from his Dead Alewives period, which lambasted the 1980s Satanic Panic by vocalizing the hobby's dorky reality ("Where are the Cheetos?")—and how focused *Community* was on notching off the major touchstones of late-twentieth-century geek culture, it's surprising that it took until Season 2 for *Community* to get to rolling polyhedral dice. Less surprising, perhaps, is that NBC wanted nothing to do with this concept, that many of the D&D books on set were from Harmon's own collection, and that the episode would later get pulled from rotation because of Chang.

Other television comedies had referenced D&D, particularly the final episode of *Freaks and Geeks* in 2000. But *Community*'s intent was to use the inherent, group-based drama and conflict of the game as integral to the story rather than just as a nod to geeks. It's a densely plotted episode with onion-skin layering. Guilty over saddling "Fat Neil" (Charley Koontz) with his depression-inspiring nickname, Jeff frantically tries to boost the spirits of the D&D–loving Neil by asking him to game with the study group.

Everyone plays to their essence. Abed orchestrates the storytelling as the Dungeon Master (drawing on Pudi's knack for nuance). Britta gets sidetracked trying to liberate a gnome from his fantasy world caste system. Chang arrives in blackface as a Dark Elf (a particularly deep cut that would only make sense to viewers who spent their childhood mining the D&D *Monster Manual*), prompting Shirley to comment, "We're going to ignore that hate crime?" That line makes clear that the writers understood the implications of blackface, but this being 2011, they believed it could still work as a joke as long as they acknowledged it was offensive. (Rob Schrab's experience with a similar episode on *The Sarah Silverman Program* did not appear to have been instructive.)

Director Joe Russo (who later called this episode his favorite in the entire series) shoots parts in *Lord of the Rings* style (complete with mock heroic Cate Blanchett–esque narration about "the balance between good and Pierce"); sound effects from the imaginary game; and looming zooms on Pierce as the Sauron figure. Oddly, there are no more Gollum moments from Chang. Once again the group overcommits, making Neil feel condescended to. In a gymnastic twist, the episode uses Pierce first as the foil—spiteful over initially being excluded from the game, he insults and goads Neil while cheating to win—and later on the accidental source of Neil's reason to live.

This is a tough episode to watch with "Pierce the Dickish" sinking to new depths of antisocial vileness. But the emotional payoff is unexpectedly touching once Neil uses his turn in the game to "feel sorry" for his tormentor, Pierce. Rather than make Pierce a two-dimensional villain, the episode finds his vulnerability and then gives the grace note not to a main character but to a bit player like Neil. Though riddled with geek lore that can be hard for some to decipher, "Advanced Dungeons & Dragons" is

Meanwhile, Off Campus . . .

As of the writing of this chapter, "Advanced Dungeons & Dragons" is most easily available the old analog way: on DVD. Though Season 2 sets still include the episode, because of Chang's blackface appearance, some (but not all) streaming services pulled it from their lineup during the industry's 2020 reassessment of diversity and bias issues. Around the same time, other sitcoms with some absurdist crossover appeal with *Community* (*The Office*, *30 Rock*, *Scrubs*) also pulled or edited episodes featuring blackface.

not just a highlight of the season but a strong response to the critique of *Community* as all snark and no heart.

Episode 40: "Early Twenty-First-Century Romanticism"

The Valentine's Day hook provides some opportunities here but it is ultimately something of a distraction. Once again there is a Greendale dance only somehow Dean Pelton isn't hosting it in an over-the-top outfit and nothing much of consequence befalls the study group.

A couple of romance-linked subplots converge at the dance but end in misunderstandings. Britta goes to the dance with her new friend Page (Brit Marling), who she thinks is a lesbian. Britta discovers Page is also straight and that they were both just trying to get attention by having a lesbian friend, but this is only made clear after a wildly uncomfortable dance-floor kiss. Troy and Abed, after agonizing over who should ask out the cute librarian Mariah (Maite Schwartz), invite her to the dance together so she can choose there. However, when she selects Troy after deeming Abed "weird," Troy decides friendship is more important.

Jeff avoids the whole scene and watches *futbol* with Duncan, who assumes that Jeff as an American knows nothing about the sport (Jeff's retort: "I'm a *stylish* American, professor. I've been forcing myself to be into soccer since 2004"). The perpetually uninvited and apparently now homeless Chang weasels into Jeff's apartment and invites half the campus over for a party.

While the Chang-needs-a-home subplot is not mint, it does at least provide a launchpad for the introduction of Magnitude (Luke Young-blood), the little dynamo cooked up as an inspired commentary on sitcom catchphrase machines and who kicks the party off with his signature "Pop! Pop!"

Taking a step back from evil plotting, Pierce slides further into opiate addiction spurred along by his imaginary bad influence (a very tiny Andy Dick who fits in Pierce's palm). It's a fairly slight part of the episode but memorable for what happens after Jeff mocks Pierce for listening to the Barenaked Ladies. This spurs a comically overblown response from the group, especially Troy: "Pierce is our friend and the Barenaked Ladies are triple platinum. Are you?"

Wait! I thought you were . . . but I'm not . . . NBC/PHOTOFEST.

Episode 41: "Intermediate Documentary Filmmaking"

A more thematically repetitive and dramatically inconclusive episode that stands out for the shot-perfect homage to and satire of faux-documentary comedies and an explosively funny storyline for Troy.

Set entirely in a hospital and seen through the lens of the camera Abed is using to shoot a documentary, Pierce appears to have been hospitalized after passing out on a bench at the end of the last episode. One by one, he calls the group in for his "bequeathings," which appear to be gifts but are all vulnerability-triggering mind games. Some are simple (e.g., a $10,000 check to Britta for the charity of her choice, which makes her feel guilty for wanting to spend it on herself). Others are more byzantine (e.g., a CD Pierce says is recordings of people talking bad about Shirley but that turns out to be the opposite, which Shirley only discovers after assuming the worst and telling everyone she forgives them). Pierce sends Jeff into a spiral by claiming to have found the father who abandoned him. All of this involves a low-key, more calibrated performance than Chase tends to give on the show. But it remains nevertheless hard to swallow the conceit that Pierce is at once a befuddled baby boomer, pill addict, and carefully conniving Machiavellian manipulator.

Pierce aims his antisocial anger at Troy in very targeted manner by hiring LeVar Burton (playing himself with a clever glint in his eyes) to hang out with superfan Troy. But the appearance of his childhood hero sends Troy into paralytic shock. A cutaway by Abed shows Troy screaming about how he wanted a signed picture of Burton but not to meet him in person because "you can't disappoint a picture!"

Although Abed realizes that his documentary is turning out messier than he had hoped, he knows that he can just "wrap it up with random shots which, when cut together under a generic voiceover, suggest a profound thematic connection." This is right after the episode has done just that in a metafictional mirroring that Jesus Abed from "Messianic Myths and Ancient Peoples" would have applauded.

Cool Cool Cool

Although Magnitude will remain among the immortals of sitcom history, it is worth noting that among the other and possibly better names considered for his character was *Event Horizon*.

Episode 42: "Intro to Political Science"

Although it concludes with Jeff learning his lesson yet again about being overly domineering, this episode reaches its pinnacle when Jeff is at his worst. The setup is straightforward: Vice President Joe Biden is touring community colleges and is supposed to meet the head of Greendale's nonexistent student government. This leads Dean Pelton to throw together a last-minute debate to elect a president. In full Tracy Flick mode, Annie throws her hat in the ring. Jeff then jumps in after Annie mocks his cynicism about the election.

The debate shows Annie and Jeff at their best and worst while also revealing that Pierce, when limited mostly to one spiteful gag, can potentially work better as a minor character. Annie is idealistic, high-minded, and well-prepared while also over-eager and even entitled. Jeff cuts to the heart of what is most fatuous about representative democracy though he does so only because of Pierce-ian childish resentment. Reflecting a lot of Harmon's own cynicism about politics, Jeff channels his old ambulance-chasing lawyer persona to pump the crowd up with patriotic gibberish barely discernible from many a post–Tea Party Republican stump speech: "I think that beer should be cold and boots should be dusty. I think 9/11 was bad. And freedom, well, I think that's just a little bit better." Though

In "Intro to Political Science," Britta fails once again to rage against the machine . . . dying of the light . . . something. NBC/PHOTOFEST.

Inspector Spacetime

Attentive listeners will have noted that part of Annie's presidential platform was bringing to justice "the assailant known only as the Ass Crack Bandit." Happy to let good ideas ferment, the show did not circle back to this heinous criminal until Season 5's "Basic Intergluteal Numismatics" tries to solve the case once and for all.

Annie shivs Jeff by showing his audition tape for MTV's *Real World: Seattle* and they have a rapprochement, his mocking jabs have an impact and relevance ("For my closing statement, I'm thinking about smashing a watermelon") that overshadow anything happening in their relationship.

Once again operating somewhat in his own orbit, Abed has a touching almost-romance with Vohlers (Eliza Coupe), one of Biden's Secret Service agents. Stoic behind her aviator shades and clearly landing somewhere on the same spectrum as Abed, she treats him like a security threat only as an excuse to spend time with him. Noticing Abed's flirtation, Troy asks, "Do you just constantly have your own side adventures?" When Abed replies in the affirmative, a suddenly vulnerable Troy weakly claims, "Me too." Fortunately the show is confident enough in their dynamic that it feels no need to find something else for Troy to do. Troy might be the neurotypical part of the duo, but to some degree he is also the sidekick. This may be the moment when he discovers that.

Episode 43: "Custody Law and Eastern European Diplomacy"

Rarely have A and B plots operated more in their own universes. Taking centerstage is Chang's continued efforts to convince Shirley what a great dad he would be. This is primarily an excuse to have Chang put on a Mr. Rogers and Ward Cleaver cosplay complete with cardigan, pipe, and a performative avuncular empathy that Jeong mixes with a hint of sinister.

Chang's frantic need to belong echoes a desire that is one of the most resonant themes in the entire show, balanced right alongside the drive of the characters to create protected spaces. The audience can sympathize with the pang of exclusion felt by a Chang or Pierce while also appreciating the group's very understandable desire to avoid maniacs and misogynistic Boomers. This creates an inherent tension the show does not always skillfully navigate, too often airbrushing Pierce's miserable behavior with a generous gesture from Jeff or—in the case of this episode—dropping in a reminder of Chang's instability in a scene where he essentially kidnaps two kids whom he thinks are Shirley's.

While the B plot is seemingly a low-stakes storyline—Troy and Abed try to keep Britta from dating their new friend Lukka (Enver Gjokaj) because she always tells them things about her boyfriends they don't want to know—it takes a fairly dark turn once Britta discovers that the reason Lukka is so good at the video games he plays with the guys is because he cheerfully engaged in ethnic cleansing back in the Balkans. It's funny primarily for Britta ruining things again and having the plot turn on the possession of Abed's Blu-ray of *Kickpuncher 3: The Final Kickening*. But using genocide for basically a throwaway joke feels unsuited for a show that usually draws better lines between edgy and cheap.

Episode 44: "Critical Film Studies"

If it was still a question by this point in *Community* whether the episodes driven by Abed's imagination were more likely to soar, then "Critical Film Studies" helped put that to rest.

A Russian nesting doll of cinematic references and therapeutic dialogue, the episode begins with a sitcom-y premise of secret-keeping. Jeff is trying to wangle Abed to a nostalgia diner where the group has set up a *Pulp Fiction*–themed birthday costume party without blowing the secret. Surprised when Abed insists on first meeting at a fancy restaurant ("Wasn't his style at all," Jeff wonders in his voiceover, "There were cloth napkins, no TVs"), Jeff is more confused that Abed shows up smiling and making eye contact, and he is utterly baffled by Abed's claim to have put his old persona to rest: Abed, uncharacteristically, wants to have an adult conversation.

There are two expertly teased reveals here. The first is that Abed's soliloquy about the meaninglessness of pop culture—shaded with tender, gentle notes that are miles from his usual monomania, registering just how much the show relies on Pudi's performance to carry the stories' emotional weight—is also about how his *Cougar Town* Facebook fandom led to his being offered a walk-on extra role at which point he became so anxious he defecated on himself. The second is that it's all a bit: trying to get Jeff to spend more time with him, Abed is playing the role of a serious adult, which to him means "talking like Frasier" and acting like a character from *My Dinner with Andre*.

For "Critical Film Studies," the group recreates Pulp Fiction. NBC/PHOTOFEST.

Once Jeff discovers what's happening, he proceeds to try and shed his old persona by unburdening his own shameful experiences on Abed. But just as Abed's truth-telling was too much for Jeff, the reverse is also true. Having scared each other straight, they go to the *Pulp Fiction* party and revert mostly to their previous selves.

None of them might really be changing. But watching Abed continually and subtly readjusting his approach to better align with a group relationship whose emotional complexities he cannot fully comprehend is more captivating than any dramatic but not quite believable epiphany. This feels purposeful on the part of the writers, particularly given Jeff's advice to Abed ("Take it from someone who just had a meaningless one; sometimes emotional breakthroughs are overrated").

Better perhaps to see a character learn something small but true than pretend that a single conversation or event can alter the entire arc of their personality.

Episode 45: "Competitive Wine Tasting"

The distance between *Community*'s organic and meta moments becomes starker in this three-plot episode—thematically connected by the blowoff classes everyone is taking—where Pierce looks for love, Troy digs for emotion, and Abed discovers the class of his dreams.

The first storyline is mostly on the surface when Jeff's jealousy over getting shot down by Wu Mei (Michelle Krusiec) at an Italian wine-tasting class leads to him undermining her relationship with Pierce. Jeff discovers she is actually a corporate spy but realizes she and Pierce should probably still give romance a shot since "you're both rude, deceitful, and racist, and you both come from moist-wipe dynasties."

Troy agrees to take an acting class primarily to get closer to Britta. The bargain-basement Stanislavski technique used by Professor Sean Garrity (back to teaching real classes after his web of fakery was discovered in "Conspiracy Theories and Interior Design") has him encouraging the students to dig for personal pain. Desperate to fit in and embarrassed about his happy and well-adjusted youth, Troy pretends he was molested. Though this leads to a kiss from Britta (as Abed notes, "Britta's attracted to pain. Helps her pretend to be healthy"), Troy's guilt causes him to confess. Garrity quiets the disapproving class by telling Troy that "the pain of not having enough pain is still pain." Then in one of the show's most self-aware moments, the camera zooms in on Garrity as he says with strained seriousness, "That may sound like an easy resolution but we're not writers. We're actors. Story doesn't matter here." What it actually sounds like is a writer's room breathing a sigh of relief after getting themselves out of a jam.

In a foreshadowing of his Season 5 dive into the dark world of Nicolas Cage (in a class taught by Garrity), Abed takes a class on the sitcom *Who's the Boss?* Initially dismissed by the pompous teacher (Stephen Tobolowsky)—who wrote the class textbook *Who Indeed? A Critical Analysis of TV's "Who's the Boss?"*—Abed uses a dense lattice of textual and linguistic analysis to prove that the boss was . . . Angela. The joke works primarily due to its simplicity, the gag being almost entirely in the existence of the class. Abed's success, a kind of fanboy fantasy in which diligent application of research and dedication beats out wooly ivory tower academia, is just the cherry on top.

Episode 46: "Paradigms of Human Memory"

For some sitcoms, this Cuisinart of an episode would have been their pinnacle. For *Community*, it was just another way to turn the format inside out while not completely losing sight of the characters' emotional lives.

As with other Chris McKenna–scripted episodes ("Anthropology 101"), it's an overloaded buffet of references, in-jokes, and surprises with a kamikaze willingness to just dump it all out there because who the hell knows if there will be Season 3?

The episode has barely started and already the group is circling back on themselves by making a diorama of making their last diorama for Anthropology. After Abed's radar detects an anomaly and he announces that Jeff and Britta have been sleeping together, the episode turns into a spoof of a sitcom clip show. Characters cue up one "You guys remember when?" moment after another. Only none of those moments (excepting a live action take on "Abed's Uncontrollable Christmas" showing how it was not a Winter Wonderland but just everyone at the table playing along to Abed's fantasy) had been seen before in the series.

Some of these invented moments are micro-targeted to certain parts of the fanbase, like a brief *Glee* satire that would be expanded on in the next season's "Regional Holiday Music" episode and shots of Abed running around in a black cape and shouting, "Six seasons and a movie!" (referencing both the short-lived NBC superhero drama *The Cape* and increasingly louder calls from the online *Community* fans for . . . six seasons and a movie). A couple of segments set to Sara Bareilles's "Gravity," which had already been used to score *Community* fan videos on YouTube, spoof how selective editing and slow motion can introduce emotional tension into any random series of shots. A phenomenal montage of Dean Pelton in varying outfits (as Scarlet O'Hara, Catwoman, Tina Turner) is both gift to the dedicated and an unintended warning of the series' future overreliance on that shtick.

Many of the invented flashbacks recall episodes from 1970s sitcoms where the gang has wacky adventures in unusual locations. But the scenes we see are not just shorn of context, they appear purposefully ridiculous even by Greendale standards (investigating a *Scooby-Doo*–style haunted house, getting shot at by a prospector in the Old West, being held at gunpoint by a Mexican cartel) as a way of underlining the absurdity of the format's generally limited scope and also seeing how many gags the writers can jam into a half hour.

Many of the cutaways are thematically clever. But the moment with the best delivery comes after the group sees Annie's Boobs (the monkey last spotted stealing Annie's pen in "Cooperative Calligraphy") grab one of their paintbrushes and dash into a vent. A quick camera pan shows Chang stripped to his underwear and lathering himself with Vaseline, insisting, "I got this." That shot, and the group's accompanying scream of horror, deliver a laugh equal to any in the entire run of the series.

The episode delves deeper than others have up to this point in the group's toxicity and constant fighting but it does so with the sense that they could actually just be characters stuck inside a sitcom, meaning that if we tune in next week, they will still be together, regardless of their pain.

Episode 47: "Applied Anthropology and Culinary Arts"

One of the oldest television tropes on record—the baby who comes too early—produces a somewhat more leisurely plotted episode that never leaves the classroom in which the birth happens.

In a rather glorious final appearance of the season, Professor Duncan administers an anthropology final primarily focused on everyone in the class drinking copiously. Pierce tries again to ruin someone's fun, this time by offering Troy and Abed $1,000 for their special handshake, necessitating an *Indecent Proposal* reference (after Troy hesitates, Pierce snarls, "Make your money, *whore*"). When Shirley's contractions start, the group stumbles into action, with Jeff snarking from the sideline, straight-A Annie frozen for lack of preparation, Britta somehow pulling it together, Chang (still not in the group but at this point more like a quasi-psychotic mascot) telling Shirley stories of the horrific situations Chang babies were born into and survived, and Abed orchestrating everything because of having already done it in "The Psychology of Letting Go" (when Troy asks, "Where was I when that happened?" Abed replies, "I don't know, off in the background").

Dean Pelton exhibits yet another stupendously inept decision by failing to realize that the World Food Festival he organized has turned into "a bit of a race . . . kerfuffle." Which is handy way of ensuring that the ambulance can't get there to bring Shirley to the hospital and also gives the reporter there covering the Dean for *Dean Magazine* something to write down.

Something of a palette cleanser, the episode neatly snips off the hanging-plot thread of Shirley's pregnancy, leaves most of the group feeling unusually okay about themselves, and probably saved some money with its one-room setting, clearing the slate before the season-ending dual paintball episodes.

Episode 48: "A Fistful of Paintballs"

Years before Joe Russo showed his maximalist tendencies by codirecting the back-to-back *Avengers* blockbusters *Infinity War* and *Endgame*, he directed the back-to-back paintball assassin episodes that concluded Season

2 in a hail of paint pellets and filmic references. This was practically inevitable given the positive reception of Season 1's "Modern Warfare."

Justin Lin garlanded that tide-turning episode with stylistic touches but maintained the show's standard aesthetic in other areas, balancing the Jeff-and-Britta sexual tension plot with paintball combat scenes. Russo fully embeds "A Fistful of Paintballs" in genre territory, introducing each character in mythic Sergio Leone manner and only showing what proceeded paintball in flashbacks that echo *Once Upon a Time in the West*. True to spaghetti western form, the episode plays out in a high emotional register with looming close-ups and near-constant showdowns. While the group's toggling between intramural strife and bonding is familiar from last time, the stakes are higher: instead of priority registration, the prize is now $100,000.

Everything is hyped up, from the weaponry (the surprise reveal of a gatling paintball gun provides a dramatic conclusion) to the threat (City College secretly funding the contest under the guise of a Western-themed ice cream company in order to destroy Greendale's campus) to everyone's personas. One of very few episodes that allows Annie to get past her neuroses, it places her center stage as a double-pistol-packing gunslinger who fully embraces her character's confidence. Channeling many in the audience, Abed notes, "She's pretty awesome today." In terms of character, Abed hits the jackpot, wearing a serape and an air of chilly malevolent nonchalance drawn right from the grim shootist Clint Eastwood played for Leone. Jeff, having retrieved the cowboy outfit he wore to the Halloween dance in "Introduction to Statistics," is a study in insecurity once the group's nemesis appears. Wielding sawed-off paintguns, bandoliers of ammo, and utterly unnecessary spurs, the Black Rider (Josh Holloway, knowingly riffing on the tight-lipped, darkly romantic tough-guy shtick he had just finished playing on *Lost* the year before) threatens the group's chances to win the prize but is primarily a problem for the ever-vain Jeff because Abed identifies him as "network TV good looking."

Foreshadowing the crucial role he will play in the season's last scene, Pierce gets his day in the sun as a warlord who briefly wields power at "Fort Hawthorne" by monopolizing bathroom access ("I found that people were willing to roll bullets under the door just for the right to take a dump") and using his patented pretend-heart-attack trick to take out the Black Rider.

The over-the-top nature of the episode's fake combat scenes—which everybody, not just Abed, commits to with utter emotional seriousness—is pushed even further in the climax when the sponsoring company introduces a platoon of white-armored paintball stormtroopers to mow down the opposition at the orders of their ice cream cone–suited mascot Pistol Patty. When the Dean scream-shouts, "What kind of ice cream company *does* this?!" it allows the show to mock the absurdity of the concept while still indulging in all the fun of pretend shootouts. Instead of a Troy-and-Abed moment, the end tag serves as a high-drama teaser for the next episode, where the very future of Greendale seems to be in doubt.

Episode 49: "For a Few Paintballs More"

Like a kid who decides to switch up their action figures for genre-hopping play, the show pivots in the concluding half of Season 2's paintball extravaganza from Leone to Lucas. With the ice-cream army storming the school, a suddenly Darth Vader–like Pistol Patty is revealed as the Dean's archrival Dean Spreck, and Greendale's warring factions coalescing into a ragtag Human Being alliance, Abed notes that they've "left the Western motif and are entering a *Star Wars* scenario." That's the universe the episode remains in except for a quick callback: a close-up of Spreck's mouth during his mocking PA message ("Resistance is as pointless as your degrees") references *The Warriors*, as did "Modern Warfare."

Because the conflict is so simply defined through much of the episode and the paintball combat comes close to wearing out its welcome (knowing the risk of going to the well one too many times, Abed points out that "sequels are almost always disappointing), the main plotline is of far less interest than what happens around and after it, much like Russo's *Avengers* movies. Mimicking a common editing scheme from the *Star Wars* universe, the action scenes split in two, with Troy and some Human Beings engaging stormtroopers in the school while others led by Jeff launch a frontal assault on their Death Star: the ice cream truck. Much of it is fun if not necessarily fun*ny* (Britta and Shirley's golf-cart gunplay badassery), except for the moment when Magnitude sacrifices himself by jumping on a paint grenade and only getting out a single anguished "Pop" before fake dying.

There is richer material in the characters pursuing their own ends rather than those of the group or Greendale. Seeing the opportunities in the Lucas universe, Abed moves right into the Han Solo role with some cocky repartee and Star-Burns's vest. Annie, who seems somewhat wilted here after dropping her gunfighter persona, falls unabashedly for Abed's confident patter. In one of the season's more touching moments, Abed informs Annie with a *Flowers for Algernon* poignance that once the game

Cool Cool Cool

Seven years after "For a Few Paintballs More," the movie *Solo* cleverly cast a suave Donald Glover as the younger Lando Calrissian but handed the starring role to a mostly charmless Alden Ehrenreich. This was an unfortunate and also fairly inexplicable decision especially when contrasted with the natural charm that Danny Pudi had already brought to the character.

is over his time as Han is done. They share a first and final passionate kiss under a rain of orange paint.

Shockingly, the episode and season conclude with Pierce in the driver's seat. Having tried and failed yet again to buy friendship (his Fort Hawthorne power-mongering), he would appear to be set up for more mockery. But things finish with Pierce saving the day by shooting the last stormtrooper. Later in the library, he lets the group behind the curtain, revealing that he has been at Greendale for twelve years and explaining how he presumes rejection and goads people until they do so. The scene would reek of schmaltz but for two things: Chase's underplayed candor and the challenge he issues before walking out: "This place has always accepted me, sickness and all. This place accepted *all of you*, sickness and all. It's worth thinking about." In the final shot, the camera pulls back through the door, everyone's faces slowly registering that Pierce may actually not slink back this time seeking readmission.

This crestfallen note punctures the group's victorious mood, yanking them back to the themes of co-dependency that kept vibrating through the season. The moment does not necessarily put the viewers in a different place than after "Advanced Dungeons & Dragons," where it was strongly suggested that the group needed to beat on a villain like Pierce (or later on, City College) to cohere. But having just shown how each of the group took on various poses during the paintball combat, the episode underlines how each of them may ultimately be more comfortable playing a role, *any* role, rather than themselves.

Community 103—Season 3: 6
Physics of the Multiverse

The third chapter of a four-chapter story is always the darkest.

—DAN HARMON

AFTER THE HIGH of Season 2's concluding paintball two-parter, there was a sense that really, anything was possible for *Community* going forward. Despite once again suboptimal ratings, NBC gave *Community* another go because, really, what else was the network going to do? Despite Abed's fervent wishes, superhero drama *The Cape* was cancelled. Only two of the new sitcoms NBC launched in the 2011–2012 season survived, and neither were still on the air two years later. *Community* might have been the network's weird kid with glasses and a tree-nut allergy who had strong opinions about what was canon in *Star Wars*, but its grades were good enough to skate by—at least until the next *30 Rock* came along.

It also had something to prove.

Episode 50: "Biology 101"

And we are BACK! The third season came loaded for bear, full of merriment, snark, not-so-veiled racism on Pierce's part, and (even more) boundary pushing. For example, the first episode opens with a full-fledged musical number, reminiscent of *Greatest American Hero*, in which the cast bops around in bright primary-colored outfits while belting out lyrics that sound like lines from an essay that a producer made a misbehaving sitcom write ("We're gonna have more fun and be less weird than the first two years combined").

After the suggestion that the song was just Jeff's dream, the show proper begins. We see that time has passed at Greendale since last season. Characters have, well, if not grown, gone through some changes. The Dean, now serious, bearded, and dressed in the kind of professional attire one can imagine him thinking a serious person would wear, is trying to be the adult in the room. This will, of course, not last.

Although Pierce was out of the group as of last season, he comes back anyway, much to Jeff's chagrin. But are they a study group or friends? Will this season decide that? Read on, dear reader!

Besties Abed and Troy move in together and in a Pee-wee Herman–esque case of arrested development are later revealed to be sharing the same bedroom in bunkbeds. But at least they have a place to stay. Chang, who lost whatever limited dignity he had the last two seasons, is now living in Greendale's duct system, presumably with the thieving monkey.

Despite the opening song's insistence that everything will be Bright, Cheerful, and Very Very Not Weird, the episode dives fast into some heavy intertextuality. After Abed begins to panic, Troy murmurs "six seasons and a movie" to him as a soothing mechanism. Theoretically this is a joke for the fans who have been using the line in an insistent Twitter campaign. But it could also suggest that the characters know they are in a

"Biology 101" reveals where the true power lies at Greendale. NBC/PHOTOFEST.

TV show and perhaps know they are being watched. Or are they the ones watching the viewers?

A pair of stellar guest stars bring some sparkle and actorly pizzaz to roles designed to create tension in the group. The group's new biology teacher, Professor Kane, is played by Michael K. Williams—formerly of *The Wire*, a show that Harmon (and a large number of his fans, and the authors of this book) was inspired by—as another adult who drops into the Greendale sandbox and cuts Jeff down to size.

John Goodman is introduced as Vice Dean Laybourne, the heretofore-unknown head of Greendale's air-conditioner repair division and long-time rival to Dean Pelton. Though Pelton believes his rank gives him authority, it turns out that the air-conditioning repair division brings in more filthy lucre than all of Pelton's academics combined. (Two of your authors are college professors, and according to them, this makes absolutely perfect sense.) Thus ensues a power struggle that will run in Greendale's increasingly crowded subplot annex.

The pop culture references zoom past:

- After Abed spirals on discovering his favorite (real) sitcom *Cougar Town* might be getting canceled and that the (fake) British version *Cougarton Abbey* is also over, Britta delivers a rare save by presenting Abed with a new mollifying show, the (fake) *Inspector Spacetime*, a cheap-looking and campy-seeming reference to *Doctor Who*. (Though funny, the scene still has its disturbing side given that the only thing between Abed and a full emotional implosion is his having a show to watch.)
- When evil Dean Laybourne lays out the cruel reality of finances at Greendale and just how little power Dean Pelton truly has, it serves as a big, sexy wink to Ned Beatty's thunderous speech about the almighty power of corporate interests in *Network*.
- Meanwhile campus security is filling the air ducts with poison to smoke out the monkey. Will the monkey and Chang succumb to the poison? Or is this subplot just an excuse for Chang to shout, "Monkey gas!" in terror.
- In a nod to *2001: A Space Odyssey*, Jeff hallucinates a scene in which he has aged and become Pierce while the study group's table resembles the monolith. Realizing what he may become, or simply panicked about the aging process, Jeff attacks the table with a fire axe before being brought back to reality.

Jeff and Pierce look to wisdom from Star-Burns (not the best idea). The dealer of illicit goods suggests what he calls a *Breaking Bad*–type situation and is rebuffed by the rest of the group. Chang, in a plot development destined to go south in the most spectacular fashion, is made Greendale's newest and most terrifying security guard.

Episode 51: "Geography of Global Conflict"

The third season has barely started and the show is challenging different characters' assumptions about themselves. In "Biology 101" it was Jeff's belief he could snow any professor and the Dean's newfound (and short-lived) confidence in his new Dean-ing abilities.

For the second episode, Annie starts out excited by her new history class and its nerd-hip Professor Cligoris (Martin Starr). Meanwhile, Britta is getting serious (for her at least) about her newfound passion as a budding psychology major, a setup that for a character specializing in self-sabotage nearly writes itself.

Annie is first to get knocked out of her comfort zone. That disruptive event arrives in the form of history classmate Annie Kim (Irene Choi), a fellow study grind whom Annie takes under her wing. Despite warnings from the study group (Jeff: "How progressive of you to have a multi-cultural evil twin"), Annie blithely ignores signs that her new friend is a saboteur until "Asian Annie" (as Pierce, being Pierce, labels her) steals her idea to have a Model UN. Annie then insists on having her own.

Deciding that the only way to resolve the problem of two United Nations (a situation Abed excitedly seizes on and asks, "Does two UNs mean there are two Earths?" before launching into a potentially lengthy exploration of free will in parallel dimensions, suggesting the fractured reality of the upcoming "Remedial Chaos Theory" episode) is a debate, Cligoris announces there will be the first and almost certainly last "Model UN Battle Royale." The rest of the study group happily signs on to help out, which even though it leaves most of the cast with relatively little to do at least provides an opportunity to hear Troy (representing the nation of Georgia in the debate, which he completely misunderstands) talk in a Southern accent straight out of *Designing Women*.

Like *Community*'s other debate episodes—Season 1's "Debate 109" and Season 2's "Intro to Political Science"—this one provides an opportunity for Annie to show how spunk can eventually win out in the face of cynicism and manipulation. But in this episode, Annie's determination does not quite manage to defeat evil Annie's even more monomaniacal zeal for victory in the first debate. The resulting tantrum (though controlled, Annie is generally closer to tripwire mental and emotional meltdown than any other character) sparks an unexpected public revelation by Jeff: "You're acting like a school girl and not in a hot way!" Just by bringing their long-running flirtation into the open, that moment seems to finally kill it, the "Ew, gross" factor proving unexpectedly powerful.

The great debate of the Annies hoovers up much of the episode's dramatic oxygen. But somewhat funnier is the B plot in which Britta is pitched into a dark well of self-disillusionment when she discovers an old activist friend of hers is still raging against the machine. "I haven't been tear-gassed in so long," she says in melancholy fashion. Unsure how to get back on the road to oligarch-destroying activism, she stages a comically ineffective symbolic protest and art performance piece by putting herself in a cage and pouring ketchup over a globe that she also hits with a hammer.

Nobody pays attention.

Fortunately for Britta's sense of self, Chang's new position as security guard means there is a power-hungry authoritarian roaming the campus looking for a hippie's head to bust. He hauls Britta away as the soundtrack plays Lionel Richie's "Hello," indicating in heavily ironic tones that the two have found a sense of purpose in opposing the other. The jab at performative activism is a particularly cynical moment in a cynical episode that elsewhere made sure to jab at the United Nations ("a fundamentally symbolic organization founded on the principles of high-minded rhetoric and empty gestures").

Episode 52: "Competitive Ecology"

Professor Kane's irritation with the study group hits new heights in this manic episode where none of the major characters seem able to get out of their own way. The group turns themselves inside out to find the right lab partners after discovering Kane wants the class to pair up and make terrariums. After convincing Kane to let them partner up with other members of the group rather than dreaded strangers—*"who are these people?"* Troy asks Abed, honestly confused by the prospect of interacting with somebody not in the group—they turn to infighting. The squabbling is driven by insecurity over popularity, procrastination, and an intense desire to not be the one forced to pair up with non-group member Todd (David Neher). The group's issues with intimacy, manipulation, and insularity are hinted at early on by Kane ("You guys have weird reactions to stuff") and are

Cool Cool Cool

"Competitive Ecology" contains one of the more obscure callouts to the inner workings of Dan Harmon's psyche. Early in the episode, Chang tells the Dean that he is in a relationship with a mannequin leg he found in the boiler room. Later he will look stricken when the leg (which he has named "Veronica") is unceremoniously dumped into a trashcan after being damaged in a fire. This mildly disturbing (even for Chang) character wrinkle derives directly from Harmon's one-time attraction to mannequin legs, which he openly discussed on his podcast *Harmontown*. Years later, Harmon's possession of a sex doll would inspire his girlfriend Cody Heller to write the comedy series *Dummy*.

later fully laid out by Todd, a genial and long-suffering type who finally explodes after Britta almost sets his turtle on fire.

> I thought you were supposed to love each other? Your love is *weird*. And toxic! And it destroys everything it touches.

Instead of showing the group learning anything from being branded as weird, toxic, and destructive, the episode has them lean into it.

Potentially annihilating everything in a more real sense is Chang, whose tenure as Greendale security guard is largely as delusional in nature as the study group's belief that they will be able to talk Kane into giving them special treatment after wasting an entire night arguing rather than building terrariums. Chang's belief in his own importance is rendered as a kind of interior movie. He spins elaborate universes of conspiratorial drama in his mind (replete with faux hardboiled dialogue: "She was all dame, legs that went all the way to the bottom of her torso") while to the world he appears to be just a small man murmuring to himself and staring blankly. Nearly burning down the school, Chang decides that the problem is not that he has made something out of nothing but that he hasn't yet gotten to the bottom of the mystery.

As ever in *Community*, when the choice for a character is between re-examining one's choices and tripling down on an obsession, the obsession always wins.

Episode 53: "Remedial Chaos Theory"

If the paintball episodes revealed the extent to which the makers of *Community* were eager to cross-pollinate in order to fold, spindle, and mutilate the sitcom genre, then the fourth episode of Season 3 made clear just how much the show was ultimately a sandbox for Team Harmon's science fiction–inflected philosophical and moral scenario-spinning. A hall of "What if?" mirrors that reflects back on the participants more than helping them achieve a breakthrough moment, "Remedial Chaos Theory" is structured as an exploratory bottle episode where the characters physically never leave one apartment but are seen inhabiting completely different lives.

A close-to-perfect episode, it starts with a premise that would make a perfectly good story on its own without any meta-narrative garnishing. Troy and Abed have moved in together and are having the group over for a house-warming party. Being arrested adolescents inhabiting the role of adults as though in a game, they wear blazers and try to act mature but don't get everything right (when Britta notices a bowl of olives next to the toilet, Troy admonishes her as though the reason were obvious: "It's a fancy party"). At the start of the party, there are several unacknowledged tensions in the group: irritation with Shirley's baking obsession; Jeff and Annie making "googly eyes" at each other; Pierce's hurt feelings over Troy moving out of his mansion to live with Abed.

But rather than surfacing these issues through sniping or surprise revelations, writer Chris McKenna breaks the episode into a *Rashomon*-style narrative revolver. Jeff proposes rolling a six-sided die to determine who has to meet the pizza delivery guy despite Abed's warning that doing so will create "six different timelines." The moment repeats seven times: one for each roll of the die—with variations ranging from the slight (Troy and Britta being a bit flirtatious) to the major (Pierce is shot in the leg)—and the last where Abed, realizing that Jeff has gamed the role so that there is no chance of him having to get the pizza, grabs the die before it lands and delivers a short statement of purpose.

> Chaos already dominates enough of our lives. The universe is an endless raging sea of randomness. Our job isn't to fight it, but to weather it— together on the raft of life. A raft held together by those few rare, beautiful things that we know to be predictable.

The episode is impressively dedicated to the concept at the risk of turning off viewers looking for a higher shenanigans quotient and less metaphysical speculation. It repeats the same moments in each of the

In "Remedial Chaos Theory," Abed tries to keep things from spinning out of control. NBC/
PHOTOFEST.

six timelines (buzzing doorbell, rolling the die, Jeff hitting his head on
the ceiling fan, Britta singing along to "Roxanne") before making the
seemingly banal fractal shifts (Shirley's pies get burnt, Pierce gives Troy
a housewarming gift) that create larger changes like the flitting of a but-
terfly's wings. The result is a fine balance of disorder and precision that
treats Abed's "sci-fi crap" (as Jeff puts it) viewpoint that the multiverse is
a real thing with complete seriousness. The end tag—a fanciful spin-off
revealing that in the "darkest timeline" Pierce dies, Annie goes insane, Jeff
loses an arm, Troy has to speak through a voice box, and Shirley returns to
drinking—is largely a gag revolving around Abed making fake goatees (for
embracing their "evil" identities). Still, it establishes a baseline of grim possibilities against which the season's darker developments can be measured.

Despite the complications, everything in the episode makes sense,
especially for people given to science fiction speculation about decision
trees, alternate universes, and how bringing an improv comedy mindset
(the "Yes, and" rule) to storytelling explodes possibilities. A little tricky
for everyone else, including the creators. Harmon posted pictures of the
writer's room white board for the episode. It looks like a quantum physics
textbook was hit by a grenade.

Like in McKenna's "Paradigms of Human Memory" from the previous season, "Remedial Chaos Theory" is less about moving things forward than deepening well-worn character grooves and reinterpreting the frame in which the show operates. (One can imagine a different sitcom that follows one of those timelines, checking back on the others occasionally, and possibly even arranging cross-over episodes). It is also a complex statement about what that lack of change means.

Right after Abed's speech about the benefits of predictability, he calls for people to accept each other's "flaws and virtues." Though a generous sentiment, it seems less positive as he goes on.

> Annie will always be driven. Shirley will always be giving. Pierce will never apologize. Britta's sort of a wild card, from my perspective. And Jeff will forever remain a conniving son-of-a-bitch.

Awards Corner

"Remedial Chaos Theory" was immediately hailed as a near masterpiece, the kind of episode that critics and dedicated viewers were going on about for weeks afterward in an attempt to convince as many people as possible to seek it out. The episode garnered *Community* its second and last Emmy nomination. Though the show ultimately lost the award for Outstanding Writing for a Comedy Series, it was to a second-season episode of *Louie* and the other nominees were *Girls* and *Parks and Recreation* so the competition was at least worthy.

More surprisingly, "Remedial Chaos Theory" was nominated for a Hugo Award, the annual science fiction and fantasy award that primarily focuses on literature but also nods to film and television. The award for Best Dramatic Presentation, Short Form commonly goes to heavy-hitting genre shows like *Battlestar Galactica* or *Game of Thrones*—in 2012, *Community* lost to a Neil Gaiman–scripted episode of *Doctor Who* (no surprise there). Starting in 2017, though, another sitcom started making regular appearances in the Hugo Awards: NBC's meta-inventive *The Good Place*, viewed in some critical quarters as picking up the kind of freewheeling, comedic-philosophical explorations pioneered by *Community*.

In a universe of infinite possibilities, does the permanence of that kind of limitation—everyone is who they are, they will never change—seem the best thing to hope for? Or is this simply how Abed, with his love of structure and familiarity, prefers to see the world?

Questions like those (also, why doesn't Abed include Troy in his list of people's characteristics? Is what he calls "the prime timeline" the brightest? Is one-armed Jeff less attractive or more beguiling for being wounded? How many seasons did those other timelines ruin?) make the episode—which scene for scene is one of the season's *least* funny— still far and away one of the show's most rewatchable and infinitely rewarding.

Episode 54: "Horror Fiction in Seven Spooky Steps"

Already an annual tradition by this point in the series, the Halloween episode teases another great Greendale dance but slips instead into a bottle episode. The group never makes it to the party, annoying Troy (calling back to last season's spook show "Epidemiology," he mentions hearing the Dean "got free taco meat from the army"). That is because Britta, leveraging her poor attention to detail and desire to be taken seriously, declares that the personality tests she had everybody take have come back and shown that one of them . . . is deeply disturbed and maybe homicidal. Wanting to study everyone's reactions to see who the killer is, Britta tells a scary story. But because she Brittas the telling of the hook-handed killer urban legend (this is the episode where she discovers her name is a verb), everybody else jumps in to tell their kind of scary story.

What follows is a *Treehouse of Horror*-ish anthology where each story shares the same remote cabin setting but ends up being a wish-fulfillment tale that signals the teller's preoccupations and prejudices. Annie's is a heaving bosom vampire romance with Jeff as the handsome bloodsucker and Britta his "skanky concubine." Shirley's is a Christian Rapture tale where everybody speaks in *Afterschool Special* teen delinquentese and the Dean plays a version of the devil straight out of an evangelical cartoon, shrieking, "Gay marriage!" Pierce's story as usual departs from the assignment at hand and so is less horrorshow than Playboy Mansion fantasy where a brandy-sipping, non-balding version of himself beds each of the women and beats down Abed and Troy. The cleverest is Abed's, a deeply logical, counterintuitive take where he and Britta avoid every mistake of the standard slasher flick victim: "We should call 911 on my fully-charged

Annie's scary fantasy from "Horror Fiction in Seven Spooky Steps" reveals a little too much about what she really thinks of Jeff and Britta. NBC/PHOTOFEST.

cell phone, lock the doors, and then stand back-to-back in the middle of the room holding knives."

Which one is sane? Are they all mad? Does Britta know how to correctly administer a psychological profile? The truth is less in the answering than the telling.

Episode 55: "Advanced Gay"

Many of the study group's men tumble chaotically into their father issues while the one whose father-son drama was one of the show's first dynamic conflicts (Abed) steers clear. In the A story, Pierce experiences a couple of revelations, the first of which leads (albeit briefly) to something quite unusual for him: growth. Discovering Hawthorne Wipes (the source of his family millions) has a gay customer base, Pierce tosses aside his homophobia to embrace the mercantilist possibilities. He introduces a new rainbow-flagged product, Hawthorne Pride Wipes ("They may cost more, but they're gayer") and sponsors a school dance, the unfortunately named Gay Bash. Pierce briefly becomes a Greendalian folk hero to the school's gay students.

Meanwhile, Jeff's unresolved and still unadmitted father issues (even following the soul-baring of last season's "Intermediate Documentary Filmmaking") lead him to interfere after the appearance of Pierce's domineering patriarch, Cornelius (Larry Cedar), causes Pierce to ditch his brief flirtation with open-mindedness. Cornelius is an especially baroque character, imagined as a nineteenth-century-style robber baron with a sideline in eugenics ("He's the Abed of racism," Shirley marvels after he describes Britta's Swedish heritage as "tainted by generations of race mixing with Laplanders") and so fixated on an insane notion of racial purity he wears a wig made of ivory. There is a lot going on in the "edible complex" (as Britta puts it) melodrama even before Jeff berates Cornelius until the old man, who must be pushing 140 at this point given his Gilded Age outfit and speech patterns, dies from a heart attack. This ostensibly frees Pierce from his overbearing father and conveniently moves the episode past its unconcluded gay storyline

The fun, clever B story is a continuation of the *Good Will Hunting* subplot: Troy's sublime mechanical aptitude is again fought over by Jerry and the still-ominously looming Vice Dean Laybourne—respectively representatives of Greendale's rival plumbing and air conditioning repair programs. A self-parody of an ominous outro from Laybourne ("This isn't over, *Troy Barnes*") sets up the two-parter air conditioning repair school

---

Streets Ahead

"Advanced Gay" includes a couple of very under-the-radar verbal gags. When Laybourne introduces Troy to the room temperature room, he pronounces, "It's incredible. That's what we do, Troy: *In*credible, *in*visible, *in*believeable things. We're an *un*seen, *un*known, *un*vincible fraternity." Delivered whip-fast and then gone, the lines were likely only appreciated by an extremely specific slice of the audience (i.e., fans of sub rosa grammatically incorrect alliteration).

---

moral conundrum that concludes the season. But the fantastical expansion of the luxurious and secretly powerful air conditioning repair brotherhood conspiracy—introducing Troy to a seemingly simple chamber, Laybourne says, "Have you heard the expression 'room temperature'? This is the room"—remains a tantalizing tangent suggesting the further universes of possibility contained in this supposedly third-rate community college.

Does City College have a room temperature room?

Episode 56: "Studies in Modern Movement"

Are these people even attending class anymore? Shifting as it occasionally does into the territory of a sitcom where all the characters can focus on is their relationship to each other, *Community* moves on from the last few more action-oriented episodes to one where the big drama boils down to whether Annie can become Troy and Abed's roommate while staying their friend. Can she? Also, a new hashtag is born (#Anniesmove! Don't try live tweeting the episode now).

The study group gathers to help Annie move out of her skid row apartment—except for Jeff, who engineers an extremely complex pretend illness (involving a phone call to Britta complete with a faked PA announcement to make it seem he was in the hospital rather than clothes shopping). As frequently happens, Jeff gets caught in his trickery. This time it's the Dean, who blackmails the object of his extremely intense, unblinking attention into lunch and karaoke.

Annie tries to go with Troy and Abed's far more anarchic flow. While she appreciates their sweeter gestures, like the shadow puppet show that welcomes her, when discovering the apartment's other bedroom has been turned into a "Dreamatorium" (basically the Holodeck from *Star Trek: Next Generation*—which, let's be honest, seems like a necessity for any collegiate dwelling), Annie unleashes a tirade against her roommates' immaturity.

It comes together with relatively little fuss, depositing everybody not too far from their starting point and more or less unscathed—even Pierce, who wastes a few minutes of screen time ruining Annie's old apartment with spilled paint and a blown wall socket; even Shirley and Britta after passively-aggressively picking up a hitchhiker (there was an argument about religion, it got weird) who may or may not have been Jesus.

Episode 57: "Documentary Filmmaking: Redux"

The season's first deconstruction of filmmaking finds Abed behind the camera again. This time, though, unlike last season's "Intermediate Documentary Filmmaking" where he manipulated and tweaked and played with how people were being represented in the style of a mock-documentary sitcom, this time he has a very clear inspiration point. "Ever seen *Hearts of Darkness*?" Abed asks the camera, laying the episode's inspiration right out there without any subterfuge. "Way better than *Apocalypse Now*," the film whose chaotic production the documentary chronicled in gory cineastic detail.

Tasked with shooting a new commercial for Greendale to entice more youths to enter its hallowed, if black mold–spotted, halls—the last one featured pre-Internet graphics and dance moves not seen since MTV was still a cultural force—the Dean knows who he wants his stars to be: "Greendale's brightest, most coincidentally diverse—Hispanics notwithstanding—study group."

It starts off simply, with the Dean looking like he will come in well under his $2,000 budget. But all too soon he is in full creator spin-out, waxing grandiloquent in Cecil B. DeMille garb (jodhpurs, riding crop), issuing baffling dictates, and driving the cast to the point of madness. Except, that is, for Pierce, who spends the entire episode insisting he won't come out of his trailer until the situation on set is to his liking. It's a funny bit given that he has to rent that trailer that he won't leave, not to mention the suggestion that the whole thing was an elegant solution by the writers to getting Chase out of everyone else's way for a while.

By the time Greendale's most famous alumni, Luis Guzman, shows up for his part in the documentary, the Dean's madness has transformed from Coppola to Brando, which as parodies go is a bit too easy. But Guzman's words of wisdom to the Dean save the day and the commercial. Cut to reconciliation.

For now.

Episode 58: "Foosball and Nocturnal Vigilantism"

Foosball; Nick Kroll doing a *vehy Cherman* accent while decrying "Teutonic punnery"; anime; "Abed is Batman now"; Dr. Zizmor; "Daybreak"—this is a great big candy dish of an episode that even in the midst of an overly elaborate setup manages an honestly affecting moment of rapprochement.

A rare instance where both storylines are equally strong with the episode confidently toggling between (due possibly to director Anthony Russo's flair for managing complex plots and tonal shifts; this being the last time he or his brother Joe would helm an episode). The A story has Jeff getting in a snit about the German exchange students' obnoxious hogging of the student lounge foosball table. Jeff's brittle competitiveness (the shadow side of his faked nonchalance) spikes and leads to a challenge requiring mentoring by undercover Foosball expert Shirley (like her drinking, she gave it up years ago because of the demons it unlocked) so he can kick "das butt." Their training sessions turn into a titanic struggle suddenly rendered in an anime sequence where the exaggerated grimaces and flashes of lightning barely contain the emotions raging in each of them. Black-and-white flashbacks reveal Shirley was once the schoolyard Foosball bully Big Cheddar who humiliated twelve-year-old Jeff. They make up, decide competing with Germans is a sucker's bet, and walk away hand-in-hand—one of the show's sweetest, subtlest moments as for a second adult Jeff and Shirley are replaced by their childhood selves.

Tonally adventurous and emotionally intense, that storyline is largely conventional compared to the B story where the self-referentiality is dense, knowing, and knotty. Troy and Abed are in a tizzy over their $299 special "Extended, Extended Cut" *Dark Knight* DVD. But just as a rare vase in a *Three Stooges* short is destined for shattering, the DVD is accidentally cracked by Annie before they can watch it. When she frantically tries to come up with a way to hide the damage from Abed, Troy asks her, "Do you know how many sitcoms have done the 'secretly replace a broken, priceless item' thing? Because Abed does." (This again invites the question Are we watching *Community* or is it watching us?) When Annie falls into the exact sitcom trap Troy has described, Abed uses the opportunity to dress up as Batman for the first time since Season 1's "Introduction to Statistics" and go hunting for the supposed thief while Christian Bale–growling gothic pronouncements ("There can be no peace while crime spits and dances on the grave of justice"). As in most every other sitcom variation on this kind of misunderstanding, Annie comes clean and Abed pretends to be fine with it all.

But unlike most sitcoms, this one ends with a glimpse of Leonard's YouTube channel, where he rates frozen pizzas.

Episode 59: "Regional Holiday Music"

And now things get weird. Or weirder. Also dark. But quite enjoyable. How do we know this? Because in the opening segment where everybody says what they're doing over Christmas break, Abed lays it out: "This semester has been so long and dark and angry. I was thinking we could have some light-hearted fun as a family."

Much like Beetlejuice, Greendale's glee club gets called out once a season less to mock the all-too-easily mockable institution itself than the show *Glee*, which premiered the same year as *Community* and whose mix of tear-jerking sentimentality and faux-cool mashup numbers was (if possible) even more eminently mockable. Greendale's glee club made a brief appearance in Season 1's "Modern Warfare" (luring competitors to their paint-splattered demise with a peppy take on "Hit Me with Your Best Shot") and in Season 2's "Paradigms of Human Memory" (dying off-screen in a bus crash, after which the study group fills in for them).

Third time out, a brand-new glee club appears and is ever-so briefly seen performing Christmas songs and a cringey pop medley ("Elton Lil' John Lennon") in the cafeteria. They are quickly dispatched by Jeff (irritated as ever by people having fun loudly), who has Chang serve them with a cease-and-desist letter for performing unlicensed music. This leads to the club's collective mental breakdown and mass hospitalization that feels like an overreaction but such is the writing staff's sustained venom for the forced glee of glee clubs and *Glee* (the latter tagged in a joke as far back as Season 1's "Basic Genealogy").

What follows is an *Invasion of the Body Snatchers* scenario in the form of a musical. When the study group rebuffs a recruitment attempt by the glee club instructor Cory "Mr. Rad" Radison (*Saturday Night Live*'s dorkily menacing Taran Killam)—a sweater vest and a smile described by Troy as "human froyo" and Jeff as "equal parts Hanson and Manson"—he sets about picking them off one at a time. But instead of being axed to death in shadowy corridors, the group is seduced by a sweet, soulful song that appeals to each of their vanities and fears.

Victim zero is Abed, whom Cory brings on board with a smart little ditty that plays to Abed's TV holiday special–formed desire for the whole gang to be together for Christmas. Under Cody's spell, Abed repeats the trick. Troy raps. Annie indulges her love of vamping with a Marilyn Monroe-esque bump and grind (also a sharp takedown of the dumb bombshell routine). Shirley gets to rescue a children's choir whose public school refuses to acknowledge Jesus by belting out a war-on-Christmas number. Pierce is won over by Troy and Abed's honestly quite snappy "We Didn't Start the Fire"–style countdown number that is also a blatant frontal assault on generational vanity ("Baby boomer Santa / Thank you for everything"). By the time Abed realizes the extent of Cory's mania, everyone but Britta has become a glee zombie. But in a nice turnabout, she saves the day through Britta-ing the Christmas pageant. Her tuneless singing so enrages Cory that he admits he killed the Season 2 glee club by cutting their brake lines.

As Abed said at the start, "dark and angry." But while the satire is relentless and biting, the combination of tart musical parody, dense pop culture comedy, and smart character work elevates the episode above its sinister twist ending and makes it one of the season's high points.

Episode 60: "Urban Matrimony and the Sandwich Arts"

Coming back from Christmas break, the show takes a breather and indulges in a good old-fashioned sitcom ratings booster: the (re)wedding episode. It begins with a high adorability quotient. Andre (last seen being weirded out by Chang in last season's "Applied Anthropology and Culinary Arts") pops into the cafeteria with a Boyz II Men–style backup trio to serenade Shirley and ask for her hand in (re)marriage: "I've loved you ever since there was a Soviet Union and only one Damon Wayans."

In many ways, Shirley is the most consistently short-changed study group character. She often has the least developed storylines, serves largely as a reaction foil, and frequently has her larger dramatic moments end up being in service of other characters (her surprise Foosball badassery and youthful flashback in "Foosball and Nocturnal Vigilantism," for example, are largely there for Jeff's catharsis). This episode is a rare exception. The rest of the study group engage in their minor shenanigans, but really this is Shirley's story.

While the rehearsal is being planned, Shirley gets a different proposal. Fired by Hawthorne Wipes after his father's death means they no longer have to indulge him, Pierce is now a rudderless rich guy in Gordon Gekko attire looking for something to do. Seeing another opportunity for well-intentioned meddling, Britta suggests he invest in Shirley's idea for a sandwich shop in the cafeteria.

Even though there are few surprise-surprises in the episode, it's another good example of how much the writers enjoy peeking inside their characters to find new depths and hidden histories. As much as the show wants to play inside and exemplify the sitcom form, it still enjoys breaking conventions, such as by letting characters reveal different facets rather than hitting the same personality quirk–based comedic beats in one half-hour after another.

Just when the season had Britta wearing a deeper groove as the 360-degree klutz, this episode lets her break out. In preparation for Shirley's rehearsal, Annie and her snooty wedding planner pal are getting ready to look down their nose at Britta's marriage-is-for-suckers proclamations when they discover she is an ace decorator and flower arranger. Though unexpected, Britta's shame over her mastery of patriarchy-defined gender skills is both a callback to earlier episodes where she feared her rebel image was a fake and in itself another Britta malapropism ("I'm one of the Steppenwolf wives"). This pushing away of her instincts also mirrors Troy's denial of his innate mechanical repairing skills.

As for Shirley, not long after the season showed her dark childhood bully side, this episode lets her pull further away from the sweet-voiced church lady stereotype by revealing her to also be a top-notch entrepreneur. Impressed by her presentation, the Dean praises her in a very

---

Trope Talk

"Urban Matrimony and the Sandwich" provides perhaps the first Season 3 iteration of a treasured *Community* gag. Only instead of serving the line up to Jeff, who usually gets most of the more cutting zingers, Annie delivers it to Jeff when he flubs writing a toast for Shirley's rehearsal: "'Webster's Dictionary defines'? That is the Jim Belushi of speech openings. It accomplishes nothing, but everyone keeps using it and nobody understands why."

revealing manner: "I cannot believe you learned all this at Greendale. You're *very* professional."

After this validation, the rehearsal itself is somewhat anticlimactic except for when Shirley gets Andre to agree to be less sexist and let her be a wife with a life. Given the running side plot where Troy and Abed have briefly "de-weirded" themselves in preparation for the rehearsal—which, ironically, given the suits, lack of *Inspector Spacetime* references, and forced attempts at their idea of adult banter feels odder and more performative than their natural state à la Abed in last season's "Critical Film Studies"— this slightly drab ending feels like the show trying out a de-weirdification of itself.

It did not take.

Episode 61: "Contemporary Impressionists"

Picking up on "Horror Fiction in Seven Easy Steps," this is another episode suggesting—well, sending up signal flares, really—that the scrim of sanity is laid very, very thinly over most of the study group's psyches.

In short, things are getting weird. Again.

Britta's over-enthusiastic psychoanalyzing detects something off in Jeff's behavior. Oddly she is right. Much of the comedy plays off Jeff's male-model hotness now boosted by his other superpower (utter self-confidence) which has recently been augmented by therapy and anti-anxiety medication. Jeff ignores Britta's warning that anxiety was the only thing keeping his ego in check, declaring himself so confident he can now do things he "never thought possible"—like wearing aviator shades. The Dean spots Jeff in his accelerated state of attractiveness and in one of television history's great pratfalls, collapses to the floor in a paroxysm of desire. This is not a subtle episode, but what works, works.

The B story continues another running discussion in the study group: How long do we continue coddling Abed? In an easy setup for another dance-and-costumes climax, the group discovers Abed owes thousands of dollars to a celebrity impersonator company run by an out-of-work French Stewart impersonator (played by a very tetchy French Stewart). To pay off the debt, they agree to work a bar mitzvah in a range of costumes that recall glorious episodes of Halloween past: Shirley as Oprah; different stages of Michael Jackson portrayed by Troy (early Afro stage) and Britta (disturbingly dead-on with the late stage paleness and cheekbones); Pierce as "fat Brando"; and incredibly Abed in tight cocktail dress and slicked-back hair as Jamie Lee Curtis in *True Lies*.

The party builds to a wacky crescendo when Jeff, drunk on psychotropic medication and being told he is a more attractive Ryan Seacrest, goes Incredible Hulk by ripping his shirt open and demanding people look at him. Chang, recently empowered by the Dean to offer college credit to unpaid security interns, finds several eager pre-adolescent boys willing to join his ersatz army and "chang the world."

While Jeff's issue seems fixable and Chang's likely to implode, back at Troy and Abed's things turn more dire. Recalling other episodes where characters despaired of balancing being Abed's friend with the costs of indulging his manias, Troy blows up on discovering that Abed hired more celebrity impersonators just after they paid off his debt. The two make up and Abed agrees to be more considerate. But then Abed enters the Dreamatorium alone, imagining himself on a spaceship only to find Evil Abed from the "Remedial Chaos Theory" darkest timeline waiting for him like a devil of solitude: "There are many advantages of traveling by yourself." Sounding like notes from an unconvinced critic or annoyed network executive, Abed pushes back, "This is really crazy, and inaccessible, and too dark." But still, the two Abeds fly on into the imaginary galactic night, suggesting an inner turmoil between the compromise of friendship and the purity of isolation.

Episode 62: "Digital Exploration of Interior Design"

This is possibly the highlight of the season with one of the series' most imaginative science fiction plot devices and a fracture within the study group's sturdiest relationship that is never quite recovered. Also "corpo-humanoid" is uttered for the first time on network television and an international sandwich franchise corporation willingly presents itself as a sinister cabal straight out of a crummy VHS–only movie that Abed would have loved.

At the start of the episode, things appear to be proceeding at a moderate level of Thursday night pre-watershed tomfoolery. Shirley is upset about the Dean selling out her cafeteria sandwich shop idea to Subway. Annie is overly invested in Jeff's needy desire to find out why a woman named Kim left a hate note for him. Troy and Abed, always looking for ways to do a smart sequel, try to one-up their school-spanning blanket fort from last season's "Conspiracy Theories and Interior Design" by building a massive pillow fort so they can get into the *Guinness Book of World Records*. While the Jeff storyline is largely filler, the rest of the episode explores new territory.

Building on the previous episode's hinting that Abed's neuro-divergence could strain his friendships, the fort-construction is tangled up once Troy realizes that Abed never listens to any of his ideas. Much as Evil Abed encouraged Abed to go his own way in the last episode, this time Troy is visited by Vice Dean Laybourne, who suggests maybe Troy and Abed's relationship is less one of equal friends and "more of a self-centered nerd and his naïve, obedient lapdog." Playing both sides, Laybourne later encourages Abed not to accept any of Troy's changes with overheated rhetoric that appeals to Abed's habit of framing everything in mediated melodramatic terms: "Don't corrupt the hosts to pacify the parasites."

Seed planted. Troy and Abed have their first true fight, which is played as mock combat—Troy's blanket fort versus Abed's pillow fort—rather than the two simply talking out their frustrations with the other. Despite the surface playfulness, it is a moment neither truly recovers from.

Always looking to burnish her anti-establishment credentials, Britta jumps at the chance to help Shirley get Subway out of Greendale. She is even willing to seduce the company's on-campus student representative "Subway" (Travis Schuldt) a "corpo-humanoid" who legally changed his name to the company's and presents as a blindingly upbeat and clean-cut walking billboard who wants everyone to "Eat Fresh!" As frequently happens on the show, Subway's cheer-squad positivity is a ruse. After he and Britta bond over their love of handicapped animals and recite quotes from *1984*—"She had become a physical necessity"—like samizdat, romance is inevitable. It is also doomed, with Subway being hustled away by corporate security (again, as product placements go, it is a bit odd the company okayed being portrayed in this dystopic fashion) and Britta left yet again heartbroken and disappointed. The segment's tart repartee and deviously creative conceptualizing is made all the punchier for moving with speed, not belaboring its cleverness, and suggesting an entire dark universe of corporatized humans in the world outside Greendale that as the show goes on starts looking less appealing day by day.

Episode 63: "Pillows and Blankets"
The second half of the great pillow-and-blanket-fort kerfuffle of 2012 brings the Troy and Abed conflict to a bitter crescendo; Keith David auditions for Season 6, and the Dean asks a question that becomes more pertinent with each passing season: "Do people go to classes?"

Because the episode is done in the style of Ken Burns's *Civil War* documentary, it tends not to get as much attention as the other parody episodes (perhaps the PBS demographic was watching nature documentaries or a Peter, Paul, and Mary concert when *Community* was on). But even when veering away from their pulpier mainstream parodies (*Law and Order*, *GoodFellas*), the show's makers still produce an episode that neatly threads a note-perfect homage with its own specific quirks.

Troy secedes from Abed's Pillowtown to form Blanketsburg. The resulting war—basically mass pillow fights—picks up on the Greendalian penchant for sudden collapses of law and order but is this time refracted through a faux-military historical perspective. All the Ken Burns trademarks are rolled out, from the careful study of maps to slow pans across still-frame images, eyewitness testimony (in this case text messages given the importance of letters home to widows), mournful music, and sonorous narration by David, whose gravity underlines the comedically low stakes of a giant pillow fight "lasting days, costing hundreds of dollars, and resulting in over twelve transfers."

As ever at Greendale, the chaos provides an open landscape for everyone to let their freak flags fly. Shirley joins Blanketsburg convinced that Britta might get Troy hooked "on the weed." Signing up with Pillowtown because "Abed is weirder and more foreign," Pierce is soon strapping on dozens of pillows and charging into battle like a creepy Stay Puft Marshmallow Man. As ever, Britta freelances poorly (ostensibly a combat photographer, none of her pictures turn out); Annie tries to help (tending to "soldiers with broken glasses and lightly grazed testicles" as the war's Florence Nightingale); Jeff manipulates through cynical rhetoric ("critics suggest he merely improvised hot-button patriotic dogma in a Ferris Bueller-ian attempt to delay schoolwork"); and Chang turns warlord with his band of pre-teen enforcers christened "the "Changlorious Basterds."

Also, Star-Burns reminds everyone his name is Alex.

A *Waiting for Guffman*–style turn of events suddenly sucks the energy out of the conflict, leaving Troy and Abed in desultory single combat. The Winger save—retrieving the pair's invisible magic "friendship hats" that he had sarcastically invented earlier in the episode to get them to compromise—works, and peace is restored.

But like the actual Civil War, dissension remains.

Episode 64: "Origins of Vampire Mythology"

Are hard-to-quit, bad relationships analogous to drug addiction? Is it funnier that Britta once went out with a carny or that his name was Blade?

How many times do people need to say "Blade" before Troy and Abed decide to watch 1998's Wesley Snipes vampire-hunting classic *Blade*? (Side question: did the writers give that name to Britta's ex just to include that reference?) Was there any reason to make Chang and Pierce best friends for a day besides giving them something to do while everybody else was dealing with the Blade issue? Who is more unsure of themselves: Britta, Jeff, or the Dean?

"Origins of Vampire Mythology" contains not just many unanswerable questions but a fistful of gimmicks that would have sunk it were the writing not so strong. After the high-concept civil war two-parter, the show gets back to basics by dredging up a trough of characters' insecurities and using them for one of the season's more touching episodes.

After recovering from mocking Britta's romantic past—the carnival is in town (gimmick no. 1) with Blade manning the duck shooting booth—the group shifts to helping her steer clear. Putting Annie in charge due to her past with addiction, Britta hands over her phone and demands that she be handcuffed "to the radiator like a mother-flipping carny-banging werewolf." Annie does as asked, successfully at first. But a gambit in which Annie lets Britta sneak her phone back so Annie can text Britta as

---

Inspector Spacetime

The end tags in "Pillows and Blankets," "Origins of Vampire Mythology," and "Virtual Systems Analysis" are somewhat earlier season throwbacks. Both feature Troy and Abed in dense game-play constructions where everybody else is merely a walk-on character. In the first, they put a bow on the episode's public television reenactment as they pretend to be running a fund raiser, expertly mimicking awkwardly grinning time-filling banter. In the second, Abed performs a stand-up comedy routine (suit jacket with rolled-up sleeves, fake brick backdrop and all) in the library to Troy, Jeff, and the Dean, only every single gag is specific just to him and his roommate ("Ever notice the difference between me and Troy brushing our teeth?"). In the last, *Troy and Abed in the Morning* broadcasts from their apartment in an initially jovial mood but turns dark after Annie rearranges the boys' sleeping area and Abed emits the high-pitched keening indicating an incipient short-circuit brought about by an interruption of the natural order.

Blade saying mean things just inflames Britta's desire. Annoyed that Annie doesn't understand Britta's self-hating need to be in bad relationships, Troy texts something nice (as Blade), instantly breaking his hold over Britta. The look on Troy's face as he taps out the unseen message to Britta is all the more heartachingly romantic given that the two of them never quite manage to openly express themselves to each other.

Laybourne bullies the Dean—now into model trains as his obsession of the week (gimmick no. 2)—into putting some pressure on Troy to bring his virtuosic repair skills over to the air conditioning annex cult.

After going to the carnival to see Blade (Kirk Fox) and spending hundreds of dollars shooting fake ducks and trying to discover the secret of his appeal, Jeff returns to Britta with the answer: Blade had an accident where "the part of his brain that feels shame" was destroyed, removing the need to prove anything about himself, explaining his confidence and irresistibility (gimmick no. 3).

Once again Jeff is assigned final summation speechmaking duties. Rather than bring the whole group together, though, this time he is speaking to Britta about the two of them and their self-destructive patterns: "Stop making our hatred of ourselves someone else's job and just stop hating ourselves."

Good advice if they could ever follow it.

Episode 65: "Virtual Systems Analysis"

Romances are teased—Troy and Britta, Annie and Jeff, the Dean and a new schizophrenic clothing scheme—but largely left unfulfilled in favor of extended time inside Abed's imagination.

In a half-hearted swipe at reminding viewers the study group is still theoretically a study group, the episode opens with the gang grousing about cramming for their . . . biology test. Given a reprieve by a last-minute class cancellation, they break for lunch. Noticing the residual flickers of Troy and Britta's maybe-kind-of-sort-of romantic connection from the last episode, Annie maneuvers them into having lunch together, promising Abed she'll play with him in the Dreamatorium.

The rest of the episode scans like an extended and emotionally heavy *Star Trek: Next Generation* Holodeck riff by way of Christopher Nolan with Abed's "simulations" uncovering his anxieties about the group abandoning him once they lose patience. Annie makes a poor *Inspector Spacetime* substitute for Troy; her "temporary constable Geneva" goes overboard on the Cockney whimsey, causing a rift in the Dreamatorium.

Abed's simulations become increasingly complex albeit pegged to recognizable TV scenarios. In one, Abed voices Jeff in a *Grey's Anatomy*-esque hospital drama ("It's a sexy, emotional school where doctors save lives and make love"); Troy is injected with truth serum and starts spitting out secrets ("I'm more turned on by women in pajamas than lingerie. I just want to know they feel comfortable. I didn't get *Inception!*"); Pierce shows up as a "tragic, heart-wrenching Alzheimer's patient and Emmy contender"; and the vending machines only sell Abed's favorite food: buttered noodles. In the meta variation, Abed reimagines Jeff and Annie in their unexpected kiss from the end of Season 1, the potential of which has been hanging out there ever since.

Ultimately Annie breaks down Abed's defenses by convincing him to not see every unexpected behavioral change in his friends as a threat ("You don't have a patent on being a control freak") and reminding him that his mental predictions are like great science fiction: "They're impressive and detailed and insightful. But they're not accurate for crap."

Episode 66: "Basic Lupine Urology"

The first *Community* episode directed by Rob Schrab resembles the Channel 101 satire videos he used to make—only with a budget, network permission, and fewer robots.

Although this *Law and Order* parody aired two years after the original had gone off the air following a twenty-year run, the source material's taut predictability, repetitiveness, and specificity made it not just an easily replicable style but something that the pop culture–besotted characters of *Community* would have known well. It's all here: the opener with the *chun-chun* sound effect; darker and richer lighting; the intense but quip-ready detectives pressured to get more evidence; the walk-and-talks; the culminating courtroom showdown where the suspect tearfully confesses; even a street scene where the campus of a suburban Colorado community college somehow has crowded sidewalks and a hot dog cart.

Everything is Harmonized just enough, finding the comedy in the self-aware space between the gravity of the Dick Wolf format and the story's sandbox silliness while still showing a forensic dedication to mimicking the original; it's clearly a parody made by fans. The opening narration is tweaked (explaining itself as stories of "the goofballs who run around starting trouble, and the eggheads who make a big deal about it"); detectives Troy and Abed try to one-up each other with jokes about the crime until Abed reminds him that (per *Law and Order* style) "we can't both do the zinger"; and the forensics expert who examines the body (in this case a murdered yam) and declares the intensity of "smushing" intentional.

(These TV-as-TV episodes again invite the question, Are we inside Abed's imagination, seeing the world as something constructed according to a script between commercial breaks, or is the reality of Greendale just that fungible? Is the entire school a kind of pop culture Dreamatorium in which the characters twiddle with the settings? Style: Dick Wolf New York procedural. Mood: Serious but wink-y.)

It appears as though the study group is on the verge of for once getting some school work done when their biology project—growing a yam in a glass jar—is ruined after a mystery assailant stomps on it. Despite the reservations of Professor Kane, an investigation is launched and everyone plays to their strengths. Abed jumps into the role of cynical street cop with the same ease that he imitated a police chief in Season 1's "The Science of Illusion." Shirley tries to keep things calm and organized. Annie and Jeff bring back their debate team skills to lead the prosecution in the faux trial—Annie doing most of the work, Jeff delivering the coup de grace ("boiled water is the icicle stabbing of yam killing," calling back to the old murder mystery riddle)—that Kane appears baffled to be conducting. Other minor characters are woven in from the ever-put-upon Todd as the prime suspect to Star-Burns as the dirtbag informant. The Dean largely gets in the way but is there to deliver an astounded "*Awesome*" after Kane concludes a gripping monologue (again, at a pitch wholly inappropriate to the investigation of a smushed yam) with his character Omar's trademark line from *The Wire*, "A man's gotta have a code."

Unlike *Law and Order*, though, this episode ends on a cliffhanger: the death of Star-Burns. By meth lab explosion. Naturally.

Episode 67: "Course Listing Unavailable"

Given that it has been a while since Greendale had a good riot, it might make sense that an otherwise unremarkable event like the death of Star-Burns would push the school over the edge. Again. But in truth the passing of the top-hatted bottom-feeder is as good a spark as any for the uprising that sets in motion a linked storyline that builds though the remaining episodes toward the season's conclusion.

After mocking Britta's psych-major attempts to force everyone into grief counseling over Star-Burns, the group finds their grief when the Dean announces Professor Kane is gone, biology class is canceled, and they will all need to attend summer school. It makes for one of the inflection points that crop up throughout the show's first half: the institution's chaos and lack of professionalism is generally treated as part of its scrappy underdog charm (City College, boo!). But every now and then, students start wondering what they are paying for. Which is why Star-Burns's memorial pivots to a litany of grievances about Greendale: "This Fallujah of higher learning" (Jeff); "Warped me like a Barbie in a microwave" (Annie); and "Let's burn this mother down!" (Pierce, channeling his generation's love for trashing campuses).

Despite some double-entendre attempts at asserting authority ("This is my school and I'll enter whatever I want"), the Dean's attempts to maintain control fail, leading to his giving full Patriot Act–level authority to Chang and his pepper spray–wielding child minions. Chang's tranquilizer

Cool Cool Cool

Those with a good eye for couture noticed that on a scale ranging from Last Minute Halloween Outfit to Full Lady Gaga, the Dean's outfits had been steadily increasing in complexity during Season 3. As the show's most obsessive character next to Abed, the Dean (who did seem to be getting his Dalmatian fetish under control, limiting it in Season 3 largely to the occasional desktop toy) used fancy dress-up as a stress-relieving way to maintain some control amidst the chaos that his poor Dean-ing led to especially when he put a suit on to help be a more "lean, mean, Dean-ing machine" in "Biology 101." He was gaining some self-awareness of the problem by the time he appeared as "Duali-Dean" (normal Dean attire on the left side of his body while the right was half a dress and a long wig) in "Virtual Systems Analysis," at first showing off his look but later breaking down, "I think I went too far with this one. *I have to go to the bank today* . . . Come on, Craig, get your life together."

But two episodes later in "Course Listing Unavailable," we see behind the scenes how the Dean uses dress-up to deal with conflict. Having to break some bad news to the study group, he goes to his happy place—the overstuffed costume wardrobe (so many feather boas)—and comes out as a Moulin Rouge dancer to soften his message that biology class "has been can-can-cancelled!" It might not have been the most psychologically healthy way to handle the moment, but the outfit was killer.

gun (teased earlier in "Contemporary Impressionists") is used to take down the Dean and replace him with a doppelganger Dean (J.P. Manoux).

Given all that, the episode would seem to end darkly. But the conclusion brings a clever and slightly cheerier twist that calls back to the forking multiverse possibilities raised in "Remedial Chaos Theory." The group is back in Troy and Abed's apartment waiting for a pizza delivery and listening to Abed wonder whether they are in the best or darkest timeline. He answers his own question in an uncharacteristically emotional manner: "We're together. That makes this the perfect timeline."

Episode 68: "Curriculum Unavailable"

Another clip show packed with memories of moments that we have never seen before that suggests the showrunners could be going back to the well one time too many, but when the material is this strong it hardly matters.

The reign of Chang continues at Greendale, which the group has not been back to in two months. Unknown to them, he and the Doppel-Deaner have arranged an elaborate ploy by which Abed (who has been dressing up as Inspector Spacetime and sneaking around Greendale trying to prove the real Dean is missing) will not face charges if he attends a session with fake therapist "Dr. Heidi" (John Hodgman) whose real mission is to convince the whole group they are not students but former asylum inmates sharing a delusion about an invented place named Greendale.

Their experience at Greendale having made them all susceptible to outlandish theories, this works initially. Most of the episode is filled out by their giving the doctor memories of moments the audience has never seen à la "Paradigms of Human Memory," many of which could have served as raw material for a better Season 4: Britta on peyote; Jeff and Annie at the Wigging Out dance; a paintball episode done as 1930s gangster flick; inexplicable classes (Baby Talk; Advanced Breath Holding; Can I Fry That? and Ladders, the last of which would be brought back in Season 6), and the Dean's human chess game.

Once they discover Dr. Heidi's psy-ops campaign, the group tosses aside the relevant points he brought up—how come none of them can speak Spanish? Why are they still attending? Why do they overlook Abed's more troubling breakdowns—to do what they are best at: Ignoring their problems by focusing on an external threat and finding new ways to tweak existing formats (in this case, *Troy and Abed in the Morning* moving to a *Playboy After Dark* format).

Episode 69: "Digital Estate Planning"

A peak in *Community*'s concept episodes: inventive, spit-take funny, structurally audacious, plus Giancarlo Esposito (as his frequently ominous self). The show would have trouble repeating this formula of success in later seasons even when it swung for the fences. This episode also sets up some of the more unfortunate aspects of Season 4.

As in the other animated episodes, this one contains a small amount of live-action framing. In this case, the study group has gathered per Pierce's late father Cornelius's instructions. Arriving at a high-tech gaming studio, they are informed by Cornelius's suspiciously serene assistant Gilbert (Esposito) that a video game has been specially designed for them all to play. Once play begins, the show is rendered as a fourth-generation console game: plinky 8-bit music, blocky characters, and a lot of leaping around. Discovering the point of the game is for them all to compete for Pierce's inheritance, he withdraws into a despondent funk while the others rally to help him win.

Cornelius's past as a ruling-class industrialist with a pathology for racial purity and toying with Pierce's emotions hangs heavy in the game from the not-so-veiled symbolism of its goal (freeing the "white crystal of discipline" from "the black caverns") to the form of their enemies (hairy

Fans at the 2012 San Diego Comic-Con show their love for Troy and Abed's 8-bit avatars from the "Digital Estate Planning" episode. PAT LOIKA—SDCC 2012, CC BY 2.0/WIKIMEDIA COMMONS.

Different Timelines

After being let go from *Community* in 2012, Harmon convened a somewhat bittersweet Reddit AMA where he held forth on several topics including what might have been. He acknowledged writing at least part of Season 3 in the belief that he was going to be fired or the show would be canceled, which explains the series-ending feel of the last episode. Harmon also describes the original end tag Adam Countee wrote for "Digital Estate Planning." In that scene, Abed re-programs the Hawthorne video game in a way he thinks Pierce would prefer: every time Pierce's avatar throws a baseball at the floating head of Cornelius, he gets a thousand points and hears, "Great job, son!" Pierce plays it for a minute, then gives Abed a hug. It's an absolute heartbreaker of a scene and could have helped silence the "too cool for school" jabs at the show. But Chase refused to shoot the tag.

hippies) and even the paperwork (a wildly racist NDA). That legacy of manipulation and spite is manifested by Gilbert's reveal of a decades-long resentment of the Hawthornes and his jumping into the game to compete for the prize. Things go poorly at first in 8-bit world with Pierce unable to work the controls, Annie and Shirley accidentally killing civilians, and Abed being distracted by a female NPC whose binary thinking makes her his most enticing possible love interest since the Secret Service agent from Season 2's "Intro to Political Science" (he's enthralled enough to download her onto a thumb drive before quitting the game, suggesting that the entire episode might have been better framed around Abed than Pierce).

Eventually the study group gets their act together—teaming up more efficiently in the game than the real world largely due to the power of Abed's logic brain to game the game and Pierce's last-minute *Dr. Strangelove* nuclear-warhead-riding gambit. The second reveal, that Gilbert is actually Pierce's half-brother, is somewhat less surprising (what with die-hard racists' history of hypocrisy regarding racially mixed offspring and all) than Pierce's change of heart about letting Gilbert win the game.

Some heel-face turns are just easier to swallow than others.

Episode 70: "The First Chang Dynasty"

Back in analog world for the conclusion of the Chang-as-evil-mastermind storyline (and none the richer, with Pierce having given his inheritance to Gilbert), the study group is still locked out of Greendale. Chang is running the school as a kind of higher education North Korea complete with fear-based rule, ubiquitous propaganda, and children signing hagiographic hymns to his glory ("Chang eats the sun and drinks the sky"). Unable to convince the police that the Dean has been replaced by a "Doppel-Deaner," the gang decides it's intricately planned-heist time though why they did not resort to this right after the Dean's kidnapping is anybody's guess.

A moderately fun send-up of heist plots follows with over-the-top costumes and campy overplaying. The jokes come more from the call-outs—Troy and Abed's broad white ethnic repairman shtick is gold, as is Jeff's Criss Angel–like magician and Chang's Napoleon outfit though his extended keytar solo feels a touch hack—than the writing.

Where the episode comes together is the hero's sacrificial bargain that Troy makes to join the air conditioning repair school in exchange for Laybourne's help rescuing his friends after their sub–*Ocean's 11* heist is discovered.

Episode 71: "Introduction to Finality"

Troy might be gone but the study group soldiers on toward their . . . summer credit for biology. Season 3's conclusion is well-constructed, funny, and able to tie off plot strands while splitting off the new ones necessary for a show moving into its fourth season. This is typically when more experimental series tend to settle down somewhat, pare things off and focus on essentials—a maturing process overtly signaled in the episode's conclusion.

That doesn't mean, though, that the show has abandoned the multiverse, mirror selves, secret society arcana, Star-Burns, or (heaven forbid) jokes at the expense of Jim Belushi.

Jeff is again trying to actually study with the study group. This is a quest that seems ever more impossible with each passing episode and one he abandons once a tangle of sandwich-related events (Subway pulls out of Greendale, leaving an opening for Shirley to open her shop in the cafeteria, which Pierce as the entitled investor insists on having full ownership of) leads to a lawsuit that entails his putting on a suit again and confronting his old law firm betrayer Alan (Rob Corddry). As with any of the courtroom proceedings at Greendale, it's only a somewhat legal-ish event with presiding Dean Pelton primarily interested in what to wear (holding up two robes, he asks the courtroom's opinion: "*Judging Amy* or *Judge Judy*?").

With the dynamic duo split up by Troy's sacrificing himself to be an air conditioning repair man, Abed goes into a bit of a tailspin and is over-taken by the Evil Abed personality he last wrestled with in "Contemporary Impressionists" and who now wants to make the prime timeline (the reality we are watching, apparently) match the darkest timeline (the one with all the goatees and evil-ness). As a result, when Britta shows up to "therapize" him (she's the worst), the now-goateed and sinister Evil Abed reveals his heel turn by bad-mouthing his "Lame Abed" personality. He uses his observational skills to identify her weaknesses as in last season's "Aerodynamics of Gender" only with a culturally specific Abed twist: "You're average . . . You're VH1, *RoboCop 2*, and *Back to the Future 3*."

While Jeff parries with Alan in the courtroom and Evil Abed embarks on a comedically ineffectual attempt to sever Jeff's arm (an extension cord is involved) just as it was in the darkest timeline, Troy is acing air conditioning repair school. The school has an extensive mythology suggesting Troy might be their messiah per Laybourne: "The true repairman *will repair man*." Laybourne dies in an apparent accident, new Vice Dean Murray (Dan Bakkedahl) takes over, and Troy challenges him to an air-conditioning duel in the so-called "sun chamber" (two repairman race to fix their unit before passing out from steadily increasing heat) to discover the truth: that Murray killed Laybourne. It's all a lot of plot to just bring Troy back into the study group fold and shows the diminishing returns of learning too much about some of Greendale's secret societies. But the segment concludes nicely with a self-aware dig at the writers' tendencies to get lost in the weeds when developing these complex subcultures: when the repairmen cheer Troy's victory and demand Murray be punished in something called "the Infinite Labyrinth of Eternal Ice," Troy (for once the sensible voice) says no: "Take him to jail! You guys are weird."

Troy and Abed have not noticeably de-weirded themselves again since prepping for Shirley's re-wedding in "Urban Matrimony and the Sandwich Arts." But the dark turns they took at the end of the season, despite turning out for the best (Evil Abed pulled back from the brink while Troy exposed a murderer and didn't let being an air-conditioning messiah go to his head), suggested it was time to put away childish things.

The season concludes with a montage that includes suggestions of adulting: Jeff gets excited about his grades; Troy and Abed shut down the Dreamatorium (though Abed secretly maintains a smaller one, just in case); and Shirley and Pierce open their sandwich shop. It also suggests mystery

Industry Corner

Season 3 of *Community* came together quite nicely if (like most normal people) viewers were simply paying attention to the show itself. But that was not how popular culture functioned by 2012, a year in which the world survived annihilation from disasters foretold by a Mayan prophecy but also started using Twitter a lot more, suggesting that "survived" can be a relative term. At the time, many of the show's highly online audience were checking in on the year's Dan Harmon drama. There was a lot of it. In spring 2012, the buzz around *Community* was that it was both on the "bubble" (maybe- or maybe-not being renewed) and that Chevy Chase was feuding with Harmon and others. Then in mid-May, just as the last episodes were being aired, there was a good news and bad news development: it was announced that the show was renewed but Harmon would not be back as showrunner.

(Star-Burns: alive!); a threat (City College's Dean Spreck appearing to plot an armored assault on Greendale); and promise (#sixseasonsandamovie).

What it does not reveal, since nobody knew at the time, is that this is the end of the original iteration of *Community*. Other seasons followed, but it would be a different show.

Community 104—Season 4: 7
Biology of Zombies

⊞

*I'm sorry I pooped on your work . . . Don't tell anyone
I said this but all writers are better people than all non-
writers. Nobody read that unless you're a writer.*

—DAN HARMON, APOLOGIZING FOR WHAT HE SAID ABOUT THE
SEASON 4 WRITING STAFF.

THERE MAY EXIST a *Community* timeline where Jeff, feeling a strange disturbance in the force—as some possibly dipsomaniacal motor-mouth with a thing for self-sabotage and clever dialogue does himself in with the executives of the show that nobody else but Abed understands they are all part of—rolls the multisided die and everything goes dark. They are off the air. No more Greendale. No more *Troy and Abed in the Mooooooorning*. No more Leonard to shut up. Nothing else for Britta to Britta. Never another outfit for the Dean. Not a single reassuring word of reunification from Jeff.

In that timeline, think pieces appeared at regular intervals describing how the great three-season arc of *Community* ended with the self-immolation and firing of its showrunner Dan Harmon. Each of those articles ask, in a plaintive fan's voice, What if? What if there had been more? Sure, Harmon landed fine and was doing great work with *Rick and Morty*. And okay, the "Three Seasons and a Movie" *Community* reunion special took a bad turn when he got into a slap-fight with Chevy Chase. And well, yes, the long-awaited six-episode run of *Heat Vision and Jack* on Hulu didn't turn out so well after Ben Stiller was replaced by Pete Davidson and Michael Bay was brought in for reshoots.

Also in that timeline, everyone agreed to just not talk about *Scud: The Musical* (though it was generally agreed that Frank Black's songs were killer, the Twyla Tharp choreography was viewed as ill-matched for the subject matter).

In this timeline, though—the one where you are reading this book, trying to figure out which streaming service *Community* has shifted to, and wondering why you didn't just buy the DVDs already—the die landed differently. When Season 3 ended, *Community* was only halfway through its run.

But when Season 4 started shooting in August 2012, Harmon was no longer involved. After his very public auto-da-fé, the ex-showrunner doubled down on podcasting (see the *Harmontown* chapter). There he explored at length all the corners of his Id that had never worked their way into a *Community* script. This was not the first time that a TV show had lost its creator but carried on regardless. Aaron Sorkin left *The West Wing* following the fourth season. Frank Darabont created *The Walking Dead* and was fired after one year. Amy and Dan Sherman-Palladino dropped out of *The Gilmore Girls* before its last season.

For Season 4, *Community* had brand-new showrunners: David Guarascio and Moses Port. Generally well-thought-of industry veterans who had worked on the very 1990s sitcom *Just Shoot Me!*, they had later produced the short-lived but critically approved fish-out-of-water CW sitcom *Aliens in America* and worked on *Happy Endings*, a smart three-season sitcom that shared directors (Anthony and Joe Russo) and composer (Ludwig Göransson) with *Community*. NBC and Sony could have done far worse than Guarascio and Port. The pair promised to stay true to Harmon's vision and appeared unlikely to Jim Belushi the show. At the same time, their work was extremely down the middle with little evidence of an interest in scrambling the format. That tension between their more conventional instincts and the show's penchant for arcane metafictional digressions did not augur well.

So what if Season 4 was just . . . not that great? What if there were some good jokes but not nearly enough and not a single riot? Isn't more *Community*, even at a somewhat subpar level, better than no *Community* at all?

Season 4 would make that a difficult question to answer.

Episode 72: "History 101"

A shift in tone, viewpoint, and purpose is immediately apparent in Season 4's first episode. Many of the beats and types of jokes have a similar ring but the edges have been dulled and smoothed. Even regular viewers who had never heard the name "Dan Harmon" (more likely than it seems; how many people watched $M{\star}A{\star}S{\star}H$ for years and never noticed it was developed by Larry Gelbart?) and could not care less what a showrunner does could pick up on the change.

It was not for the better.

That being said, the episode begins promisingly. The study group enters the library in ones and pairs at the start of another year at Greendale. But something is off. The lighting is bright, everyone is hitting their lines a bit too broadly and playing less to each other than some imaginary audience. There's some forced business about everybody wearing the same glasses; "Pierce" shows up in the form of Fred Willard; and a standard-issue laugh track is running behind the whole thing.

A quick zoom-out reveals this is all in Abed's head. In real Greendale, there is study group anxiety over it being their senior, and so final, year. (But aren't most community colleges just two years? Details, details.) Another year, another blow-off class: this time it's History of Ice Cream. Excess exposition by the Dean reveals that the registration system hack

In "History 101," Abed imagines the study group as a rebooted sitcom. NBC/PHOTOFEST.

that over-enrolled the class was actually his plot to ensure that Jeff (who only needs one more history credit to graduate) will remain at Greendale forever.

This leads to an *American Ninja Warrior*–like contest for registration called "Hunger Deans" because, well, somebody likely thought it would be funny and relevant to reference *The Hunger Games*. It is neither. However, if the non-canonical introduction of a tango dance contest was slotted in because somebody thought it would be funny to see the Dean strip to a tight dress and slink passionately around Jeff, in that case, at least, they were correct. Also, the competition being over who can win the most "red balls" is either an arcane joke referencing *Homicide: Life on the Streets* and *Minority Report* or some very low-bar testicular humor; either way, jokes!

Elsewhere the episode ticks some of the characters forward. Britta and Troy hold hands but there is no spark or conflict there of interest. Annie and Shirley engage in some highly nerdy pranking that ends up just highlighting tension about the group possibly breaking up. Chang has returned, only now claiming to have "Changnesia" and saying his name is "Kevin."

Every now and again we pitch back into (as the narrator in his head announces) *Abed's Happy Community College Filmed in Front of a Live Audience inside My Head*. The device is so thumpingly obvious—Abed escaping the reality of change in the real world to the happy pop culture zone in his mind where everything stays the same in reruns—that it lacks any punch. And that is before the utterly unnecessary *Muppet Babies*–esque animated sequence. (On the plus side, the invented TV shows being teased at the bottom of the screen, like *American Sword Cooks*, look fantastic.)

This is normie *Community*. If the entire episode had been done in the faux-sitcom format with only the occasional nod to it being a figment of somebody's imagination (like the animated episodes), that could have been something. Heck, an interdimensional something-something that swapped out the Willard from Abed's imaginary *Community* with the prime timeline's Chevy Chase for the rest of the season would have been appreciated. As it is, much of the episode feels like the characters are acting out the ironic "We're Gonna Finally Be Fine" song from the start of Season 3 ("We're gonna have more fun and be less weird") with full sincerity.

The episode hits all the major points: the Dean screws something up; a contest is structured around a pop culture reference; Abed wrestles with reality; Chang puns.

The new crew definitely did their homework. Maybe too well.

Episode 73: "Paranormal Parentage"

The humor and plotting in this season's sophomore outing feels a bit spiffier, assured, and less like somebody had binged the first three seasons and thought, "What would a *Community* writer write?" It is credited to longtime series writer Megan Ganz whose specialty had been complex homages (*Law & Order* in "Basic Lupine Urology" and the take on *Modern Family* in "Intermediate Documentary Filmmaking"— whose success may have been part of why Ganz left to work on that show following this season of *Community*). The cultural references are somewhat more slapped on the surface here. It's a Halloween episode (though broadcast in February) so everybody is in costume getting ready for a party when they get word that Pierce has locked himself in his panic room. They head to his spooky mansion to help the old geezer out.

Not long before Jeff asks, "What in the *Scooby-Doo* is going on here?" the group breaks into pairs. This means they can get terrified more easily as Pierce haunts them, part of another elaborate revenge plan caused by his feeling left out. There are a few good lines. Pierce's 1980s décor, a lot of neon and Patrick Nagel–style art is described as "like David Lee Roth threw up *Miami Vice*." Abed—annoyed at not being able to watch *Cougar Town* reruns then finding Pierce's security monitors and deeming them a worthy TV substitute—watches his friends panic and bicker, drolly commenting, "I remember when this show was about a community college."

Abed's line is a halfway decent wink and valid, of course: *Community* stopped being about a community college long before this. But the show had changed in the interest of exploring the nature of group sociology, the attraction and trap of belonging, and the shared mythos and meaning of pop culture, among other things. Under the new management, though, this season was specifically turning *Community* away from all that and devolving into another semi-wacky sitcom about a group of friends in semi-curious circumstances.

Which is fine as far as that goes. But it was not the ride that the audience had bought a ticket for.

Episode 74: "Conventions of Space and Time"

Abed would have *hated* this one. And for good reason. That does not mean there were no laughs to be had. But the episode is broad where it needs to be clever, and its perspective on geek culture is that of the quizzical outsider rather than the ironically self-satirizing insider.

Even though Troy and Britta are dating, he makes her sneak out the window every morning so Abed will not find out. After she goes through a comedically gymnastic scramble to dress on the fire escape and circle back to the front door pretending she is just now showing up with doughnuts, it turns out Abed was already aware they have been having sex.

The A plot pivots on Troy's anxiety that Abed will have a problem with the relationship. He is somewhat proven right. For reasons that make little sense except that the story demanded everyone be in the same location, the whole group attends the *Inspector Spacetime* convention (InSpec-TiCon, if you must know, and looking a whole lot like Comic-Con). There it is revealed Abed also has a secret friend, only his is Toby (Matt Lucas), a fan whose dedication to the show matches Abed's so completely the two barely need to speak. "They could just touch tentacles and download," Britta jokes before telling Troy he is not crazy, "That dude is trying to steal your boyfriend."

Before Toby's creepily suspect Tom Ripley tendencies are revealed and Troy and Abed are happily reunited in deep codependency ("*Toby and Abed in the Morning*? That's ridiculous!" Troy shouts), there is some highly unessential B plot to get through.

Annie is back at the hotel where, because the staff calls her "Mrs. Winger," she pretends to be Jeff's wife. At the convention, Jeff's resemblance to *Inspector Spacetime* villain Thoraxis briefly gains the interest of superfan Lauren (the statuesque Tricia Helfer only a few years removed

---

Inspector Spacetime

Inspector Spacetime matches *Doctor Who* in often obscure ways (the "Quantum Spanner" that Troy wields as Reggie is similar to the BBC show's "Sonic Screwdriver"). One of the few key differences between the shows is that the former pairs the male time-traveling hero Inspector with a male sidekick Constable while in the latter the Doctor traditionally gadded through space and time with a female sidekick. "Conventions of Space and Time" includes several references to the show's Dunkirk: the introduction of a female Constable, Minerva. "Everyone hates her," Troy explains to Britta. Abed follows up, "Not because they're sexist. Because she sucks." Despite Abed's slightly hard-to-swallow claim, *Doctor Who* would introduce its first female Doctor four years after this episode aired.

from her iconic Cylon seductress role in *Battlestar Galactica*). Pierce and Shirley are nearby watching an American adaptation of *Inspector Spacetime* for a focus group. In a decent parody of how these things seem to end up, the people running the group eagerly jot down all of Pierce's suggestions to make it less confusing.

Each of his ideas (spell out everything about the concept, leave nothing to the imagination, make the inspector's male constable sidekick into a hot blonde with a tennis racket) are then visualized in the end tag, which shows an episode of the American version starring *Beverly Hills 90210*'s Luke Perry and Jennie Garth.

But while that looks like a nightmare for any dedicated *Inspector Spacetime* fan and is duly derided, the irony is a little too hard to overlook. Almost everything in the episode before the end tag is over-obvious, painstakingly explained, and tied up very cleanly so that there are no bad feelings. "Conventions of Space and Time" ends up doing exactly what it is supposedly satirizing.

Episode 75: "Alternate History of the German Invasion"

Going back to the well again with a sequel of sorts to last season's "Foosball and Nocturnal Vigilantism," this episode once again uses a trio of "Düsseldorks" to unintentionally provide moral tutelage. Only this time instead of teaching Jeff the peril of competitiveness and value of forgiveness, the hooting and obnoxious German students remind the entire study group what entitled jagoffs they can be.

Stymied again from taking History of Ice Cream (apparently the final is a sundae bar), the gang mooches gloomily over a real history class. Another sterling addition to the list of great actors who have played Greendale's downtrodden instructors, Malcolm McDowell infuses Professor Cornwallis with a snappy vigor that has yet to be crushed by the school's ineptitude or its students' low aspirations. Meanwhile the study group zeroes in on something far more important than learning: getting "our study room" back from the Teutonic threesome who seem always able to get to the sign-in sheet first (it's their damn "perfectly crafted timepieces").

The group resorts to their usual approach when facing a minor obstacle: invent an elaborate scheme for getting back something they don't really deserve. While Jeff's invocation of *Hogan's Heroes* (which taught him that "the lovable misfits always win") is a bit on the nose, it does at least set up a gag reveal that the Germans call the old sitcom *Hogan's Villains*.

Cool Cool Cool

When Dan Harmon complained on *Harmontown* about how it felt for him to watch Season 4 ("It is very much like an impression, and an unflattering one. It's just thirteen episodes of 'Oh, I'm Dan Harmon. Derpy, derpy, durr! *Die Hard!*'"), it is possible "Alternate History of the German Invasion" might have been on his mind. Its German students are no longer led by Juergen (Nick Kroll) as in their first appearance but instead his brother Reinhold (Chris Diamantopoulous). The rematch between a mouthy American who has bested one arrogant German only to be matched against his just-as-arrogant brother is a clear nod to *Die Hard with a Vengeance* (Jeremy Irons hunts down Bruce Willis in revenge for having killed his brother Alan Rickman in the first movie).

Harmon's *Community* would have let it go at that: anybody who needs to get the reference gets it, and for those who didn't, the show was already on to the next joke or three. But Guarascio and Port's *Community* always skews obvious, and so Abed directly mentions *Die Hard 3*, taking the air out of a sly moment that does not require footnoting.

Though their fake Oktoberfest ruse (didn't Halloween already happen?) and invocation of an obscure Greendale regulation technically wins the day, the group ends up being protested by the other students who are sick of their "hogging" the study room.

Which is not bad as a comeuppance goes and ties in nicely with Cornwallis's instructions to not study history only from the victor's perspective, with flashbacks showing the other students' annoyance at the room being occupied for entire bottle episodes (the pen hunt, Dungeons & Dragons) that had nothing to do with studying.

The entire group realizes the error of their ways and Jeff gives a speech about forgiveness, declaring in neon: Lesson Learned. (Another few episodes like this and the group will be completely healed of all moral flaws.)

The episode finishes with the Dean introducing "Kevin" to the group. Everybody screams. The end tag reveals that Troy and Abed have a podcast. Because of course they do.

Episode 76: "Cooperative Escapism in Familial Relations"

Jeff's long-delayed outreach to his father, teased at the end of the last season, is now teed up in an episode that shows him to be nearly as torn up by parental issues as Pierce. Using Thanksgiving to put everybody in awkward family situations, the group is split between two dinners. Shirley invites everyone to her house in order to have a buffer with her judgmental relatives. Jeff reunites with the father who abandoned him in childhood and his (up to now unknown) half-brother. Neither plot leads to much.

Jeff's father Will (James Brolin) turns out to be a silver-haired man of few emotions who wants nothing to do with the past and is highly disappointed in his other son, Willy Jr (Adam Devine, hamming it up as an insecure basket case). At first this is fine with Jeff. But urged on by Britta, Jeff finally has it out with Will, delivering a pained soliloquy about how as a fatherless child he was so desperate to have somebody to worry about him that he faked an appendectomy: When another kid asked to see the scar, Jeff then gave himself one with a pair of scissors. Though well-delivered and poignant at times, Jeff's father reunion is all too neatly resolved. Even less forgivably, Britta came along with Jeff to this highly sensitive personal scene and never Britta'd a thing.

Shirley's Thanksgiving storyline does not fare much better. Her holiday seems more awkward than most not least because of the antics of a certain "crazy white guy" (Pierce). Abed tries to turn the study group's hiding out in Shirley's garage into a *Shawshank Redemption* prison break—with him in the Morgan Freeman narration role, of course. The break never quite materializes as each tries to leave but cannot. This only adds to the episode's ho-hum feeling.

Episode 77: "Advanced Documentary Filmmaking"

Another mock documentary episode that while definitely weaker than the series' other entries in this format is more comedically and stylistically coherent than what we have seen so far this season. Abed is behind the camera again. He is ostensibly telling the tale of poor "Kevin," aka Chang, and his struggles with "Changnesia"—which his doctor notes is a mystery, particularly how it "affects the memory but not the ability to make forced puns"—but really showing once again how the study group, for all its unity, falls apart rather quickly under stress. Obsessed with proving that

Chang is merely pretending to be a Changnesiac, Jeff becomes a pariah while the target of his animus is elevated to hero status. Obsessed with getting a $40,0000 grant from the MacGuffin Neurological Institute for the study of Changnesia (thus paying for Abed's documentary), the Dean goes too far and gets too little.

Unlike other documentary-format episodes like the Ken Burns-ian "Pillows and Blankets," this does not have a consistent stylistic or thematic focus. The references are sometimes clever (Abed filming himself watching "ugly" unseen footage much like Werner Herzog did in *Grizzly Man*), sometimes overt (Abed footnoting *Capturing the Friedmans* for no good reason), and sometimes funny but off-topic (Chang writing notes to himself on his arms à la Guy Pearce's character in *Memento*, which is very much not a documentary, including, "Rent Memento").

Despite some clever lines (Britta being identified on screen as "Basically a Therapist"), Jeong's as-ever full-bore commitment to the crazy, and the Dean's summary of Chang's post–Spanish instructor track record ("disgraced student, psychopathic music major, homeless vent dweller, security guard, keytarist, power-hungry warlord") the Is Chang Faking? plot becomes a virtual cul-de-sac.

As for Pierce's "blackface Señor Wences" hand-puppet bit (just what it sounds like), what is there to say? At this point, the show does not seem to know whether to treat Pierce as a racist buffoon or as a sad and needy soul who deserves sympathy; vacillating between the two keeps him from being more than an adjunct to the study group rather than their in-house saboteur as earlier in the series. This lack of clarity likely had at least something to do with Chase's erratic behavior, with eruptions of vitriol and a reported tendency to walk off set before filming was done, leaving the crew and cast to shoot around him as best they could.

Episode 78: "Economics of Marine Biology"

Jeff loses more of his edge and Abed turns closer to caricature but Shirley finally gets something to excel at that does not involve baking or Jesus. The setup has strong possibilities for antics, or as Abed excitedly (as he can get) declares, "Sounds like a romper." Doing his best impersonation of a serious person, the Dean enlists the study group to recruit a potential new student whom he terms a "whale" for having the perfect mix of attributes ("low intellect, high lack of ambition, and limitless parental support") to sustain a funding-starved community college. Their whale, Archie (Zack Pearlman), is a stoned underachiever who is already being scouted by City

College. Beer-blitzed "school board guys" Carl (Jeremy Scott Johnson) and Richie (Brady Novak) pressure the Dean to pull out all the stops with "Hookers! Blow!" among their suggestions for party-themed recruitment. He eagerly goes along with the recruiting blitz while failing to see the many warning signs flashing the question What price Greendale's soul?

Some of what the Dean has the school go through to secure the whale seem innocuous, like appealing to Archie's party dude instincts with blatant lies (Professor Ed Hardy's class on bikinis, a "Mountain Dew Cool Zone"). Less defensible is Jeff pretending to be Pierce's buddy for a day so he won't ruin the Archie campaign with his usual jealousy over not being the center of attention; but as usual, after-the-fact attempts to solicit sympathy for Pierce rarely impact his relentless awfulness.

But the request that crosses the line is Archie's demand that Magnitude give up his catch phrase. Magnitude covers multiple whiteboards with ideas, but "Diggidy doo" just cannot compete. This leads the Dean to show a rare fortitude and insist that "Pop, pop!" remain Magnitude's intellectual property. Archie's last-minute conversion to the Greendale cause is mawkish ("It would be pretty sweet to be treated like a normal dude") and misses an opportunity to bring City College back into the mix as the show's archvillain, a role the season is sorely missing.

Of the two side plots, Troy and Shirley taking physical education is the funnier: Shirley shows her natural coaching aptitude, and the last bits of Troy's jockish arrogance are scoured away when he miserably fails the "mocker room" challenge. Abed's attempt to capitalize on the Dean's refusal to allow a fraternity on campus to lure Archie leads to some half-hearted *Animal House* hijinks. But Shirley and Troy are given a goofy musical montage (very *South Park: Bigger, Longer and Uncut*) in which they teach Chang how to do things like drink from a water fountain.

Episode 79: "Herstory of Dance"

A return to the energy, emotion, and snark that's been missing from the season up to this point. Establishing the setup in familiar but brisk fashion—the Dean distracts from the CDC's confiscation of Greendale's drinking fountains by announcing a Sadie Hawkins sock hop—the study group launches into action. Annoyed by constricting gender roles, Britta announces her Sophie B. Hawkins "protest dance" then–rather than admit she meant to say Susan B. Anthony–she insists she was right the first time. This leaves Jeff spending most of the episode waiting for Britta to be embarrassed when Hawkins herself (a radio mainstay from the mid-1990s, which the Dean notes is the time period after which most Greendale students "sort of gave up," meaning she is the most recent music they know) does not show up. Later Pierce engages in another unusual burst of humanity by secretly paying Hawkins to show up to keep Britta from being embarrassed.

But truly the episode belongs to Abed. He starts the episode announcing his desire to grow by avoiding "capers, romps, and exploits" and even stopping "filtering everything through TV." But once Shirley and Annie both try to set him up with a date, he cannot avoid doing the "classic 'Two Dates in One Night' sitcom trope." Abed's juggling of dates—one a straight-arrow church lady while the other a bundle of putative adorkability (scooter, slide whistle, forced whimsy)—is just backdrop, though, for the real connection. Running back and forth from the coat check for outfit

---

Cool Cool Cool

While in Season 4 the Dean's Dalmatian fetish went largely unremarked-on, his outfits leveled up (before dropping off rapidly in frequency and fashion the following season). Was this a sign of an increasingly manic mind coming undone by the stresses of a job he was significantly underqualified for and using costumery as distraction? Or was it a shtick the writers simply couldn't break the habit of? Was there a desire to show off another physique besides Jeff's? Whatever the reason, here is a thoroughly scientific ranking of that season's greatest outfits.

1. "Herstory of Dance": As "Deana Reed," the Dean pays homage to 1950s sitcom housewives with a grey shirtwaist dress and eerie grey face makeup to approximate black-and-white television.
2. "Alternative History of the German Invasion": The best part of his sexy nurse outfit (complete with stethoscope and kicky red high boots) is the incongruity of his wearing it at the jail when bailing out "Kevin."
3. "Paranormal Parentage": Trying to pair himself with Jeff's Halloween costume (boxer), the Dean comes as a ring girl complete with "Round 1" sign, bare midriff, and sparkly hot pants. Once seen, it cannot be unseen.

changes, Abed enlists the help of coat check girl Rachel (Brie Larson). Abed is so committed to the first trope he fails to appreciate another (the girl for him was right under his nose all along). Close enough to Abed's wavelength to pick up on everything he is about and yet distinct enough to provide him the opportunity for growth, Rachel brings out a warmth and excitement in Abed that feels unprecedented so far in the show and still wholly true to his nature. Even when he launches into a public apology to her as a grand gesture (a romantic trope joked about only minutes before), it plays as both pop culture reference and fully sincere.

The episode closes out again with several Important Lessons (Abed: "It was wrong and hurtful"; Pierce: "Cut [Britta] some slack") that grate less for the sentiment than seeming forced and perfunctory.

Episode 80: "Intro to Felt Surrogacy"

Exhibit A for episodes that aim for the creative spark of earlier seasons and cannot quite manage it. Discovering that the study group has been sitting in awkward silence, the Dean arrives with a boxful of felt hand puppets in each of their likenesses. Why did he already have these ready to go? No reason, except for his unhealthy emotional investment in the study group's predicaments (which is highlighted when Garrett has news of a cafeteria fire and the Dean nearly screams, "*Not now!*"). Is this an all-too-apparent excuse to do an entire episode with puppets? Absolutely. Is there anything wrong with that? Not at all.

The source of the group's awkward silence turns out to be a patently absurd adventure they all took that only makes sense when visualized with puppets and musical numbers. Feeling they needed an adventure to get out of their rut, the group took a hot-air balloon ride (their guide played by a sweet-voiced Sara Bareilles, calling back to the use of her song "Gravity" in Season 2's "Paradigms of Human Memory"), crash-landed, ate psychedelic berries offered by a chipper mountain man (Jason Alexander), told embarrassing truths about themselves while tripping, and then felt embarrassed once coming to. Only it turns out that only Shirley told a humiliating story. So then the whole group contributes their own tales of shame, in song form.

High points: The Dean taking the nose off his "Dean-occhio" get-up every time he's upset; Jeff declaring, "The problem isn't us. *We're awesome.*"

Mid-points: This is the last sequential episode with any noticeable Pierce.

Low points: After the crashlanding, Abed says they need to split into two groups, "the survivors and the others," leading Shirley to snap, "Stop it with your *Lost* references"—another bolting of training wheels onto a line that needed no explanation.

Episode 81: "Intro to Knots"

A nifty play on an *Alfred Hitchcock Presents*–style bottle episode that might have gone further with the premise. Wielding secret intel that Cornwallis is going to fail them on their joint history paper, the group agrees to invite him to a Christmas party for wining, dining, and hopefully a slightly improved grade.

As parties on *Community* do, this one turns sideways fast. The initial annoyances are over Annie decorating Jeff's apartment like she's playing house and everybody breaking the No Presents rule. Cornwallis arrives and is briefly wined and dined. This is quickly followed by some testy exchanges that lead to the professor being tied to a chair and threatened (albeit in very G-rated fashion). Once Cornwallis realizes how easy it is to play on the group's not-so-hidden rivalries and resentments, he starts finding the cracks and looks for a turncoat to set him free.

The Christmas party–turned hostage scenario in "Intro to Knots" went poorly but check out Abed's wicked, authentic John McClane T-shirt (yes, Die Hard *is a Christmas movie).* NBC/ PHOTOFEST.

The situation is over before it quite gets started, however, leading to another Winger unity speech and the realization that Cornwallis—though seeming like an arrogant and handsy academic washout—is just another vulnerable and lonely soul looking for community.

Despite the chipper conclusion, threats still lurk. Kevin-or-Chang tells his unseen conspirator everything is going to plan. In the darkest timeline (as imagined by Abed), Evil Jeff gets Evil Annie released from Greendale Insane Asylum and vows to destroy the "prime timeline," which is funny enough except that once again the season is simply building on earlier themes and storylines rather than crafting anything new.

Episode 82: "Basic Human Anatomy"

A late-blooming academic rivalry between Annie and Shirley and an extremely lengthy breakup between Britta and Troy (the show's most overt and least-interesting couple) serve as the dramatic backdrop for an episode that is largely about two questions: Is Troy better at imitating Abed or Abed better at imitating Troy? And how did Leonard finally become front runner for valedictorian after being a Greendalian since 1968?

Troy and Britta's relationship is running on fumes, signaled in this episode not just by their not remembering their one-year anniversary but also by an entire season showing little interest in anything the two do together. Before the couple can rekindle it with a romantic anniversary dinner at Señor Kevin's, though, an elaborate routine involving a six-pack of body-switching movies and flickering lights (the custodian doing a "routine light switch check"), appears to result in Troy and Abed swapping identities à la *Freaky Friday*. This leads to Britta having dinner with Troy who is acting as though he is Abed. Meanwhile, in deep dedication to the bit, Abed acts like he is Troy (for the record, Pudi's imitation of Glover is ever so slightly more pinpoint than the reverse).

All of this is a very lengthy and not terribly amusing build up to the reveal that Troy wants to break up with Britta and is using the *Freaky Friday* routine as emotional cover.

The semi-meta end tag is one of the season's best, with Troy and Abed running lines of dialogue in the study room and breaking up laughing before Jeff interrupts what appears to be a credits outtake scene with "Dorks! Stop doing outtakes."

Episode 83: "Heroic Origins"

Showing that Season 4 was starting to run out of ideas just before hitting the finish line, this episode circles back on itself to create answers for things that never needed answering rather than move the characters forward. Pierce's absence is explained by his donating a kidney to Gilbert. At the same time, the episode does reveal the school has a paper called the *Greendale Communist Worker*, so not a complete loss.

For his graduation gift to the group, Abed has crafted an elaborate story map plotting out "our origin story." Despite Jeff's pushback (partially due to irritation at Abed going through his things to find clues about the past), Abed launches into a series of monologues, accented by comic-strip illustrations, that kick off flashbacks showing how the group impacted each other's lives long before they became a study group.

Gimmicky without bringing much new to the table, the flashbacks draw dotted lines from one crucial event to the next. Britta's "an-*her*-chist" group is protesting at the courthouse where she congratulates hot-shot lawyer Jeff on just winning a case for Misty the Stripper who will meet Andre later at a bar where he has just been left on their anniversary night by Shirley who had to pick up her kids from the mall where they were being lectured about *Star Wars* by Abed.

And so on.

Annie and Troy are involved largely to expand on the aspects of their shared high school experience. Further revelations show the group was all at the mall and feeling at loose ends on a day when Chang and the Dean were passing out Greendale recruitment flyers. Answering a question that was better left unresolved, one scene illustrates where Magnitude got his catch phrase from.

It is arguable that the most entertaining sections involve Abed stationing himself at movie theaters to warn people away from seeing *The Phantom Menace* (told by his father to apologize to a theater manager, Abed just spits out *"Midi-chlorians!"* with the kind of outrage only a socially maladroit nerd could muster).

Nevertheless the episode pivots on whether or not Jeff is the group's supervillain. Despite Shirley blaming Jeff at first for encouraging the stripper to go out with the married guy who turned out to be her Andre, she eventually forgives him. Then everybody has frozen yogurt and ponders if they were fated to be together.

Meanwhile the true villain reveals himself to be . . . City College's Dean Spreck, laughing maniacally as he plots Greendale's demise through

---

Cool Cool Cool

The absence of Pierce from "Heroic Origins" is possibly explained by his agreeing to leave *Community* in late 2012 when Season 4 was nearly done with filming. The official language used at the time was that the producers and Chase had come to a "mutual agreement." The unofficial story was that everybody had enough of Chase's reportedly entitled and abusive behavior, which could be why—even though all the other characters in this episode get an origin story—we only see an elderly white man, face obscured, ruining a frozen yogurt machine and then faking a heart attack. Classic Pierce.

---

the deployment of a massive mechanical spider because, well, who didn't love *Wild Wild West*?

Episode 84: "Advanced Introduction to Finality"

The imposter *Community* syndrome reaches its climax in a low point not just for the season but possibly for the series.

The dramatic crux of the episode is Jeff finally graduating and the tailspin of sadness and reflection that this sends the study group into. Apparently following through on his original plan to get back to lawyering once he has a real degree, Jeff accepts an offer to work at the firm of Mark (Joe Lo Truglio), whose blithe sleaze comes across like a blurred Xerox of Rob Corddry's Alan character.

Meanwhile the group scrambles to put together a graduation party for Jeff. Abed refers to it as "boring but grounded," admitting he was "hoping for more" in his sitcom view of their lives. The "more" turns out to be a jumble of callbacks to better episodes, a wan kind of fan service that fundamentally misunderstands the show's appeal.

The group's party plans are threatened when in a poorly considered move (both by the character and the writers), Jeff throws a twenty-sided die like in "Remedial Chaos Theory," this time to decide who brings the soda. Unlike in that episode, though, it lands on its side in a crack of the study table. Naturally this opens up some kind of portal to the Darkest Timeline. Evil Jeff and Evil Annie appear, doing their best to ruin the Prime Timeline by causing dissension in the ranks and using modified paintball guns that transport people to the Darkest Timeline.

Evil Jeff and Evil Annie plot dastardly deeds in "Advanced Introduction to Finality." NBC/
PHOTOFEST.

Or something. There is some fun to be had in the concept of a mostly identical Jeff and Annie sneaking around and causing problems. But the result is a mediocre mishmash of *Terminator* and *The Matrix* references (Jeff gaining Neo-like powers to stop interdimensional paintball pellets mid-air and such) that is neither funny, inspired, purposeful, nor true to any deeper sense of the characters. Skipping across timelines provides some laughs, from Evil Troy and Evil Abed's morning show being dedicated to Emperor Chang to Troy and Britta's baby having been given the "traditional African name" of Chewbacca (per Troy, it means "He who hunts bounties").

Granted, the nobody-wants-Jeff-to-graduate storyline is a bit thin to hold up an entire episode. But *Community* at its best knew how to channel an excess of imagination into a tightly edited less-is-always-far-more. *Matrix Paintball* was far, far less.

Community 105—Season 5: The Science of Syndication

> *I'm not gonna say, like a phoenix rising up from the ashes of unemployment, I have created a machine that eats pain and craps joy.*

—DAN HARMON ON BEING REHIRED AT HIS OWN SHOW

SO. THAT WAS WEIRD.

After Season 4 finished with the last episode's rote *Terminator/ The Matrix* paintball mashup homage and autopilot "Will he or won't he?" Jeff departure melodrama, Sony and NBC could have cut the cord completely and just let *Community* go. The show's fan base, both dedicated and less so, had been torching the thin simulacra whipped up by interim showrunners David Guarascio and Moses Port as being an uncanny valley of comedy (similar to the first three seasons only . . . not). The ratings were tumbling as was to be expected for a cult comedy without the writer responsible for what got it noticed in the first place. There was little expectation that the network would bother going back to the well for such little reward. This was especially the case given that in 2013 NBC had largely gotten out of the comedy business, turning its signal over mostly to ninja warriors, Chicago firefighters, and amateur singers eager to grab that brass ring.

But in June 2013, about a month after "Advanced Introduction to Finality" broadcast and following months of lobbying by Joel McHale and Jim Rash, it was announced that Harmon and Chris McKenna were coming back to run *Community* again. The show was picked up for a half-season run of 13 episodes starting that January.

The whole fracas, from Harmon's patented combustible mix of public feuding and self-examination to the studio and network's about-face was a fairly unprecedented episode (if you will) in the history of broadcast television. Previously the firing and rehiring of a showrunner would attract little notice. But given the high dramatic gloss that legacy news publication gave at the time to even a relatively minor media dust-up, this was Big News.

Especially when the showrunner kept making news, which showrunners are not supposed to do. Then again, showrunners before 2013 tended not to have their own podcasts (which at that time was still a medium that needed to be explained to many people: "It's like a radio show, Dad, but you have it on your phone. No, it's not on the radio. *Your phone*").

Harmon decided to finally watch what had been done with a whole season of his brainchild while he had been fired. Nobody would have suggested this was a good idea; in fact, one could make the argument that his going in cold as though Season 4 had never happened might have been the best approach.

The result was a predictable chain reaction of Harmonia. It started on his podcast *Harmontown*, where Harmon unleashed his hurt feelings (primarily anger over what he saw as an "unflattering" and poorly done impression of his interests and style) and an obscene rant. This was followed by a self-effacing apology to the writers. The difference was that this time, he was not fired again.

Maybe because he didn't say anything about Chevy Chase—who was in Season 5 but only briefly and only as a hologram.

This left Harmon, McKenna, and the rest of the writers to put the somewhat battered show back together and hope they could regain the fans who had drifted away. Though it entered syndication just before Season 5 started airing, *Community* never became a success of the kind that NBC was looking for, like *30 Rock*, which had a similarly busy weirdness but inside a more traditional format. But the re-Harmon'd *Community* did repair the damage and moved ahead by trying to top itself: more animation, the secret history of Greendale, an amplification of the corporate authoritarian nature of Subway. At the same time, Season 5 also showed the writers making themselves work without the safety nets provided by easy repeatable gags: cutting back on the Dean's over-the-top outfits, not relying on a chaotic disrupter like Pierce to get everyone's blood boiling, avoiding the temptation to give Abed another buddy to replace Troy.

Because there was no replacing Troy.

Episode 85: "Repilot"

It seems fair to assume that leading up to the January 2014 premiere of the Season 5 opener, anticipations were high. Given the show's tendency to respond in very specific ways to criticism and the spectacularly off-key, Harmon-less Season 4, the premiere could have been a doozy. Harmon and McKenna (his co-writer for that episode) might have gone full snark like the brushback musical number that kicked off Season 3 ("We're gonna get more calm and normal . . . "). They could have layered high-concept ideas one inside the other in an *Inception* of comedy that would have sent the crowd at San Diego Comic-Con into a frenzy of delight and made the suits at 30 Rockefeller Plaza wish they had just slotted in a game show as a midseason replacement.

But the Season 5 writer's room seems to have become a calmer place than the angsty place it frequently resembled before Harmon was fired. If reports can be believed, there was less drinking, less sleep deprivation, less waiting until the last minute for Harmon to deliver scripts, all leading to a generally happier and more Adderall-free vibe. This could have helped produce a season that may have had fewer fence-swinging gonzo escapades but also enjoyed a more even tone.

In short, the first episode that Harmon and McKenna delivered was a thoughtful, somewhat downbeat exploration of both the limitations

For hire: Lawyer with degree from Greendale and expensive Scotch habit. AUTHOR'S COLLECTION.

of what Greendale could offer and the dim prospects awaiting the study group off-campus.

Having bet everything on making it as a lawyer in the outside world, Jeff begins the episode in full collapse. As his office furniture is hauled away by repo men, Jeff is approached by his old law firm nemesis Alan (Rob Corddry) with a proposition to help him out with a juicy lawsuit against Greendale by stealing incriminating documents before the Dean can shred them. It's yet another moral test for Jeff to determine whether he falls back into his old larcenous ways or stays true to the ragtag band of community college misfits. But unlike many such challenges previously set for Jeff, the outcome of this one does not feel preordained.

What follows is a tidy bit of sitcom reformatting that wrangles the Pierce-less group back together around the old table like a team of cinematic heroes reuniting for a sequel and falling right back into their expected roles. It does not waste too much time on reorienting the audience, limiting itself to an inspired yet casually offhanded critique of Season 4 in which Annie blames her diminished energies on "that gas leak last year." (Following that line, "gas leak year" became the standard shorthand for fans to refer to Season 4, which most agreed was best left undiscussed.)

The storyline is dealt with in perfunctory fashion, with Jeff first feeling betrayed by the Dean (discovering he *was* shredding the documents even after Jeff had defended the school's honor to Alan as a place that would not do that) and then realizing Greendale was ultimately worth saving. This is thanks to a pitch made by an Obi-Wan Kenobi–style blue flickering hologram of Pierce announcing a Pierce Hawthorne Museum of Gender Sensitivity and Sexual Potency donated "in compliance with a court order I'm not allowed to discuss" and nodding to a real-life agreement supposedly made between Chase and Sony that he would not return to the studio—which argued that while Greendale was a "crappy place" that was only because "it gives crappy people a chance to sort themselves out."

Most of the episode follows the study group starting to do just that. The group's initial giddiness on reuniting under the manufactured pretense of a Save Greendale Committee melts quickly under Jeff's questioning. None of their lives have gone well off-campus. Each has seen their dreams wither away like Jeff's. The depth of their disillusion leads the group to set their iconic table on fire in a symbolic protest that, like many such actions on the show, serves as ironic joke on the futility of grand gestures.

The group realizes that Jeff was initially manipulating them in order to file a class-action suit against Greendale. But the fact remains they feel

Never leave the table. AUTHOR'S COLLECTION.

safer inside an educational institution so derelict it has hired back Chang as a math teacher, a thwarted arsonist who knows as little about arithmetic as he does Spanish.

The artificial nature of how the group has been brought back together is again clearly understood by Abed. He sees the scaffolding of a sitcom repiloting itself to get back on track or try something fresh ("This could be like *Scrubs* Season 9," he ponders). This neatly sets up an end-of-episode gag in which a voiceover appears to be used as a generically soothing wrap-up only to reveal that the narration is actually that of Zach Braff from the

---

Meanwhile, Off Campus . . .

Harmon's tendency to view comedy through a lens crafted by a slate of pre–Will Ferrell *SNL* alumni comedies can be spotted in the "More Fletch or Clark Griswold?" discussions he would have on set with Chevy Chase. There was also the fact that Jeff Winger's last name was a homage to Bill Murray's character in *Stripes*. That led to Harmon unsuccessfully trying to bring Murray in to play Jeff's father (which involved his leaving a message on Murray's 1-800 number, the only way at the time to reach the inscrutable Zen comedy master) at a low point while watching Season 4.

end of *Scrubs*' Season 9 premiere episode, which Abed is eagerly explaining to the group.

But Abed's outside-the-narrative viewpoint also continues *Community*'s recurring theme of using the artificially generated problems and dynamics of a sitcom as a frame through which to better understand and manage the challenges of life. Even as the episode is ever-so-slightly mocking the overused *Scrubs* concluding narration bit, it is also acknowledging the soothingly tidy nature of such writing. And refusing to be above it.

Episode 86: "Introduction to Teaching"

Not high concept by any means but a sharp and confident return to form that showed just what *Community* had been missing during the gas leak season. Busy without trying too hard, "Introduction to Teaching" features well-calibrated character work and thoughtful writing alongside full-bore anarchic absurdity.

The episode goes heavy on Jeff and Abed, bringing in the rest of the group in only limited fashion after an opening sequence gag where they ooh and ahh over "Table Mk II," trying not to dwell on the fact that they burned the first table in the last episode for . . . reasons.

Jeff has decided to recommit to Greendale as a law professor. But being still fundamentally a slacker, he struggles with caring enough to keep up appearances or even learn his students' names ("Ski Cap" or "White Dave" being the best he can muster). He finds guidance in the form of his new office mate, Professor Hickey (Jonathan Banks). Though seemingly introduced to fill the void of entitled boomer left by the departure of Pierce, Hickey serves less as a figure of mockery than as an avatar of grumpily stolid stubbornness in a landscape of flighty characters whose anxieties have anxieties.

Hickey takes Jeff under his wing, introducing the novice educator to yet another secret Greendale underworld: the teacher's lounge. A smoke-filled oasis of free-flowing cocktails and cynicism where Hickey's announcement that Jeff is "having trouble planning his curriculum" gets a roaring laugh and some advice from Chang about how to teach without doing anything: "Break into groups, grade each other's papers, and please enjoy the seven-disc edition of *Planet Earth*."

Though providing little in the way of character development, the B story is rightfully the more remembered. Calling back to Season 2's "Competitive Wine Tasting" where Abed aced a class on *Who's the Boss?* this time he seizes on a seminar by the serenely pompous Professor Garrity

(Kevin Corrigan) that seems tailor-made for a movie obsessive like himself: "Nicolas Cage: Good or Bad?" There is even a note on the chalkboard that reads "ABC" for "Always Be Cageing." But the class turns out to be a sinkhole for Abed. Used to easy dichotomies ("Robert Downey Jr., good; Jim Belushi, bad"), Abed fails to wrap his head around Cage's manic and seemingly random swings in mood, volume, and quality of film. He ultimately leaps onto Garrity's desk and performs an unhinged imitation ("I'm a cat! *I'm a sexy cat*") that is simultaneously an homage to a subgenre of YouTube Cage supercuts, a glimpse into the at-times fragile state of Abed's equilibrium, and an acknowledgment of Cage's camp genius years before the actor leaned into it himself with films like 2022's meta-comedy *The Unbearable Weight of Massive Talent*.

Chaos reigns elsewhere in the school when Jeff lets slip a secret Hickey has told him: teachers invented minus grades to drive students "nuts." Since Greendale is apparently an overflowing powder keg of rage, barely a second after one student shouts "Minuses are made up!" Neil (Charley Koontz) declares, "It's riot time!" and chaos erupts. Magnitude (Luke Youngblood) gets in on the action, hurling a brick through a window and screaming "Pop! Pop!" in battle-cry fashion like he was leading a phalanx of protestors in Chicago circa 1968.

Cool Cool Cool

According to Harmon, the staff had spent a couple of seasons pushing an episode where Jeff invented a class called Nicolas Cage Appreciation and the Dean's punishment was making the study group watch every one of Cage's movies in a row. That (tragically) never happened though Abed's Cage seminar is just fine as a consolation prize. For anyone thinking Harmon was just another smartass chortling while watching Cage supercuts on YouTube, this is what he said at the *Community* convention in 2013.

> Unless you're a total cynical dick, you have to embrace the fact that Nicolas Cage is a pretty good actor. He's done a lot of weird, dumb movies, but that was supposed to be the point of the episode: that Nicolas Cage is a metaphor for God, or for society, or for the self, or something. It's like, what is Nicolas Cage? What is he? Is he an idiot? Or a genius? Can you write him off or is he inexplicably bound to your soul?

While things are brought under control by the end of the episode, the Dean acknowledges, "I don't think we can eliminate riots *completely*," giving an indication of just what a razor's edge the school is sitting on.

The rest of Season 5 would continue proving that point.

Episode 87: "Basic Intergluteal Numismatics"

A cool, controlled send-up of David Fincher and the entire post-*Se7en* serial killer chic genre, this episode delivers overtly juvenile humor (the title meaning, in essence, basic butt-crack coins) in a fairly subdued manner that amplifies the oddity of the storyline while also showing that Harmon et al. could have had a decent sideline in formulaic murder procedurals.

Continuing the season's penchant for building off earlier plots, the plot features the return of the never-identified Ass Crack Bandit from Season 2's "Intro to Political Science." As in that episode, the bandit's crime generates a response in keeping with the mournfully tragic sensibility of the genre being satirized but wildly disproportionate to what was actually done (dropping a quarter between people's exposed butt cheeks when they bend over). The notes left by the bandit are cryptic and clue-filled but show less Zodiac killer–like sinister intent than a Troy-ish level of immature imitation: "I am the mad hatter, if hats were butts."

Annie, the bloodhound seeker of truth whose interest in forensic investigation was in fact sparked all those years ago by the bandit (and would later lead to her getting an FBI internship), diligently pursues clues with Jeff at her side. Unlike most of their escapades, Annie leads the investigation with Jeff acting as backup. While there is limited smolder, their re-pairing finally leads the Dean to point at them in exasperation and ask, "What is this creepy business?" He then suggests a theory (correctly, based on Annie and Jeff's overwrought denials) that their relationship is based on liking "to partner up on cutesy capers so you can hold hands in the dark and address your urges in semi-acceptable scenarios."

The episode is littered with self-aware moments like this though generally more in the service of imitating the serial killer genre than exploring character dynamics. Those genre cues range from the visual (the cinematography has a chilly, green-blue filter common to gloomy procedurals) to the audio (Shirley's boys perform an eerie cover of Radiohead's "Creep" that recalls Fincher's similar usage of the song for *The Social Network*) to the plot (Abed has a brief, on-point, somewhat heartfelt monologue about the overuse of "mildly autistic super detectives" in shows that use "a social disorder as a procedural device").

Inspector Spacetime

Though *Community*'s bag of cultural references is heavily Abed-centric (movies and TV), occasionally the lens widens to music. In "Basic Intergluteal Numismatics," jokes revolve around Radiohead and Bach. A key plot point hinges on knowledge of Dave Matthews, whom Jeff very uncharacteristically turns out to be a hardcore fan of, declaring "excuse me for being alive in the '90s and having two ears connected to a heart." Additionally, the musician Ben Folds not only plays a professor suspected of being the bandit but wrote and performed the song "Ass Crack Bandit" that plays over the episode-ending montage.

The surprise reappearance of Star-Burns, thought to have died in the last season, seems to solve the crime only to be revealed as another red herring. While the episode ends without revealing the coin-crack culprit, suspicion falls heaviest on Annie, who comes very close to outing herself when the bandit comes up in Season 6's "Emotional Consequences of Broadcast Television."

Episode 88: "Cooperative Polygraphy"

A tightly packed bottle episode with a delayed-fuse payoff, "Cooperative Polygraphy" presented the best of what peak *Community* had to offer. It is as good a standalone argument for the weird greatness of an ensemble show that was willing to strip its characters down to the things they were most ashamed of and still find room for grace not to mention what was likely the longest running joke about sperm ever seen on a network sitcom.

While most sitcoms who lose a major character tend to move on after one Very Special Episode, *Community* did not shed itself so easily of Pierce, whose absence hung nearly as heavily over the show as Coach's did in *Cheers*. Four episodes into Season 5 and the study group has just truly started getting over the death of the man Jeff called back in Season 3's "Biology 101" episode "our closest, oldest, craziest, most racist, oldest elderly crazy friend."

They start the episode filing into the study room still wearing the bright blue outfits from Pierce's cult funeral. After a few mournful cracks about Pierce's Laser Lotus beliefs—its mix of Scientology pyramid-scheming and bogus Buddhism forming a rich trove of material that the show would miss—the group faces an expected visitor. Mr. Stone (Walton Goggins), a mysterious, black-suited man with a monotone delivery like the very voice of fate itself, tells them he is there for an inquest at Pierce's request to determine who murdered him. Everyone agrees to be polygraphed and Stone begins, reading from Pierce's questions with enough accuracy that he remembers to mis-pronounce Abed's name "Ay-bed."

After just a handful of initially innocuous but cutting queries that lay open each character's most shameful secrets, the group descends into a maelstrom of accusation, denial, and denunciation that recalls the to-the-death bickering of Season 2's recrimination fest "Cooperative Calligraphy." The fighting is both bitter and joke-packed, punctuated by deadpan announcements from the polygraph team about who's lying. The increasingly tense back-and-forth pitches from minor discoveries like Troy and Abed stealing Jeff's Netflix account to more serious ones such as Shirley's sandwich shop using a tofu substitute called "meatfu" for the supposedly vegetarian sandwich Britta likes; then there is the downright disturbing revelation that Abed put tracking devices on everyone. Confused about why that's a problem, he asks, "You guys are changing your faces. Are you mad at me or hungry?"

Though Jeff does his best to keep everyone from falling into another of Pierce's manipulative traps (shades of "Advanced Dungeons & Dragons"), the lure of riches from the estate pushes everyone onward. The secrets keep coming. Annie secretly slipped everyone speed to keep them studying. Shirley gives money to a pro-life group, the revelation of which leads to one of the season's great Britta-isms: "If I wanted the government in my uterus, I'd fill it with oil and Hispanic voters!" Chang declares that yes, he *did* in fact masturbate in the study room (and everywhere else).

Just when everyone looks faded and shamed by all the truth telling, the process takes a surprise turn. Pierce, via Mr. Stone, turns from provocation to benediction, bestowing gifts on and praising each sour-faced person around the table. The punch line in this surprisingly moving montage is that just when the spirit of Pierce appears to be behaving in somewhat decent fashion, it becomes clear that he has also given each member of the study group a vial of his sperm for safekeeping . . . or procreating.

After yanking the audience one way and another to test their loyalties to this increasingly flawed-seeming group, the episode drops another reason for gloom: Troy surprisingly takes up the challenge dropped by Pierce to pilot his boat the *Childish Tycoon* (a play on Glover's musical moniker Childish Gambino) around the world in exchange for several million dollars.

An emotional whipsaw in the final analysis, "Cooperative Polygraphy" easily stands next to if not above many of the more frequently lauded episodes.

Paintball is great. Truth is better.

Episode 89: "Geothermal Escapism"

Some of *Community*'s high-concept, school-wide, action episodes used the chaos to embed dramatic character wrinkles: Jeff and Britta sleeping together in "Modern Warfare"; Annie and Abed making out in "For a Few Paintballs More." But when Season 5 went back again to the concept episode well in "Geothermal Escapism," the action scenes served a different purpose. This time instead of Greendale transforming into a combat zone because of the Dean's mistake or City College sabotage, it comes about because one character needs something to mask their emotions about another character leaving. And how better to do that than Hot Lava?

Things begin as they usually do with goofy patter around the study table. Only this time, there's a "Bon Troyage" banner signaling Troy's going-away party. The potentially maudlin goodbyes are interrupted by the Dean announcing that per Abed's request there will be a school-wide game of Hot Lava, "the sweet, classic children's game in which you are not allowed to touch the floor, or you're dead." The prize? Abed's *Space Clone* comic book, worth $50,000. Following the by-now established template of the paintball episodes, Greendale is transformed nearly instantaneously into a lawless hellscape populated by fractious bands with stylized outfits and fanciful names. Unlike the paintball episodes, the drama is centered less on who wins than determining how long Abed can go without facing the reality of his best friend's departure.

Having already done homage to spaghetti westerns and *Star Wars*, the style is less specific for this combat episode, using a general, post-apocalyptic vibe with a few specific *Mad Max beyond Thunderdome* touches thrown in. The comedy derives largely from the ridiculous efforts the players put into inching down a hallway without touching the imaginary lava, as well as the instant mythologizing ("You have *gods*?" Britta asks incredulously after hearing a reference to "the Vapors of Magmarath"). Chang is of course a warlord (if given to puns, one *might* say the collapse of civilization indicates that it's time for a Chang), leading a band of mohawked guerrillas who attack their prey from lockers.

Streets Ahead

In "Geothermal Escapism," Chang admits that his "same-sex celebrity crush" is Nathan Fillion. Besides showing unusually non-insane good taste for Chang, this is also a call-forward to the next broadcast episode "Analysis of Cork-Based Networking" in which Fillion makes his first appearance.

Having the students and faculty—Jeff and Hickey jump right in without hesitation—battling with brooms and simply pushing people onto the floor rather than wielding non-lethal guns gives the whole episode a more purposefully childlike feel. This, along with Britta's determination to put her badly remembered psychology classes to work by getting the group to acknowledge their feelings about Troy, keeps the focus less on the play-fighting than on why Abed cannot let it stop. When Abed is finally forced to confront the loss of Troy, his usual reticence cracks and he pretends to sacrifice himself (dropping into lava à la Ripley's death in *Alien³*) to let Troy go. When Britta suggests that it isn't Troy who is leaving but his clone—another example of the group rallying quickly to protect their friend from emotional pain—Abed pretends to believe the fiction in order to maintain his frazzled composure.

The pivot from hardcore, geek imagineering and self-immolation to the soppy conclusion in which Troy leaves on the *Childish Tycoon* while Styx's "Come Sail Away" plays is so awkwardly handled it feels like a Season 4 leftover. *Community* is always more impactful when managing emotion on its own terms, not cloning an ending from some other sitcom with an entirely different sensibility.

Episode 90: "Analysis of Cork-Based Networking"

A walloping classic that may get overlooked for not having an over-the-top concept powering things along, this episode hinges on how systems of bureaucratic power-grabbing can turn institutions into feuding fiefdoms where it is impossible to accomplish even mundane tasks.

But, you know, funny.

Things start with the first official-ish meeting of the Save Greendale Committee, finally allowing the show to cut ties with the study group concept as a reason to keep everyone together. Chang and Duncan put in appearances, but nobody besides Annie wants to actually do anything of substance. The others prefer to jabber about *Bloodlines of Conquest*, the *Game of Thrones*-esque HBO show everyone is watching. Abed's testier side comes out as Britta insists nobody talk about it because she's several seasons behind.

This leads into the episode's low-key B story in which Abed avoids the spoilers Britta tries to throw his way by wearing noise-canceling headphones only to inadvertently attract the attention of Carol (Katie Leclerc), who is deaf. Reading the audience's mind, Britta asks Abed, "Are you going to have another intense burst of compatibility with a girl we never see again?" showing once again how the writers of *Community* could act just as much like fans of the show as they were its makers. The almost-romance fizzles once Abed, who has learned ASL in a quick Abed-ian burst of autodidacticism, discovers Britta paid off Carol in order to hit him with a *Bloodlines of Conquest* spoiler. But the wrap-up is neatly handled when Abed realizes the mysterious and quietly alluring Rachel (Brie Larson), the only new Season 4 character to return, is now back in the coat check for the first time since last season's "Herstory of Dance."

The A story is a tangled treat that begins innocuously: Annie asks Hickey to re-hang a bulletin board that fell down in the cafeteria. From there the plot twists like a snake into the dark bowels of Greendale and the subcultures residing there like Russian nesting dolls. Annie and Hickey's efforts to get someone to hang the bulletin board leads them to offer increasingly large favors to one guest star-led interest group after another: Nathan Fillion's powerful custodian union; Robert Patrick's sinister parking office; the IT administrator played by Paget Brewster (who returns the next season as a different character, Frankie Dart).

There's a lot going on in this storyline, particularly how Annie evolves from an upbeat Jimmy Stewart optimist who thinks she can get around bureaucratic obstinance with plucky charm to a fully debased cynic willing to trade away her ideals for an insignificant win. It manages to be both howlingly funny—especially in the preposterously feudalistic nature of Greendale's departments—and a thoughtful examination of how institutional paralysis leads to personal corruption.

It's a layered enough piece that the C story—a decently funny bit in which the group is race-guilted into going with Chang's terrible idea for a dance theme ("Bear Down for Midterms") only to discover that the news is filled with a story about a bear mauling kids at a birthday—doesn't have time to make much of a dent.

> ### Cool Cool Cool
>
> "Analysis of Cork-Based Networking" features a thicket of pop culture references. Some are right on the surface if not obvious to all viewers like the Dean murmuring, "This got Sorkin-y" after Annie and Hickey engage in a knock-down ethics confrontation, or the multiple callouts to Jim Henson's muppet-Bowie oddity *Labyrinth* (Hickey: "Welcome to the labyrinth, kid. Only there ain't no puppets or bisexual rock stars down here" / Dean: "What kind of labyrinth have you created? Certainly not the kind with puppets and macho rock stars"). On top of that, when Annie is starting to lose herself in the cynical game of bureaucratic browbeating and favor-trading, she answers the question "What do you mean, 'everything'?" by screaming *"Everything!"* at top volume à la Gary Oldman's spittle-flecked bellowing *"EV-ERY-ONE!"* in *The Professional*. It's the season's second Oldman nod, the first performed in "Cooperative Polygraphy" when Chang informs the group that he masturbated *"EV-ERY-WHERE!"* The last comes three episodes later in "VCR Maintenance and Educational Publishing" when Britta brings it full circle by shouting *"EV-ERY-BODY!"* at a terrified Chang.

The end tag, however, is a small piece of perfection (not a common occurrence in the immediate post-Troy era). Trying to call the number for ordering office supplies, Duncan inadvertently clicks through to a secret government number where a robot voice tells him, "Arcadia initiated," then a panicked man asks, "You really want to activate this, sir?" as what sounds like a nuclear-armed bomber roars overhead.

Ah, the apocalypse.

Episode 91: "Bondage and Beta Male Sexuality"

By this point in Season 5, the series' un-Pierced and Troy-less configuration is humming along smoothly enough that memories of the gas leak year have mostly been banished. That does not mean Pierce and Troy's absence has no impact. One of this episode's most poignant aspects is watching Abed straining to avoid dealing with the loss of Troy. But by moving confidently forward without trying to replicate the past—Hickey might be another un–PC boomer but he's also a crusty firebreather who would have eaten a pampered milquetoast like Pierce for breakfast—the series maintains the exploratory spirit that animated it from the start.

As written, the A story is a piffle, briefly returning to the Season 1 standby of Britta's hotness: Duncan decides to take a run at Britta, who reminds him of everything he loves about America: "Bold, opinionated, just past her peak, and starting to realize she has to settle for less." Trying to show himself to be the kind of charity-minded guy he thinks Britta would like, Duncan invites her to a theater benefit for starving children with cleft palates. This inadvertently rekindles Jeff's interest in Britta after she runs into some of her old activist friends and lights up the room in an unusual and brief burst of self-confidence. "Something about everybody liking her turns me on," Jeff admits. The comedy works primarily due to McHale and Oliver amplifying the worst aspects of their characters (shallow and popularity-obsessed versus needy and spineless) in a kind of onedowns-manship competition.

The B story shows Abed in a state of mind unusual for him: loneliness. Skipping the benefit to attend the premiere of the *Kickpuncher* reboot (not including clips of which feels like a missed opportunity) in a handmade cardboard "classic Kickpuncher" outfit that shoots foam instead of rock-ets, Abed walks the empty Greendale halls playing imaginative games but without the gusto that Troy's presence would bring. He happens into Hickey's office and finds him secretly working on his cartoon, *Jim the Duck*. After Abed accidentally sprays foam on the cartoons, Hickey erupts in rage and punishes Abed by handcuffing him to a filing cabinet so that he will miss the movie.

What follows is a sharp and short two-hander in which Hickey's anger over what he sees as the school catering to Abed's whimsies ("Let's eat cookies and ice cream and dress in pajamas in the middle of the day!") swivels fast to barely papered-over grief ("I watched my third wife die!"). Abed, skilled in manipulating people in order to survive a lifetime of bul-lying, tries flattering Hickey about his cartooning skills. But when that fails, Abed, furious at being kept from what to him is a pop cultural Holy Grail, erupts in the first burst of real anger the show has given him. The back-and-forth is broadly sympathetic though giving the last word to Abed in a pair of lines that paint a full picture of his childhood: "You're not the Marco Polo of bullying me. You're just another tourist taking pictures of a great big wall."

The episode's adroit balancing of relationship drama, introspection, and verbal comedy already puts it in the season's top rank before even con-sidering what is arguably the most memorable sequence. A semi-detached storyline follows Chang as he goes to the benefit and wanders accidentally into a small, black-box theater with a waiting crowd. Taking the opportunity, he launches into an improvised one-man show: "Hong Kong! 1964 . . . " The ghost-story twist comes when he runs into a janitor who tells him the space has been closed since a fire killed twenty-four people there. Chang runs screaming out of the theater but nobody notices. The concluding shot of the episode, a slow pan and zoom into a black-and-white photo showing Chang in a group of people in period dress. But the punchline pulls it back from an over-obvious *The Shining* joke by revealing the photo's caption: "Old Timey Photo Club, 2014." The piece not only plays to Jeong's subtler skills but also, as with Abed and Hickey's story, reveals a bit more depth in a character who often skirts cartoonishness.

Episode 92: "App Development and Condiments"

At this point, some might argue that Season 5 is frittering away any forward narrative momentum with standalone episodes like this that do nothing to advance the overall storyline. No character is truly changed or even deeply affected. Even at the conclusion of the main conflict between Jeff and Shirley, the two end up in essentially the same spot of semi-distant but warm regard they were at after their last big blowup in Season 3's "Foosball and Nocturnal Vigilantism."

Those people would be wrong.

One of the season's last truly inspired episodes, "App Development and Condiments" plugged a bitingly funny satire on the oppressiveness of popularity and social media into a loony *Logan's Run* design scheme while letting Britta (finally!) lead a revolution.

As often happens, disaster is announced by the Dean announcing a new idea for raising Greendale's profile. Doom arrives in the form of two developers—Steve Agee and Brian Posehn who along with episode director Rob Schrab worked with Harmon on *The Sarah Silverman Program*—offering Greendale the chance to beta test a new app. Harmon's original vision was simple: Jeff panders to his intro to law students so they'll score him higher on a Yelp for Teachers–type app. It morphs into something funnier and more malevolent.

The app MeowMeowBeenz comes with a diabolically simple hook: rate everybody for everything. Within a day, almost all of Greendale is hooked. Most people are addicted to the dramatic spikes and crashes of everyone else's approval and disapproval. Abed, mostly absent for this

Who wore it better: Star-Burns or Sean Connery? NBC/PHOTOFEST.

episode, chimes in that he loves the app because it "takes everything sub-
jective and unspoken about human interaction"—which he has difficulty
following—"and reduces it to explicit, objective numbers."

Everyone else, though, seeks status. And as every time when all of
Greendale is engaged in competition, the campus descends once again into
a dystopic hellhole.

By the second day, the students have already divided themselves into
a five-tier caste system corresponding to the number of stars given in
MeowMeowBeenz. By the eighth day there are security guards, ostraciza-
tion, caste-denoting outfits, and a desolate, barbed-wire-laced region in
the parking lot evocatively termed "the outlands." The outfits and décor—
jumpsuits, Roman-styled flowing robes, white backdrops, and disco-ish
design—plus aggressive social role-playing produce an effect akin to the
Stanford prison experiment crossed with *Buck Rogers in the 25th Century*
by way of *Hunger Games* cosplay with Star-Burns in a *Zardoz* outfit for no
earthly reason except the retina-searing impact of the thing itself.

As she did a few episodes earlier in "Geothermal Escapism," Shirley
climbs to the top of the pack and is again relishing not being the overlooked single mother. Jeff and Britta revert to type as snarky manipulator
and rebellious refusenik who try to expose the authoritarian insanity into

> ## Cool Cool Cool
>
> Fan appreciation art for *Community* generally took the form of memes, T-shirts, and the like. However, the episode "App Development and Condiments" was given a different kind of honor. Just a couple of weeks after the episode about a fictional malevolent social rating app called MeowMeowBeenz first aired, at least one real fan-created app by that name was available for download.

which everyone has descended. Each has a moment of triumph: Jeff rocketing up to five-star status by dint of a hacky stand-up set and Britta by spitting some choice one-liners ("I'm a psych major, words are my weapons!") and leading the uprising of one-star untouchables only to become a vengeful dictator once she has power.

It would be going too far to say that this episode was particularly prescient. When the episode was broadcast in 2014, Facebook was already a decade old and well on its way to cementing the dehumanizing mob potential of social media. Nevertheless it was another two years before *Black Mirror*, that barometer for millennial techno-angst, produced an episode (Season 3's "Nosedive") imagining a creeped-out future with ubiquitous adoption of a MeowMeowBeenz–like app. Also, in real-life 2020, the Chinese city of Suzhou introduced a "civility code" to monitor and score its citizens' model behavior through a smartphone app.

What did neither *Black Mirror* nor Suzhou have that "App Development and Condiments" did? Koogler! He is the episode's smarmy, college-flick frat dude (played with sublime self-aware chill by *Arrested Development* creator and occasional *Harmontown* guest Mitch Hurwitz) whose only purpose is to remind people to party. The end tag, a fake trailer for a movie starring Koogler, is a deeply meta masterpiece homage to the 1980s summer party movie aesthetic but also a reminder of a simpler, more rockin' time before MeowMeowBeenz.

Episode 93: "VCR Maintenance and Educational Publishing"

A very lengthy setup for Britta's Season 6 move into the emotionally fraught territory that is apartment 303. Originally occupied by Troy

COMMUNITY 105—SEASON 5: THE SCIENCE OF SYNDICATION   175

and Abed, it became Annie's home in Season 3 after "Remedial Chaos Theory."

In this episode, Annie and Abed finally realize they need a new roommate to split the rent after Troy's departure. The result is a highly manufactured standard sitcom hidden-agenda scenario—which could be called "classic" or "hack" depending on the viewer's mood—in which each of the two brings a guest over for what is ostensibly dinner but is in reality an awkward audition. Abed pushes his girlfriend Rachel while Annie stumps for her brother Anthony (Spencer Crittenden, a cohost and occasional Dungeon Master on the *Harmontown* podcast whose comedic mileage comes directly from his monotone delivery) in a secret competition that only succeeds in making their guests highly uncomfortable.

The hook for Annie and Abed's skirmish is a gift he receives from Rachel: an interactive VCR game called *Pile of Bullets*. This leads to some very detailed satire of a thankfully moribund genre that quickly exhausts any comedic possibilities even with the game's rootin'-tootin' host (*Breaking Bad* creator Vince Gilligan) hamming it up like Slim Pickens. Annie alienates Anthony with her manipulation. Abed wins back Rachel with a "third-act apology" referencing every romantic comedy stored in his mental hard drive, and like many of his successful gambits, it manages to be both fully artificial (his old dorm mate Pavel pours water over Abed during the apology so it looks like he is standing forlorn in the rain) and yet fully sincere and winning.

The B plot is one of the season's more forgettable even though it gives Shirley the rare chance to drive the action. She, Jeff, Hickey, and Britta engage in a *Treasure of the Sierra Madre*–style roundelay of greed and betrayal after discovering a cache of old chemistry textbooks they think could be worth thousands on the black market. Initially resisting the allure of sinful greed, Shirley quickly shifts into boss mode, leading the conspiracy until it turns out the books are misprints and worth nothing.

While somewhat unremarkable, the episode still deserves canonical recognition for providing a standout moment of Dean-ing. He tells Hickey and Jeff their paychecks will be late by delivering a "freestyle rap apology" while wearing a Payday candy bar costume. This starts as just another routine in which a somewhat nerdy white guy raps in comedically stilted rhymes ("I'm a peanut bar and I'm here to say / Your checks will arrive on another day"). But just seconds into the number, the Dean's lyrics and delivery toughen and tighten, spitting out angrier lines that don't mesh with his personality, to put it mildly ("Criminals, Wall Street, takin' the pie / And all the black man gets is a plate of white lies!"). Then in one of the season's most comically ineffable moments, the Dean drops the mic, seemingly to conclude the rap but in actuality because he's scared of it, shaking and nearly sobbing as though recently possessed: "I don't . . . *I don't know what that was.*"

Years later on the joke dissection podcast *Good One*, Harmon would talk about that scene and what he referred to as the "tax" that needed to be paid for using standard-issue gags like white guys rapping badly. He meant that to make it worth even lightly invoking the latent racism embedded in such gags (suggesting black people are naturally gifted rhymers and performers), the joke needs to earn its place. While the rest of the episode did little to justify reliance on old sitcom tropes, the Payday Rap pays its tax and then some.

Episode 94: "Advanced Advanced Dungeons & Dragons"

When everyone else (actors or characters) is losing their way or maybe just phoning it in, Abed and Annie can always be counted on to function as the spine of the series. This truism becomes even more clear in later Season 5 episodes like this one.

At this stage the characters are somewhat less committed overall to the school itself—despite being at least theoretically responsible for saving it by committee. Without Pierce and Troy they are facing a diminishment of both positive and negative intensity. This gives the episodes more freedom to meander down different narrative alleys. But the low-stakes atmosphere, while common for most sitcoms, can deprive a show like *Community*, which was willing to mix up its comedy with full-tilt melodrama, of some of its sting.

This is where Abed and Annie come in.

In this self-aware revisiting of Season 2's "Advanced Dungeons & Dragons" episode, the group digs out its character sheets and twenty-sided dice to insert themselves into another personal issue nobody asked them to help with. Hickey is grumbling about being shut out of his grandson's life by his son Hank (David Cross), who just so happens to play what Hickey calls "that crap with the dungeons and the dragons."

Annie leaps at the chance to play father-and-son matchmaker. Abed comes onboard as well only after delivering a meta side note that feels drawn from his Season 2 Charlie Kaufman phase.

Cool Cool Cool

At one point during "Advanced Advanced Dungeons & Dragons," Hickey threatens the group by saying that if they lose the game (meaning he loses the chance to visit his grandson), "I'm gonna punch each of you in the heart." Supposedly this is a version of a line that Banks himself would say on set in response to direction, apparently tongue-in-cheek. If true, this means that Harmon was pulling a Pierce by using combative, real-life lingo from an at-times crotchety actor for their character's dialogue.

A satisfying sequel is difficult to pull off. Many geniuses have defeated themselves through hubris, making this a chance to prove that I'm better than all of them. *I'm in.*

Just as with Neil in the earlier AD&D episode, the group's intentions go quickly awry. Father and son end up using the game to maximize their competition. As Hank, Cross proves to be a valuable cameo addition. Bristling with intensity (like most of the best guest stars, Cross plays the role straight), Hank unloads grievances on his father as they reluctantly play the game. Banks returns the favor by amplifying Hickey's usual grumpiness to full-on fury.

As the other characters' characters are killed off, they end up watching Hickey and Hanks wrangle and bicker their way back into some form of a relationship. While Annie set up the scenario that made it possible, Abed was the one who kept cool amidst the chaos.

Just as a Dungeon Master should.

Episode 95: "G.I. Jeff"

The last and possibly greatest of *Community*'s animated episodes, "G.I. Jeff" features some of the same elements that made Season 2's "Abed's Uncontrollable Christmas" work on so many levels. It takes a classic style of animation religiously consumed by adults of a certain age in their youth and uses it as a safe-seeming pathway through which the characters can address anxiety or trauma. In this instance, Jeff comes to grips with turning forty years old—which he had been lying about to the group—by downing a fifth of scotch and some "youth pills" he bought in Koreatown, passing out, and coming to in a hospital after dreaming he was in a G.I. Joe cartoon.

The episode primarily plays out within the framework of the imagined cartoon. Its aesthetic is painstakingly copied from the choppy, inadequately lip-synched, mid-1980s action-figure advertainment series *G.I. Joe: A Real American Hero*. The spirit ranges from broad comedic exaggeration (including some homoerotic overtones that recall *TV Funhouse*, another affectionate animation satire worked on by this episode's writer, Dino Stamatopolos) to thoughtful deconstruction.

The story turns each character into a G.I. Joe action figure whose exaggerated codename and outfit satirize both an aspect of their personality and the original series' dated mentality: Jeff as Wingman the hero; Abed as wisdom-spouting, generically Eastern ethnic Fourth Wall; a ludicrously buxom and short shorts–wearing Annie as Tight Ship; Britta as Buzzkill (circular saw hand, very cool); and Shirley as Three Kids (as in saying "I've got three kids!" regardless of the situation).

Things start in typical *G.I. Joe* fashion with terrorist organization Cobra attacking some random location (in this case the Taj Mahal) and the Joes fighting back. Fighter planes zoom and bullets blast but—as in the original series—there isn't a single casualty. Then when Wingman kills Cobra villain Destro, the unexpected fatality brings everything to a halt. Buzzkill, Three Kids, Tight Ship, and Wingman are put on trial for "violence, suggestive language, and mature situations unbecoming of G.I. Joe."

After that the group keeps poking holes in the confusing and weirdly bloodless cartoon warfare erupting around them. Wingman makes the logical argument that since the Cobras are ruthless terrorists, "if we never kill them, are we not basically on their side?" Buzzkill wonders why they are all dressed "like serial killers and strippers." After Fourth Wall appears

Cool Cool Cool

The attention paid to verisimilitude in "G.I. Jeff" included animators actually tracing over drawings from the original show to get the look right. Despite the satirical under- (and over-) tones, the episode was approved by G.I. Joe's owners Hasbro and generated genuine excitement in the G.I. Joe fan community and convention world (which somehow is a real thing that exists). Some fans even took to cosplaying as Tight Ship.

as the stereotypical dispenser of wisdom (wearing a confused ethnic mélange that Wingman calls "three layers of racist"), what he refers to as "this medium's lack of internal logic" begins to break down even more.

Those clues to the artificiality of this construct start drawing Jeff out of his dream world. The fake G.I. Joe ads sprinkled throughout (again, dead-on stylistic imitations of 1980s child advertising) become increasingly odd. In the last one, the narrator finishes his "Everything sold separately" spiel with an existential flourish: "Everyone dies eventually, nobody gets out alive." that feels like a precursor to similar ruminations in Harmon's *Rick and Morty*.

Finally the episode breaks fully back into live-action *Community* reality and everyone is gathered around Jeff's hospital bed, faces dark with concern. Jeff's worry over his age is neatly diagnosed and put away, everybody smiling at his telling them how they were in his dream like *The Wizard of Oz*.

Episode 96: "Basic Story"

The first half of a season-concluding two-parter, this episode throws a knotty conundrum at the Save Greendale Committee: What happens after they finally save Greendale?

Annie notes that there is not much left to do though as usual her status reports present more questions than answers ("According to the demonologist, the gymnasium is clean!"). Abed begins to fret, but everyone else seems content—at least until the Dean rushes in to announce that an insurance appraiser is coming and if Greendale is found not up to scratch, then they are "doomed!"

As generally happens, Jeff correctly identifies the problem ("This school is addicted to chaos") but is unable to convince the group to follow his laissez-faire lead, the Winger charm and the power of the Winger speech having been depleted through overuse. Panic ensues.

While the group works to get the school in shape, Abed peels off on another fourth wall–breaking internal spiral. This time he realizes that the long-running community college–set sitcom he feels he has been living in could be coming to an end.

Rather than discovering that Greendale is a garbage pile that just needs to be put out of its misery, the appraiser (*MadTV*'s Michael McDonald), a curiously affable sort who enjoys quoting Dante, declares that it is actually worth money. The ironic twist is that by improving the school, the Save Greendale Committee made its real estate valuable. This leads the

> ## Cool Cool Cool
>
> In the episodes "Basic Story" and "Basic Sandwich," Abed is wearing a T-shirt with the logo of the Dead Alewives. This was the Milwaukee improv comedy group where both Harmon and Schrab (who directed "Basic Sandwich") matriculated before heading west.

ever-inebriated school board frat bros Carl and Richie to realize that they can sell the place. Which they do. To Subway. For a sandwich university.

It is hard to imagine the series improving on working a sponsor into an episode's storyline than Subway's introduction in Season 3 with Rick (aka the "corpo-humanoid" legally named Subway). But this episode still neatly uses the corporate takeover for background snark: when a Subway executive tries to convince Jeff to teach a course in "sandwich law," he entices him with a Subway Black Card, intoning, "$5 footlongs for life, Mr. Winger . . . *for life*" as though offering a sack of gold doubloons.

The episode concludes with something of a Hail Mary from Abed's perspective. Poking around in the Dean's office just before the unmentioned Dalmatian posters are packed up, Abed (who had been repeating "buried treasure" earlier in the hope that it would happen) finds a hidden map. He, the Dean, and Annie jump immediately to thinking they could discover buried treasure left behind by the school's idiosyncratic founder and really save Greendale; meaning, of course, that the three need to dash back to the library—where Jeff and Britta have just decided on a whim to get married, something they keep to themselves—and do a short song-and-dance number on the theme of buried treasure.

Almost more than ever, this episode suggests that all of Greendale is very much like Abed's Dreamatorium. It's a place where in actuality nothing that amazing can ever truly happen. But at the same time, Greendale also provides a space in which people can at least imagine that anything can happen. Somewhere between those poles of realism and dreamland lies the spark of possibility, which is where much of the show's magic is contained.

Episode 97: "Basic Sandwich"

The concluding episode of Season 5 shows the writers' full-tilt commitment to *Lost* fandom and an uncertain mindset about where to take a show that was yet again on the brink of cancellation.

An opening monologue by the Dean accompanies a scratchy filmstrip about the life of groundbreaking computer engineer Russell Borchert (Chris Elliott). A bearded and corduroy-clad embodiment of 1970s Silicon Valley hippiedom who looks very much like he might have been behind the Dharma Initiative on *Lost*, he originally founded Greendale as a computer training school after getting rich inventing the nine-track cassette tape. Dedicated to inventing a computer that could process emotions, Borchert went a bit barmy. He decided that the computer's circuitry needed to be gold-plated ("It was a weird time," the Dean notes to Abed and Annie, "*The Bionic Woman* won an Emmy," which is as good a way as any to explain the decade). Borchert also became physically attracted to the computer, which sets up the Dean for the episode's most rim-shot-worthy punchline: "Hence the legend that he died of the first computer virus." Borchert disappeared, his research lab was sealed off, and his body and fortune never located.

All this backstory is less to fill out the history of Greendale than it is to engineer a caper that requires the whole group to band together and find a solution to a seemingly impossible problem. Transparent plot device or not, this is ultimately a positive development given the season's relative paucity of bonding moments (not to mention the disappointingly limited number of school dances).

The caper itself is set off by an extremely enthusiastic Dean, Annie, and Abed. They convince everyone else to join their manic-seeming scheme to locate Borchert's hidden treasure so they can buy Greendale before Subway can close on the purchase.

The resulting hijinks rate somewhere around a 3 on the Greendale Chaos Meter (see sidebar). Hickey smashes through a wall with a pick-axe. Duncan gets electrocuted, after which he looks like a Looney Tunes character who just stuck a finger into a wall socket. Jeff throws out the bombshell that he and Britta are engaged.

Following Abed down a secret trapdoor and through a hidden entrance opened by choosing the right song on a jukebox, the group finds themselves in Borchert's time-capsule of a computer lab. A filthy, bearded loon with creepy long fingernails and a clear sexual fixation on his computer Raquel, he agrees to give them his fortune if they leave him alone. When Carl, Richie, and their unexpected new sidekick Chang (whose madness has been recently notching back up toward Truly Dangerous) find the group in the lab, they steal the millions and trap the group there. It turns out that the only way the group can reopen the door is to reboot the mainframe with "a blast of human emotion."

This highly convoluted and goony scenario is resolved by Jeff connecting himself to Raquel, telling everyone to turn around, and then looking at Annie even though he's supposedly about to marry Britta. The door opens, and they march upstairs to present a contract showing that Borchert retains the right to be vice dean. One look at him scares off Subway (their representative defines the corporation as a conflict-avoidant entity since they are "but simple sandwich artists who want the world to eat fresh"), leaving Greendale once again in the Dean's extremely incapable hands.

The episode concludes with celebration and the suggestion that either everything will be resetting to normal at the start of the next season or this will be it. Jeff starts a fight with Britta in an obvious ploy to break off the engagement as he is still vacillating between her and Annie. There's a callback (Star-Burns cranking up Dave Matthews and everybody dancing) whose frequency of usage has by now become the joke more than the song itself.

Abed continues to speculate on their life as a sitcom only now he's considering whether it is coming to an end. He apologizes for not wishing Annie happy birthday "or Halloween, or Christmas, or any other specific calendar event," nodding to this season's lack of holiday shows. As usual, Abed tries to engineer the outcome, this time by telling Annie, "We'll definitely be back next year" (she's talking about the school year, he's talking about the 2014–2015 NBC season) before giving the caveat that "if not, it'll be because an asteroid has destroyed all of human civilization." Abed punctuates that line with a meaningful look and comment ("and that's *canon*") as though he's trying to define that aspect of the show's universe for the viewers he imagines are there but whom Annie of course cannot see.

That underlining of Abed's life-is-TV fixation pushes the show closer than it previously had to suggesting that nothing happening on screen is quite real.

Still, the end of Season 5 has a heavy TV-about-TV theme. At one point, after hearing about Jeff and Britta's engagement, the Dean snipes like an over-tired sitcom writer: "What does this look like, an hour-long episode of *The Office*?" Abed and Annie take a quick tiptoe through the fourth wall when they briefly look at the camera (he knowingly, she confused). The end tag is a montage of promos for fake, awful-seeming, and inexplicable but quite real-looking NBC shows like Questlove in *Celebrity Beat-off* and *The Office*'s B. J. Novak dressed up as a mummy for *Mr. Egypt*, which is promised to air in either the fall, winter, or spring, "depends on what fails!"

Inspector Spacetime

The (Unauthorized) Greendale Chaos Meter

1. Pillow fort.
2. Britta leading protest.
3. No more chicken fingers.
4. Paintball.
5. Ladders! (see Season 6).

This is what it looks like when a sitcom comes to grips with its own mortality.

Community 106–Season 6: Theories of Closure

9

Everything we complained about for five years is finally solved.
Now it's just us—and we're falling apart.

—DAN HARMON

W HEN NBC DROPPED the long-dreaded ax on *Community* in May 2014 just a few weeks after Season 5 concluded with "Basic Sandwich," it was practically an admission that the network was giving up on sitcoms as a living, breathing format.

NBC's 2014–2015 schedule leaned heavily into hour-long dramas and competition reality programming of the *America's Got Talent* variety. Sitcom offerings included the occasional old favorite like the final season of *Parks and Recreation*, but they were mostly short-lived, fling-it-at-the-wall shows that seemed to exist in a kind of time warp (wacky families, stand-up comedians working too hard under bright lights). In a shoot-the-moon attempt to (yet again) bring back the long-faded NBC sitcom magic, the network even hyped a brand-new show starring Bill Cosby before nixing it after sexual assault allegations stacked up too high for the network to ignore.

CBS was not trying to reinvent anything either. But with seemingly unkillable shows like *The Big Bang Theory*, they appeared to have at least remembered the recipe for half-hour comedy and didn't want to rely on, say, accused serial predators for a living. ABC and Fox were smartly splitting the difference by airing shows (*Brooklyn Nine-Nine*, *Black-ish*, *New Girl*) that tweaked the sitcom format and were unafraid of bringing the strange to Middle America while generally keeping things bright and likeable.

Ironically, by the time *Community* ended its long-running will-it-or-won't-it-get-cancelled? industry soap opera, the show had already eased into a more relaxed and less aggressively antagonistic mood that should have made it more palatable to a network uninterested in breaking new ground. But the departure of stars Donald Glover and Chevy Chase—plus stubbornly un-stellar ratings—made a sixth season ever less attractive. It was also possible that Harmon's interests had wandered somewhat with his animated show *Rick and Morty*, which was getting all the cheer, support, and renewals he could ask for over at Adult Swim.

Given the strength of *Community*'s support in online and convention fandom, it was not a surprise that less-risk-averse streaming services were interested in grabbing the show. Hulu, which had already been showing *Community* reruns, made a bid. But ultimately sixth season rights were snapped up by a service that very few people were aware even existed. Yahoo! Screen was a short-lived and abysmally conceived attempt by the floundering early Internet company to get into the original video business. The sixth and last season of *Community* ran thirteen episodes on Yahoo! Screen from March to June 2015. In January 2016, the service shut down, and so did Greendale.

During its short lifespan, Yahoo! Screen appeared to be a don't-bother-the-creatives operation. They gave Harmon and his crew room to maneuver plus the money to do it. In an interview with *Vulture*, Harmon expressed relief about not being at a network that saw *Community* as a problem "that they wanted to either 'solve' or get rid of." But as he later noted, not having an authority to fight against may have drained the last season of the scrappy ingenuity and combativeness that made the earlier seasons more electrifying. In a commentary for the last season's seventh episode, "Advanced Security Features," Harmon sounds drained, honestly conveying how he no longer had the "hunger" of the guy "who loved TV so much" he would fight to the death for his vision of what the medium could be. His commitments to other projects, his occasional absence from the set, and his sporadic delivery of timely scripts is too often apparent during the last season. While still relentlessly metafictional, *Community* became narrower in its comedy and generally stopped using Greendale as a place for conspiracy-laden side plots, cartoonishly pointless classes, and not-infrequent riots.

What is immediately noticeable at the start of the season is how much tighter the bond has grown between the smaller core of original study group members. Whereas the show once spent a good deal of its running time creating and healing and re-creating fissures in the group then bringing in outsiders to comment on the dynamic's unhealthily incestuous nature, now there are just four core members (Abed, Annie, Britta, and Jeff) and an auxiliary (Chang and his posse of personalities) holding court around the battle-scarred table. Though new characters Frankie and Elroy integrate into the dynamic better than expected—in the last episode, Frankie even congratulates herself for being "a humble outsider that came in and nailed it"—outsiders they remain. The group's unity leaves little room for Troy and Abed's playacting or the clashes between the group majority and chaos elements like Pierce or Chang.

But by narrowing the show's previously sprawling story arcs and over-the-top interpersonal conflicts, Season 6 also makes it easier for creators and viewers to get ready to say goodbye.

Episode 98: "Ladders"

The last season of *Community* begins with a moment that seems determined to undercut the significance of everything that follows. A student-flung Frisbee floats up to the roof of a Greendale building, already several layers deep in flying discs. The roof collapses and Frisbees pour into the cafeteria carrying a screaming Garrett into the hallway and casting a decades-old disc into Leonard's hands, spurring him to flashback to decades earlier when—as a longhaired hippie—he accidentally tossed it onto a then-empty roof. Leonard ponders his past, murmuring "like tears in rain" as the Frisbee disintegrates in his hands.

One of the show's more inspired openers, it knits together a few familiar themes—canonical science fiction (Leonard's dialogue referencing Rutger Hauer's famously improvised *Blade Runner* death speech) and the decrepit nature of Greendale (it's later noted that "80 percent of the rubble was Styrofoam")—while not bothering to have anything to do with the primary characters or storyline. It could be read as a quiet acknowledgment from Harmon that whereas previous seasons had worked overtime to push every boundary in order to create a densely realized alternate universe, this time out he would be content with embracing a looser randomness.

At the table, the Save Greendale Committee is depleted and in disarray. Annie is adrift without a cause, Abed is disturbed that Shirley has "spun off" into an inferior show, Britta is running Shirley's sandwich shop into the ground, and Jeff is even more disengaged than usual. After Chang suggests a conspiracy behind the departures of Shirley and Troy ("Any of you white people noticing what's happening to this group? Do Abed and

I need to be concerned?"), the Dean introduces a consultant he wants to join the committee: Frankie (Paget Brewster).

A tight-wound, white-collar type with a steely intensity who is fluent in bureaucrat-ese, Frankie seems a poor fit for the committee's anarchism and no substitute for Shirley, who previously provided the show's moral center. But unlike most new Greendalians who are assessed by the core group and found wanting, Frankie proves the value in her self-described "exceptionally boring" nature. She suggests they all lean into the three attributes that her marketing study found that people identified with Greendale: "weird, passionate, and gross" (which honestly reads like a somewhat self-mocking description of the show's fan base). Although unable to understand Abed's belief that they are all characters on a show, Frankie connects with him through a shared desire to bring order to emotional chaos. Abed's approval is clear after she says, "I don't own a TV" and he replies, "You're the first person to say that that I didn't immediately delete from my brain."

Once Frankie is introduced and given a scrap of back story—"I come from a big family of people who are literally insane. I moved down here to take care of one of them"—the show shifts into a more freewheeling antic mode. Abed, Jeff, Britta, and Annie end up running a speakeasy under the

Annie and Abed carouse coolly in their underground speakeasy from "Ladders." NBC/ PHOTOFEST.

cafeteria complete with a jazz trio, small tables, fedora-wearing patrons, *Miller's Crossing* references, and a brief appearance by conspiracy-minded janitor Bob Waite (Nathan Fillion). Abed briefly loses himself playing out a series of film montages that only make sense once he edits them in his mental screening room. Rampant partying spreads across Greendale, still danger-ously susceptible to any passing fancy, and an inexplicably popular and riot-ously drunken class known only as "Ladders" (why? Because ladders!) leaves Annie (who, truth be told, would *never* take such a class) in a neck brace.

While the episode's hijinks quotient is fresh and unforced, the show is already carrying a whiff of mortality about it. As the resident prophetic voice and unpaid editorial consultant, Abed worries that the show of their lives is losing its thread. He lays out his disquiet in a short but remarkable speech to Frankie.

> My umbrella concern is that you, as a character, represent the end of what I used to call our show, which was once an unlikely family of misfit stu-dents, and is now a pretty loose-knit group of students and teachers, none of whom are taking a class together in a school which, as of your arrival, is becoming increasingly grounded.

At this moment, *Community* ceases being a show that critiques and complicates the sitcom format and moves into one that is in open conver-sation with itself about how to maintain its original animating spirit in the face of relentless change. It is hard not to hear in Abed's soliloquy a writer openly questioning what he is doing.

And why.

Meanwhile, Off Campus . . .

The end tag for "Ladders" comes across as a meta glimpse into Abed's mind. A note-perfect imitation of an NBC Must-See TV teaser, it places Shirley inside a crime drama called *The Butcher and the Baker*, which centers on a melodramatic, wheelchair-bound detective (Steven Weber). A pocket satire, it mimics the mid-2010s network TV aesthetic to a *T* while also setting up Shirley with the kind of line that network TV often doles out to black performers who get typecast as Sassy Black Lady: "I got dinner to make and you got cases to solve."

Episode 99: "Lawnmower Maintenance and Postnatal Care"

With only twelve episodes left in its entire run, there does not seem to be much reason for *Community* to bring in another new addition to the study group. There is even less reason for that character to be introduced by way of a riff about the brief but scarring (for science-fiction fans, at least) vogue in the 1990s for movies about virtual reality. But since the character, washed-up VR designer Elroy Patashnik, is played by the inimitable Keith David, any potential awkwardness is quickly forgiven.

Although it could have spent screen time carefully introducing Elroy to the remaining core players, the episode mostly dispenses with such formalities. This suggests that either the committee is more mature than the study group of three seasons ago (who would have already tried to get Frankie fired and Elroy brought up on fraud charges) or they are so traumatized by the departure of their friends that they have practically given up. With the normally stressed-out Jeff and Annie now taking such things more in stride, some of the tension is drained out of the introduction of new characters, resulting in a noticeable decrease in mania.

This episode is largely built around the comedic potential of recreating the kind of stodgy graphics and pointlessly baroque operating mechanisms favored by inexplicably popular movies like *Lawnmower Man*, *Virtuosity*, and *Disclosure*. To put a finer point on it: the episode is really about watching the Dean strap into a clunky VR rig and letting hilarity ensue. He flings himself about in spasmodic rhapsody as he walks through a sub-Salvador Dali virtual landscape and bellows self-important dialogue ("Jesus wept! For there were no more worlds to conquer!") of the kind favored by movies that overestimated the appeal of moving objects in virtual space rather than clicking a mouse ("I put a tilde on this *N*—I can do *anything!*").

In this season, Britta is seen more on her own terms outside of flirtations or conflict with her friends for perhaps the first time since Season 3's "Geography of Global Conflict" (when protesting gave her and Chang a purpose). Dead broke and crashing with Annie and Abed, Britta realizes that demons from her past still haunt her. Of course her emotionally fragile need to rebel against *something* means those demons are in fact just her parents (Martin Mull, Lesley Ann Warren). Far from the Reaganite monsters one might imagine Britta raging about, they seem to be nothing more than charming hippies-turned-yuppies who committed the sin of secretly helping Britta out financially.

Even though the confrontation ends in Britta flailing through yet another failed grand statement—storming out of her parents' house, she steals a boy's Green Machine bike and pedals off in a huff—it gives her character a touch more grace than the show normally allows. While still mocking Britta's posing, the scene introduces a subtler critique when her father, who blames ravaged brain cells for his inability to determine whether her claims of horrible parenting are based on reality, suggests that "us being bad parents" was as formative for her as Woodstock was for them. This makes Britta for once less a figure of ridicule and more a character with a damaged psyche that prevents her from growing up.

This puts her in good company given how much of *Community* examines the positives and negatives of arrested development. After all, this is an episode that includes a fully realized trailer for a fake Portuguese knock-off of *Gremlins* that Abed brandishes (he explains the gnarled plot as "a metaphor for World War II") and a freeze frame of Jeff and Elroy laughing repurposed as an ad for a fake 1970s-looking show *Hard Drive and Wing Man*, illustrating just how much the show is still living in that Gen X TV obsessive-with-a-budget headspace. The episode's comedic moments are bright and sharp but echoing familiar themes of immaturity and adult-world avoidance. When Jeff realizes once again just how trapped he might be in the delayed-adulting vortex that is Greendale and asks, "I'm never getting out of here, am I?" the Dean responds, "I haven't met many who do."

Episode 100: "Basic Crisis Room Decorum"

There is one fundamental question that the characters in *Community* keep circling back to without ever quite resolving: Is Greendale worth saving? Those unconvinced of the school's value can pull out several arsenals' worth of smoking guns to prove their point (black mold, monkeys in the ducts, no apparent connections between teacher's class assignments and their ability or willingness to teach said class). Those arguing for the school's value tend to fall back on appeals to emotion and the airy notion of Greendale as a place of acceptance whose low standards and chaotic structure make it less an educational institution than an island of and for misfit toys to shelter from the brutalizing storm that is reality.

That debate plays out again in the final season's third episode. A few token gestures are made toward integrating new characters Elroy and Frankie, but "Basic Crisis Room Decorum" is mostly structured in such a way that it could have been dropped with minimal editing into just about any season. The premise is familiar: an existential threat from City College pushes the committee to fight back while also wondering just how hard they should be trying. Annie gathers everyone in the library in the middle of the night to brainstorm ways to combat the attack ad that City College will show in the morning . . . which alleges that Greendale graduated a dog.

Everyone splits off into expected roles as Annie launches into overkill mode. She builds a "situation room" filled with unnecessary white boards and clocks showing the time in different places, suggesting how she imagines problems get solved when viewed through an Aaron Sorkin lens; Annie and Frankie hunt for evidence that the allegation is false while Jeff plays sarcastic foil to their earnestness; Chang lobs non-sequiturs from the fringe; Abed serves as A/V support tech; and a drunk Britta manages only to soil herself.

The crux of the conflict pits Jeff's legalistic relativism against Annie's moral absolutism. As ever, this fight is more about his giving up on getting anything meaningful from Greendale while Annie holds out hope the scrappy underdog school will prevail (the harder-nosed Frankie tries to keep Annie from deluding herself: "I never hope. Hope is pouting in advance. Hope is faith's richer, bitchier sister").

But rather than dig deep for a grand statement about the necessity of Greendale, the episode solves the crisis with an upbeat, owning-our-mistakes ad (which repeats the slogan used by Harmon in the web shorts advertising the show before its first episode: "You're already accepted"). This leaves more time for the outlier subplots.

One, in which Britta briefly bonds with Elroy over their shared love of 1990s alternative-rock band Natalie is Freezing, feels a bit perfunctory but at least includes a brief clip of Britta's dream in which she twirls like Stevie Nicks in the band's music video.

The other is a more fleshed-out joke. Some Japanese school boys pretend to be Jeff in a texting chain so they can prank the still-besotted Dean with nonsensical requests and claims of true devotion hidden by surface disdain ("It's only my style to be secret; please bring me five can of olive"). While this last bit could have been another jab at the Dean's infatuation, it turns to something more interesting in the end tag, which packs an entire film's worth of drama into scant minutes: after being viciously lectured on the cruelty of the world by his father, one of the Japanese boys reaches out to the Dean for support. But the agony of the boy's solitude and inability to break through the Dean's delusions ("I am not Jeffrey . . . Now I need a friend") becomes an origin story for his becoming a future yakuza leader.

It's a brazenly baffling gambit to pitch to viewers right at the end and concludes the episode on an uncertain note.

While *Community* appeared at this point less engaged with advancing the characters, it remained committed to their usefulness as springboards to other story possibilities.

Episode 101: "Queer Studies and Advanced Waxing"

A flurry of pop culture referencing and some more-committed emotional character-work threads together this episode, making up for a somewhat drifting plotline. The callouts are even more 1980s-centric than usual, hitting mall-culture mainstays like *Donkey Kong* (in Elroy's first scene, he is trying to talk Jeff into helping him sue the designers, claiming they ripped off his game *Construction Site*) and *The Karate Kid* (Annie helps Chang run lines for his audition for a stage adaptation of the movie).

Chang's audition process is a highlight not just of the episode of the season. Initially upset for being cast in the "Asian part" (Annie reassures him that that's okay: "Like Sidney Poitier or Meg Ryan before you, you were cast for race"). And Chang endures abuse from the director Matt (Jason Mantzoukas)—"You're the worst actor I've ever directed, and I've directed *both* Wahlbergs!"—who seems to favor Annie. In a fierily written pivot that Mantzoukas supercharges with bonus scorn, Chang discovers that the director's harsh criticism was actually perverse praise and that Annie (in the Danny LaRusso role) was Matt's true object of derision: "I know you're not capable of anything better, so that's why I've been so nice to you." That moment, and Chang's lauded performance in the live show, provides just about the only positive feedback the alternately mocked and feared character receives in the entire series.

While Chang finds his purpose in acting and Annie's confidence gets knocked down yet another peg, the committee is embroiled in an extremely low-stakes brouhaha over the lack of Wi-Fi on campus (a real-world complaint in most colleges, really). A gently anticlimactic storyline has Elroy and Abed seeking out the root of the problem only to trigger Abed's more childlike side when it's revealed that fixing the issue would involve moving a nest of birds. Given his unique development over the years, it's an unfortunate step back for the character and the kind of thing that feels more appropriate for an innocent like Troy, whose sweetness is inexpertly grafted on to Abed.

> ## Inspector Spacetime
>
> The lost Wi-Fi subplot of "Queer Studies and Advanced Waxing" provides one of the season's subtler meta references. When Frankie says that her emails to the IT lady keep getting bounced back, it's a clear fan nod to that fact that Paget Brewster played IT Department head Debra Chambers in the previous season's episode "Analysis of Cork-Based Networking." Since the physics of *Community* does not appear to allow for characters played by the same actor to appear in the same timeline, Frankie and Debra can never communicate.

With Chang in a more emotionally regulated headspace, wild-card responsibilities are picked up by the school board bros Richie and Carl, last seen in the Season 5 closer "Basic Sandwich" selling Greendale to Subway. This time they are trying to publicly signal their tolerance after canceling a gay pride parade by convincing the Dean to join the school board. Still susceptible to flattery and never knowing when to say no, the Dean initially goes along with the plan despite his misgivings ("All I have to do is pare down my sexuality to simple gayness"); on the plus side, he gets his own song ("Gay Dean," set to the tune of Dolly Parton's "Jolene"). But being a misidentified token quickly pales, and the Dean steps away from the school board. Though the Dean's storyline in this episode is packed with one-liners ("I make gayness look like Mormonism"), it is one of the only times during the series when the Dean's full-spectrum pansexuality is treated as more than a punch line.

Elsewhere, Britta is shown for the first time in her bartending gig at a dive called the Vatican, which makes occasional appearances throughout the season and is notable for being the show's only consistent off-campus location . . . not to mention a sign that Britta might be marginally employable post-graduation.

Episode 102: "Laws of Robotics and Party Rights"

The degree to which the showrunners have clearly inhaled science fiction from a very early age becomes clear in this episode, which has two solid, futuristic, predictive scenarios, one of which has already come true. Frankie brings the committee together to announce that the state is about to give Greendale $300,000 but with an unexpected twist: they need to enroll several prisoners. The new students will attend virtually through "telepresence bots": iPads mounted on top of a set of gyroscopic wheels, allowing these new VR classmates to motor around campus, take courses, and dramatically raise the percentage of students with facial tattoos.

Once the prisoners are at Greendale, the image of their disembodied faces impaled atop thin black poles floating down hallways and through classrooms is surprisingly spooky. Because this is never a show to ignore the law of unintended consequences, Willy (Brian Van Holt), the prisoner taking Jeff's law class (an automatic A blow-off hour where Jeff fires up *Planet Earth* and texts rather than teaches), has barely showed up before he's bullying, threatening, and ultimately trying to murder Jeff. Granted, the murder attempt is comical: Willy's stick-figure contraption wheezing against Jeff as it impotently tries to push him down a flight of stairs. But the subsequent power struggle in which Willy leverages an aw-shucks salt-of-the-earth shtick to turn the group and even the Dean against Jeff engages Jeff's rawest insecurities to a degree that the show hasn't dug into for some time.

A curiously curtailed Abed continues working his meta magic on the sidelines. Ignoring the cinematic potential of the electronically disembodied student-prisoners at Greendale, he is content with tossing in one-liners

"Laws of Robotics and Party Rights." NBC/PHOTOFEST.

Inspector Spacetime

Unexplained visual hints of hijinks from earlier seasons crop up in "Laws of Robotics and Party Rights" referencing the committee's now-somewhat lengthy shared history:

- When Annie closes her bedroom door, the shot shows a sliding bolt lock on the outside, a callback to Season 3's "Origins of Vampire Mythology" when Britta was locked in there to keep her from her mysteriously powerful boyfriend Blade.
- Abed hangs his felt goatee—signifying his going over to the darkest timeline in "Remedial Chaos Theory"—inside his locker.

(trying out a Seinfeld-style joke, impersonating "the black guy in every sci-fi movie") before helping Britta host a party at their apartment that Annie is dead-set against by pretending it's for a party movie he's shooting. There is not much payoff for this subplot, which earlier seasons could have juiced with Magnitude cutting a rug or Star-Burns giving his pet iguana a beer bong. But Abed does step outside the show's framing in one superb blink-and-you-missed-it scene. He explains to Britta that an earlier prank involving Leonard and lizards was done for his "Reverse *Godzilla*" movie and as a set-up for a "good pop-back"; Abed then waits a beat, but when there is no quick-cut Leonard-and-lizards flashback, gives a slight shrug of disappointment and moves on. Although nobody actually comes out and says it, the scene appears to be an indication that even Abed may be ready to move on.

The episode feels somewhat threadbare at times, particularly with how non-integrated Frankie and Elroy are to the action, but it does have some standout moments of the kind that are too often missing in a final season. Rob Schrab's direction provides the visual flair and percolating inventiveness typical of his episodes. Additionally, the concluding scene feels borderline prophetic in a post-Covid-lockdown world. The committee holds a virtual meeting around their usual table in which they are all only there via telepresence bots. The result is a kind of electronic chaos all too familiar to a certain class of telecommuting worker in the first days of the Covid-19 pandemic: glitchy screens, fake backgrounds, and a bathroom being used for an office. It may not be exactly Jules Verne, but the technology-fueled disconnect is nevertheless far more eerily predictive than most TV sitcoms ever manage.

Episode 103: "Basic Email Security"

It took six seasons, but this episode is about the closest that *Community* ever came to a ripped-from-the-headlines story. In a very clear nod to the hack of Sony Pictures from November 2014 (about six months before this episode aired) in which a massive trove of emails was leaked online, an Anonymous-like hacker group targets Greendale. They threaten a massive breach unless the school cancels an upcoming show by stand-up comedian Gupta Gupti Gupta (played by the episode's director, Jay Chandrasekhar), whose material they find offensive. This confuses the Dean: "How can he be racist? *Listen to his name.*" To prove their seriousness, the hackers leak the lunch lady's emails, which the committee has already been poring through for gossip.

Once again, Britta takes this as an opportunity to soapbox about the need to protect free speech even though she simultaneously finds Gupta Gupti Gupta's material disgusting and worthy of protest. She seems somewhat goaded into it by a part-Patriot Act, part-*Minority Report* proposition made by Officer Cackowski (who also introduces some timeliness with his out-of-left-field querying about who's "stoked" for *Avengers: Age of Ultron*, which opened a few weeks after this episode aired): "I say cancel

---

Metaverse

Among the many unexplored subplots teased in the lunch lady's leaked emails (only visible to the kind of people who screenshot the episode) are:

- Alan Connor (Jeff's law firm betrayer) asking her to "please stop the silent treatment."
- The death of Buzz Hickey.
- Vicki being the lunch lady's daughter, potentially explaining her continual state of mild-to-extreme embarrassment.
- Leonard's anger over her comments on his frozen-food reviews.

the performance and give the government the sweeping powers it needs to detect and eliminate people before they turn into hackers."

But even though the plan to make a grand scene out of Gupta's appearance degenerates into petty catastrophe, the episode does not use it as an excuse to pummel Britta once again, giving her a small win by letting her actually carry out her big moment without being mocked.

The emphasis is primarily on what happens when—after everyone follows Britta's "let them leak me" declaration—the hackers follow through on her dare and the entire committee's dirty electronic laundry is hung out. The scene that follows is in essence a writer's room free-fire exercise in which a deluge of dirty secrets and petty criticisms are aired at high volume.

Jeff is mocked for writing fanboy letters to astronauts; Elroy gets called out for the creepiness of making 3D models of all the women at Greendale; Britta is told that her life coach is really "just an Italian sociopath you met at a dispensary;" and an open question regarding Frankie's sexuality is raised but never answered (the descriptor "Chapstick lesbian" gets tossed into the mix).

With raw betrayal fogging the air, Annie suggests they might not be able to "bounce back from this one." This causes Elroy (who earlier asked incredulously, "This was a study group?") to ask, "*This* one?" Elroy's question then leads to Abed's meta-explanation of the scene as "the third installment of a trilogy that began with Annie losing a pen in what I've come to call 'the Golden Age.'" The frayed nerves of the finger-pointing and name-calling give the episode a more amplified energy than is seen in much of the season, but Abed's deflating comparison to Season 2 makes it as clear as can be that this is a show that has decided it is just about out of creative road.

Cool Cool Cool

When Sony Pictures was hacked in late 2014, leaked internal emails included revelations that embarrassed high-ranking executives. Some were relatively inconsequential, such as one from Joel McHale to Sony Pictures Television president Steve Mosko's assistant. McHale identifies himself ("You might remember me from such canceled Sony TV shows as—Community") and jokingly asks for an employee discount on a Sony TV.

Meanwhile back at what might be called the "main plot," Gupta finally gets up in front of one audience member—at Britta's urging to "get up there and do your stupid act for freedom"—and performs material so stale it could have gotten him an opening-act at many post–2016 Republican gatherings. The satire of that moment—a South Asian comic flatly reciting jokes about blacks and Jews while a mob of howling students pounds on the doors and a social justice warrior does her best to defend him—feels prescient given the rage-infused culture wars to come. But nothing in it carries the self-critiquing sting of Abed's "Golden Age" reference.

Episode 104: "Advanced Security Features"

While Season 6 can feel at times like an orphaned series whose creator has taken up with other interests, episodes like this one serve as a reminder of what the show is capable when all (well, most) of its elements come together.

Earlier seasons would often start an episode with the study group receiving a jaunty update from Annie or an in-group airing of grievances. Now the committee has settled into a routine of Frankie alerting them to what the issue of the week will be. This time it's the upcoming alumni dance. Previously, school functions like that were where the group went to work out their issues. Here it serves as the endpoint for a convoluted subplot about Jeff's anxiety over Elroy not liking him. This is neatly resolved at the dance when Elroy confronts the lead singer (Lisa Loeb) of the faux-1990s indie-rock band Natalie is Freezing about how their relationship went bad years before, after which he feels freed and finally warms up to Jeff and the gang.

Unfortunately, the dance is deprived of any expected Dean-terference (and thusly much of its comedic punch) because the Dean is hijacked by the episode's other storyline, which turns out to be where the episode's true resonance lies.

Following the multi-layered running gag of Subway production integration that started in Season 3, it isn't a surprise that this episode turns on a similarly winking premise. After a warning by Frankie that guerrilla marketers are on campus, the Dean races through, breathlessly expounding on Honda's new Fit in a rush of advertorial dialogue threaded with mania ("It's a *small* car with a *big* personality . . . I have to find a Honda dealer—school is canceled!"). He returns soon after, having bought a fleet of vehicles and outfitted his entire office (and body!) in Honda gear, having been taken advantage of by the automaker's on-campus representative Rick (Travis Schuldt).

The acknowledgement of the Honda material—alongside (likely non-paid-for) callouts to Windex and PowerPoint—is clever enough, with an in-your-face component that recalls other contemporary examples like Carl Weathers declaring the wonders of Burger King on *Arrested Development*; Tina Fey on *30 Rock* expounding on Verizon's amazing service before looking at the camera and asking, "Can we have our money now?"; and Danny Pudi as Buddha self-consciously shilling for Duke's Hard Cider on *Great Minds with Dan Harmon*.

But *Community*'s commitment to the gag runs deeper and darker than that, connecting the Dean's self-ruining lunatic compulsions to the kind of buying addictions corporations like Honda prey on. Embodying the advertiser in the pleasantly unassuming form of Rick—not seen since his stint as corpo-humanoid "Subway" in Season 3's "Digital Exploration of Interior Design"—makes their consumerist message seem as threatening to the still-smitten Britta as a warm bath. The nameless executive (Billy Zane) who convinces Britta to team up with Rick as a romantically linked secret marketing duo is not precisely threatening but does present an image of Honda as a secretive, all-powerful corporation manipulating people with subterfuge. When Britta and Rick's second love story falls apart, it's ostensibly a semi-comedic bit: he pretends to like *Avatar* (which Britta calls "three hours of puke") because it's a popular movie and he doesn't want to turn off customers. But when Rick explains his willful disregard of any

Metaverse

"Advanced Security Features" is one of the most inward-looking and self-referential episodes of *Community*'s entire run. Clearly aware that Elroy has not truly found his place in the committee's tangle of relationships and personal history, the writers give Chang a line when Elroy has just left the library that reflects their acknowledgement of that issue: "Is he black Pierce? Old Troy? Shirley without a giant purse?" Abed follows up by self-consciously admitting he "hasn't been a whirlwind of entertainment since Troy left." When people make polite "that's not true" sounds, he replies that it's okay, "you're boring, too." In terms of a series responding to fan critiques (which its creators were certainly reading), their own uncertainties (which Harmon was certainly riddled with), or both, this is a direct enough creator-to-audience message that it may as well have a stamp on it.

individual opinion ("We like things most people like"), the undercurrent of dehumanization is palpable.

One might wonder why Honda agreed to such a grim portrayal; one of the last shots of the episode is of Rick's tears splashing onto the steering wheel's Honda logo. But it is perfectly possible they figured the episode was just on Yahoo! Screen so very few people would end up seeing it anyway.

Episode 105: "Intro to Recycled Cinema"

Loopy, pop culture–addled, slightly despondent, and ever-so-slightly uplifting, this episode pulls together many of *Community*'s most familiar themes and gives them a spin that is fresh and funny enough that Pierce and Troy are hardly missed. (Although Troy's outfit in Abed's movie would have been amazing).

Riding the unexpected success of his *Karate Kid* star turn, Chang has suddenly become a viral catchphrase celebrity. The cold open is a disorienting commercial in which a blonde homemaker rhapsodizes about the glories of a plastic-encased pile of pig-based lunch meat before Chang pops up at her window and delivers a true "What's the Beef?" for a new generation: "*Haaaaam*, gurl!"

With Greendale yet again in desperate financial straits and Abed in possession of a few minutes of footage he shot of a pre-famous Chang for a cop movie he was making, the committee pulls together a wild plan to stretch that material into a feature film. Fortuitously, Frankie happens to know a producer (Steve Gutenberg) who claims he'll pay them a $500,000. Just like the Little Rascals (or Bowfinger), it's time to put on a show! Of course, there's a catch: the gang has to make an eighty-one-minute feature in a weekend. Roger Corman did it, so of course Abed is up to the challenge, despite his misgivings.

The shoot itself is another costume lark only this time instead of trading barbs on the dance floor the characters are reciting garbled dialogue for a craptacular science fiction movie (*Captain Starr and the Raiders of the Galaxy*). Everyone plays to type, with Jeff as a bare-chested scene chewer insecure about the attractiveness of Chris Pratt; Britta coming across as a confused New Wave wastrel who bungles her lines; and Annie playing a "pleasure droid" whose costume is so revealing that an eye-rolling Britta asks, "What is your name, Exploitia?" The production is a team effort, with Elroy contributing CG models of a "gingivitis monster" he animated for a mouthwash commercial; Abed swallowing his pride enough to not waste time making a better movie; and Frankie banging out a steel drum solo in a *Star Wars* cantina knockoff scene, a callback to "Advanced Safety Features" when Jeff pretended that the reason they missed Troy so much was that he was a great steel drum player just to get Frankie to start playing them.

Though everyone gamely pitches in for the glorified home movie, their energy is shadowed by a lingering sadness. The editing-and-effects required to turn Chang from a New York police captain into a heroic space pirate are played for comedy at first. But then mere repetition of Chang's echoing outtake dialogue ("What's my motivation?" "Why am I doing or saying anything?") begins to read as hauntingly lost. Other characters seem to have lost the thread, with Abed almost abandoning hope in the god of cinema, while Jeff reveals his true anxiety is that everyone will leave him marooned at Greendale ("Annie's going to be president, even Pierce got to die, and Chang goes to Hollywood").

But then, showing again that Jeff long ago ceded the role of moral delivery figure, Abed knits a thumbnail description of his filmic atrocity into a pop koan.

> Life is a big dumb pointless movie with no story and an abrupt ending where the hero gets shot by Dracula in the middle of a lunch order during an outtake . . . So we keep the cameras rolling and we edit out the parts we don't like and we stop thinking about Chris Pratt so much. Because it is not healthy.

Bowing somewhat to traditional sitcom convention, the episode resets everything at the conclusion with Chang back in school after blowing his shot at stardom (fired by Steven Spielberg for being a prima donna, he is

---

Cool Cool Cool

There are a lot of movies that *Captain Starr and the Raiders of the Galaxy* could have been inspired by. One of the more obscure and rarely-seen is 1994's *The Fantastic Four*, never intended for release but shot on the quick and cheap by Roger Corman just so the producers could keep the rights to the Marvel characters for a few more years. Eventually leaked online and looking like something *Mystery Science Theater 3000* would have almost felt bad for mocking, it makes Abed's work glow by comparison.

replaced by Randall Park); Greendale still in penury after the movie deal falls through; and everyone making fun of Britta.

Episode 106: "Grifting 101"

Narrowing in focus as it approaches the conclusion, *Community* was by this point starting to abandon the B plots and simply send the committee on different missions. The upside of this is fewer episodes with half-baked subplots. The downside? Roping the entire cast into a single narrative structure removes the opportunity for some characters to explore the once-mysterious corridors of Greendale and have serendipitous encounters. It also leads to episodes like "Grifting 101."

The genesis of the story feels as though one of the writers had a serious beef with *The Sting*. This is understandable given that George Roy Hill's inexplicably popular 1973 comedy about Prohibition-era con men hinged on a grift that was not entertaining or particularly clever—as Abed points out, "they basically made a fake building and hired a thousand people to cooperate in perfect secrecy." The script works out that frustration by introducing the new grifting class professor Roger DeSalvo (Matt Berry), whose white suit and flamboyant cockiness play on a particular kind of clichéd movie con-artist whose schemes would never pass muster in the real world. Of course his scam—having his students spend $150 each on suitcases that they spend the entire class practicing passing back and forth—works well enough for a place like Greendale.

The conflict starts when Jeff is once again spurred into action by the sight of another apex-level slacker who makes the double mistake of being better at it than Jeff and hunting in Jeff's territory. This has become a somewhat tired trope at this point in the series. but the episode is somewhat enlivened by the undermining of con-artist movie narrative tricks, such as people's ability to craft massively convoluted plots in their spare time. When everyone is disappointed at Jeff not coming up with a better plan to hoodwink Roger, he responds in understandable exasperation, "At what point do you think I slipped off with pen and paper and planned an entire grift?"

Episode 107: "Basic RV Repair and Palmistry"

Whatever veil was left between the show and its audience was riddled with so many holes by the end of this corkscrewing tail-chaser of an *Inception* riff that it had essentially ceased to exist. In a highly rare off-campus expedition by the committee, the episode starts with the committee packed onto

Elroy's RV and driving through the mountains with a massive fiberglass hand strapped to the ceiling. It concludes with Abed even more deeply embedded in his life-as-movie simulacrum.

The arbitrariness of the hand-on-the-RV plot device is a blatant ruse to get everyone venturing out of the library for twenty-odd minutes of bickering and bonding through various road trip mishaps. The transparency of the device is highlighted the moment after Jeff and Frankie unload a lengthy exposition tirade on the Dean—explaining to the audience that he bought the hand for reasons unknown with money Greendale doesn't have, leading the committee to haul it through the mountains to an eager eBay buyer—when Abed comments all-too-correctly that "this is a *lot* of narrative pipe."

By this point in the episode, Abed has already been creating a counter-narrative in which he puts himself in the place of the audience and keeps trying to create an explanatory flashback by saying, "Three weeks earlier." In a nod to "Remedial Chaos Theory," he mentally cuts back multiple times to the same committee meeting but tweaks the dialogue each time, trying to leverage the powers of his visualization to reorder the past and ultimately affect the future. His straining attempts to bridge the world in front of him with the world in his mind eventually fail, leaving even Jeff (normally more generous with Abed's quirks) infuriated and Abed disappointed in himself for overcomplicating things. Though even in his self-critique Abed leaves it unclear whether he is upset for not fully engaging with his existence or for making an artistic error: "A bunch of people in an RV? And I had to Christopher Nolan it?"

This thread can be viewed as the writers looping around themselves in an inside-out joke about imagining the most patently absurd way of getting the characters on a road trip (a joke they extend in the end tag when they reveal that the giant hand's buyer is a depressed father guilty after having given his young son a massive kite that tragically carried him away). But it also serves as an argument for the possibility that Abed is hardly disconnected from reality. While the rest of the committee harangues each other and is just trying to get through the escapade as quickly as possible without freezing to death once the RV runs out of gas, Abed is the one truly present character. He might be viewing what is happening to them as an elaborate science-fiction scheme, but his commitment to the moment is sincere and total.

Episode 108: "Modern Espionage"

Proving once again that nothing kills a good idea like a sequel, the last full episode devoted to paintball assassin is best remembered not for its homage to genre cinema but for the non-paintball framing device of two surprisingly related and highly unpredictable on-campus productions: Vicki's one-woman musical and Garrett's stand-up comedy routine mocking Vicki.

The paintball episodes from the first two seasons were lovingly crafted valentines to specific and highly recognizable styles of filmmaking (space opera, spaghetti western, Hong Kong action). Their chaotic choreography is nowhere to be seen in this somewhat rote return to the well. As ever, the original study group members are aware that they have done this before ("Done it to death," actually, as Annie puts it), but in this instance the self-consciousness does not inoculate what follows from the comparative lack of imagination.

The dark shadows and secretive identity of a mysterious paintball gunman (known only as "Silver Ballz") suggest that the inspiration here is a generic brand of contemporary espionage movies à la the Jason Bourne series. But the end result is more a grab-bag of references ranging from Batman to *Die Hard with a Vengeance*, *Captain America: The Winter Soldier*, and possibly even *The Simpsons* though the latter may have just been an off-handed reference by Frankie to a monorail.

The error here is not just stylistic but thematic. Without a consistent genre to commit to, the characters do not seem as committed either. Annie and Abed hint at their chemistry from Season 2's "For a Few Paintballs More" in a fancy-dress-with-guns dance sequence—nodding to either *True Lies*, *Mr. and Mrs. Smith*, or both. A squad of long-absent characters returns, from Star-Burns to Koogler, though the conclusion hinges on Deputy Chief Custodian Lapari (Kumail Nanjiani) and his betrayal of Greendale to dread City College.

This invites the question of whether "Modern Espionage" can be a true paintball assassin episode if this time Greendale avoided being turned into a paint-splattered wasteland ruled by bands of impressively costumed student-warriors. The comparative lack of anarchic overkill points to the disturbing possibility that at this late stage, *Community* may have grown past the desire for such things.

Such maturity is truly disappointing.

Episode 109: "Wedding Videography"

Perhaps feeling the show needed a gangly bit of tomfoolery before calling it quits, the writers gave the committee a timeworn setup with a welcome twist. The end-of-season wedding is a classic sitcom standby, but here it is made far more palatable by being between a couple of bit players and does not involve a surprise nuptial announcement between, say, Britta and Chang—despite the potential for worlds-colliding madness in such a pairing.

Once Garrett makes his screechy-voiced proposal to Stacy (a newcomer to the series and played by Harmon's then-wife Erin McGathy) in Jeff's law class and it turns out the whole committee is attending the wedding, the episode moves into familiar territory: pointing the gang in the same direction and watching things fall apart on the journey.

There is no real B story to speak of. But since the entire episode is framed as another of Abed's documentary projects, it allows him to shoot small asides that bring some variety to the acting-out-at-a-wedding A story. At one point, Abed films Annie being lovably silly so there will be "missing lover footage" of the kind that a moody hero watches in a movie just "in case I get kidnapped or murdered." Another neatly self-contained satirical moment has Elroy explaining his addiction to "encouraging white people." He narrates a montage of him making out-of-nowhere positive statements to random white wedding guests ("Oh now *that's* the way to handle meatballs!") before explaining it as a survival technique from being a black man working in tech during the 2000s: "This face, this voice, they're either gonna help you or hold you back. So you tap the gas because, well, why tap the brake?"

Most of the episode has far less of an edge, invested more in watching everyone pregame before the wedding with drinking games that result in them showing up late and crashing around like buffoons. Attempting to make up for their bad entry, everyone tries to be the best wedding guests ever only to inadvertently reveal that Garrett and Stacy are actually cousins. Chaos and disappointment ensue, leaving Chang to save the day with a heartfelt plea to the bride and groom to push through it. This allows the ever-put-upon Garrett to close out the show on a defiantly high note: "Everyone stay and eat cake or go to hell!"

Although Garrett asking Stacy to be his "legally incestuous wife" makes for a good enough joke on its own, the episode follows it up with an end tag that functions as a superb mock PSA. An actor identifying himself as the episode's writer, Briggs Hatton, addresses the camera in faux-earnest mode as though he is about to lecture viewers about climate change. But

> ## Metaverse
>
> When Abed is shooting the before footage for Garrett's wedding, he captures Annie and Britta talking straight to the camera despite Abed reminding them not to. At one point, Annie looks at the camera in annoyance, causing Abed to say, "Don't Jim the camera like that." Even though the American version of *The Office* had by this point been off the air for two years, the character Jim's habit of hitting a comic beat by giving the camera a certain look had embedded itself in pop culture lore and—by definition—Abed's television-attuned consciousness.

instead, he is there to explain his deep interest in incest (he is shown making a pitch to the writing staff, including a haggard-looking bearded actor as Harmon with a bottle of vodka suggestively in the foreground): "I can make love to my cousin in Nebraska, but if I take her on a date in South Dakota, I'm looking at fifteen years prison time." All that's missing is the "The More You Know" tag NBC uses for PSAs.

Episode 110: "Emotional Consequences of Broadcast Television"

By the time any series gets to its last episode, it is not exactly looking to bring new viewers in. *M*A*S*H* didn't need to communicate why Hawkeye was so traumatized. There was no reason for *The Sopranos* to spoon-feed background about Tony's moral quicksand. Viewers knew.

For its conclusion, there was less of an obligation than ever for *Community* to present a clear, linear, and structured episode. Instead, it folded back in on itself, going beyond the fan service—Leonard getting the first line ("School's out, bitches"!); Annie's forced-casual laugh at a mention of the Ass Crack Bandit clearly proving she was indeed the nefarious culprit; Jeff mocking "those boring-ass Marvel movies" that *Community* alumni the Russo brothers often directed—to produce an origami-like tangle of what-if multiverse riffing.

After learning that the Save Greendale Committee, having accomplished its task, will need a new name, everyone gathers at the Vatican bar for an end-of-the-semester drink that turns into a What now? session. Abed (whom everyone has by the point accepted for treating his life like it was a television series) takes up the offer to treat the question of their real-life future as though he were pitching "Season 7." The Dean follows with his pitch, as do Chang and Britta. Jeff pitches in as well though only after complaining he doesn't want to "spend my brief moment of humanity doing conceptual riffs, developing the imaginary TV show of our lives."

But the episode veers close to suggesting just that. They may actually be living inside some kind of show. Or they are so used to framing existence through media they can no longer see an appreciable difference between real and screened life. Each character's pitch, signaled by a quick run-through of the opening credits' paper fortune teller, is a window into how little they really see the others. Abed's pitch flattens out dialogue to factual description (Jeff: "Abusively cynical one-liner dismissing everything you just said"). Dean's has Elroy and Shirley happily listing race-coded stereotypes ("hallelujah, and church, and singing, and street wisdom"). Chang's is taken up mostly by an animated creature calling itself Ice Cube Head.

At times the episode looks likely to spin off into a vortex of self-referentiality. Ironically, Abed brings the riffing back down to Earth by anchoring them with a short speech that positively equates the alchemy of the group's friendship to that of a television show.

> It's TV. It's comfort. It's a friend you've known so well and for so long you just let it be with you. And it needs to be okay for it to have a bad day, or phone in a day. And it needs to be okay for it to get on a boat with Levar Burton and never come back. Because eventually, it all will.

At this point, Harmon and the writers are simultaneously acknowledging they have not been consistently nailing it for the past six seasons, insisting no show should be expected to, and arguing the emotional bonds created between the on-screen characters and the viewers mean something, perhaps because like everything in life, it will eventually come to an end. This creates the backdrop against which Jeff and Annie share an only slightly fraught last kiss ("I'll regret the kiss for a week," she says with un-Annie-ish nonchalance. "I'm in my twenties, who cares?").

There is not a lot of typical closure here. Several characters take off for different lives: Elroy to work at LinkedIn (in a dated piece of 2015 snark, he explains they hired him "to help figure out why people don't use it"); Abed to work as a production assistant on a television show; and Annie to intern for the FBI—all of which terrifies Jeff, who as much as he hates to admit it has made Greendale into either a home or a hideout, leading to a nightmarish *Rick and Morty*-esque vision of him imagining strangling to death a series of cloned Abeds.

"Emotional Consequences of Broadcast Television": *We're still doing a movie, right guys?* NBC/PHOTOFEST.

Streets Ahead

When *Community* moved to Yahoo! Screen, what it lacked in main-stream notice it gained in a lack of adult supervision. But despite not having any network standards and practices suits to run afoul of, *Community* resisted the urge to go full HBO and largely held to a broadcast television level of obscenity—that is, until the last episode, when Britta and the Dean both clearly say "Fuck." Does this indicate that a seventh season might have worked blue?

Though things conclude in lightly upbeat fashion with sad-happy farewells buttoning up the episode's earlier breakouts into format decon-struction, the final joke is a cold and cutting one. Following a black screen title reference to the long-running fan demand ("#andamovie"), the end tag appears to be a gag commercial in which a family plays a board game version of *Community*. Referencing the final episode of *St. Elsewhere*, the father holds up a game card showing a snow globe and says, "The whole show was happening inside this game!" When his son hands him a script "of a fake commercial at the end of Season 6 starring this family," the father has a horrifying realization.

> You stupid child. Nobody's winning anything. Don't you see? We don't exist. We're not created by God. We're created by a joke. We were never born and we will never actually live.

Following an uncomfortably long beat of the family's devastated silence, a fast-talking narrator (Harmon) hurls out a block of verbiage that toggles between mock disclaimers ("Some episodes too conceptual to be funny") and lacerating personal critique ("Life may pass by while we ignore or mistreat those close to us"). It's funny, dense, slightly bleak, and just a bit unnerving.

Is television a comfort, a trap, or a playground for wrangling with existential quandaries? That's a question this season never quite answered, much as it tried.

Advanced Acting Seminar: 10
What Can You Do with a BA
from Greendale? The Cast's
Post-Graduate Careers

TARRING ON A HIT TV series is not a bad thing for an actor, particularly once that syndication money starts rolling in. For a few years it's a gas, what with all the exclusive invites, being able to put a down payment on that place in Malibu, and appearing on the cover of *People* and *Parade*. After a while, though, it can be a bit of a challenge to outrun the shadow of a signature role and keep a career going; just ask Alan Alda, Matthew Perry, or Jason Alexander.

For an actor to avoid that ubiquity trap, it can sometimes be better to get noticed on a critically acclaimed but only moderately successful series rather than star on a smash hit that runs for eternity on *Nick at Nite*. That way, the character they play is not etched so deeply in the audience's minds that it limits future opportunities.

An ensemble comedy like *Community* with middling ratings success and infinitely passionate fandom could serve as an ideal launchpad for actors like Alison Brie, Donald Glover, and Joel McHale. It was the kind of show that might also have restarted the career of a comedic icon like Chevy Chase who had fallen off the industry's radar.

Might.

The Actors: The Greendale Seven

Alison Brie

As *Community* was winding down in the mid-2010s, Alison Brie capitalized on her big-eyed, sparkly persona to snag roles in an array of middle-of-the road relationship comedies (*How to Be Single*), comedy comedies (the Will Ferrell and Kevin Hart vehicle *Get Hard*), and even a costume drama (*Doctor Thorne*).

In 2017, though, she starred in *GLOW*, a three-season Netflix series about an aspiring actor (Ruth "Zoya the Destroya" Wilder) who takes a job with a women's wrestling league, circa 1985. It played beautifully to Brie's strengths (anxious vulnerability alternating with flinty determination). That series, a continuing run of supporting and starring film work (including some, like the suspenser *The Rental* and the romantic comedy *Somebody I Used to Know*, directed by her husband Dave Franco), and a stream of high-end animated voice work (*Rick and Morty*, *BoJack Horseman*, *Moon Girl and Devil Dinosaur*) make it less likely she would forever be listed in a casting agent's database under "edgy Anna Kendrick type."

Yvette Nicole Brown

Since Shirley often got the shortest shrift of any study group member, it is not surprising that Yvette Nicole Brown left the show with one of the lower profiles despite her precision timing and ability to mine real emotion out of potentially mawkish moments.

Being less buzzed-about, though, did not keep Brown from working "after college." A TV jobber with a strong line in children's fare, she put together a packed resume of animated and live action shows post-*Community* that was heavy on Disney and Lego. Brown kept her hand in sitcom work as well with recurring roles on more conventional shows like *Mom* and *Will & Grace* and also *The Mayor*, where she got to pull more dramatic weight as the mother of a rapper who accidentally wins an election. In an impressive display of her wide-ranging talents, Brown has put her singing skills to work in a Disney musical (*Disenchanted*), written a rom-com (*Always a Bridesmaid*), and been nominated for a Primetime Emmy (*A Black Lady Sketch Show*).

In the spirit of Abed scoring a walk-on role on his beloved *Cougar Town*, Brown parlayed her *Walking Dead* fandom into a cameo in the show's eleventh season.

Chevy Chase

By the time Chase was shuffled off *Community* in the fourth season, he appeared to have already made himself persona non grata on set. Once off the show, he was just as unwelcome in the rest of the industry. Part of the reason that he was relegated to recurring bits in below-the-radar comedies (an unasked-for sequel to *Hot Tub Time Machine*, an unwanted reboot of

Vacation) may have been his (by-all-accounts) unpleasant behavior on *Community*. But since Hollywood's memories of personal ugliness are short, if there had been a market for what Chase was selling, somebody would have picked it up (see the resurrected career of Mel Gibson). The reason for Chase's depleted post-*Community* career could very simply be that his fumbling, blowhard shtick had been played-out since the late 1980s (see *Caddyshack II* and *Fletch Lives*, or better yet, don't). If that had not been the case, it is possible he might have stayed on the show and picked up some better roles afterward instead of having his character written out in an almost Chef-esque fashion: dying of dehydration after filling containers with sperm.

Donald Glover

It would be going too far to say that Donald Glover owed his 2010s stardom to *Community*. As a writer, musician, improviser, ace comic actor, and heartthrob, he was destined to make it big somewhere. That being said, *Community* provided him with a weekly showcase where he could hone his craft and build a persona. The spirit he brought to the show was most notable by its absence after his departure in Season 5.

By the time Troy literally sailed out of *Community* with Levar Burton in "Geothermal Escapism," Glover was primed for success. He had already covered two very divergent audience demographics with a two-episode run as one of Hannah's boyfriends on *Girls* and as the alphabetically focused singer LMNOP on *Sesame Street*. His ongoing music career as Childish Gambino was significant enough to have satisfied most people on a professional and artistic basis. Moving away from the nerdy, in-joke style that had built his earlier fanbase, later Gambino music pulled in a broader and funkier feel that garnered increasing popular and critical attention. Scoring multiple Grammys, he broke most clearly from his older persona with the 2018 "This Is America," an explosive denunciation of American violence and racism.

Post-2015, Glover covered his bets acting-wise by appearing in an array of high-profile projects. He played to his earlier strengths as a nerdy researcher in Ridley Scott's *The Martian*; showed a previously unseen skill for romantic appeal as a seductive exotic dancer in *Magic Mike XXL*; played a musician opposite Rihanna in *Guava Island*; popped up in various *Spider-man* projects; and then did the almost impossible: channeled the suave charm of Billy Dee Williams as a younger Lando Calrissian in *Solo*.

Donald Glover's Atlanta *was a nearly unprecedented pivot for a sitcom star and comic to acclaimed show creator.* PHOTO FX NETWORKS/PHOTOFEST.

Though he could likely have done nothing but acting for the next few decades, Glover's restlessness led him in different directions. He created, starred in, and often wrote for the show *Atlanta*, a four-season exploration and celebration of the city's black community and hip-hop scene. A low-key, somewhat depressive, and frequently surreal miscellany of comedy and borderline tragedy, it seemed to purposefully submerge Glover's personality in order to highlight incredible performers like Brian Tyree Henry, LaKeith Stanfield, and Zazie Beetz who all built careers off the show.

In the monologue for his 2018 guest-hosting spot on *Saturday Night Live*, Glover lampooned his reputation for excelling in a gamut of creative arenas with a number called "I Can Do Anything" where he falls off a skateboard and electrocutes himself—all bits that Troy and Abed would have loved.

Gillian Jacobs

Like much of the cast, Jacobs remained part of the Harmonverse following *Community*, showing up in *Rick and Morty*, *Great Minds with Dan Harmon*, and *HarmonQuest*. Like Alison Brie, Jacobs also quickly established herself on a successful Netflix series back when that streaming service was still putting a lot of money into half-hour comedies.

Though Jacobs's character (Mickey) in the Paul Rust and Judd Apatow, three-season, sad-com *Love* doesn't exactly Britta her life, her thing for messy relationships and extremely poor decision making was not exactly *not* Britta. Afterward, Jacobs lent her vocal talents to an ever-increasing array of animated series.

Unlike many theatrical peers who take up residence in screen world, Jacobs returned to off-Broadway. She was a bright and nervy presence in the 2018 dark comedy *Kings* where she played a Washington, DC, lobbyist whose sense of morality is twisted like taffy by the compromises demanded by her world. The character was far more put together than Britta—no roach clips as barrettes—but seemed to share a fear that her world could come crashing down at any moment.

Jacobs also parlayed her skill for ensemble comedy to good effect in Mike Birbiglia's underrated look at the improv comedy world *Don't Think Twice* and broke from typecasting by playing a quite mature (for the show) frenemy of Lena Dunham's character Hannah in *Girls*. That sense of fragility that made Britta such a compellingly watchable character also informed Jacobs's genre dramatic work, starring in Netflix's R. L. Stine trilogy *Fear Street*, the horror flick *Come Play*, and the anthology *The Seven Faces of Jane* where she played the same character in eight short movies by different directors (including one co-starring Joel McHale and one directed by Ken Jeong).

Joel McHale

McHale has the chiseled looks and easygoing confidence that should augur a future as cinematic leading man. But since modern Hollywood appears largely uninterested in such stars these days, unless McHale finds a way to join the Avengers, his future seems likely to be more small screen focused.

As though understanding that *Community*, and possibly also *The Soup*, might have been the best vehicles for his talents he was ever likely to see, McHale followed those tailor-made shows up by throwing himself into whatever was out there. This meant a starring role in a run-of-the-mill sitcom (*The Great Indoors*, playing the older guy exasperated by the youth of today); short roles in random sitcoms (*Black-ish*; *Will & Grace*); comedies (*Psych 2: Lassie Come Home?*); and frequent rounds on game shows and talk shows . . . alongside Jeong; he appeared as a recurring guest judge on *The*

Stephen Fry and Joel McHale try to make something of The Great Indoors. CBS/PHOTOFEST.

Masked Singer. McHale even tried his hand at running a slightly updated riff on *The Soup*—whose name, *The Joel McHale Show with Joel McHale*, set new standards for self-aware self-celebration—which lasted for a few months on Netflix in 2018. Though there was some more interesting work here and there (*The Twilight Zone, Mystery Science Theater 3000*), for the most part, McHale's has been a resume of taking what he can get when he can get it, though always with a happy smile.

As with Jacobs, Brie, and others, McHale also loaned his voice to edgy, animated shows (*BoJack Horseman, Love, Death & Robots*). Unlike some cast members, he also had a side gig voicing videogames (*Fortnite*). Perhaps having picked up genre appeal from his appearances at various comic cons (a development foreshadowed by Jeff's unexpected stardom at the Inspector Spacetime convention in "Conventions of Space and Time"), McHale made a surprising number of appearances in properties like the animated *Mortal Kombat* movies, the revamped *The X-Files*, and—wielding a sentient staff with a straight face—the CW's tween-targeting DC Comics *Stargirl* series.

Possibly the most meta moment of McHale's post-*Community* career was his appearance in *A Futile and Stupid Gesture*, David Wain's dramatization of the glory days of National Lampoon, playing none other than

Chevy Chase. McHale said that he got the okay from Chase, and his performance is definitely more homage to the peak years of a comedic talent than a satirical takedown, but the effect is still jarring.

Danny Pudi

The Greendale study group member most at threat of being typecast after *Community* was definitely Danny Pudi. Given the unique aspects of Abed as a character and Pudi's captivating inhabiting of those quirks, there was every possibility he would be playing versions of Abed forever. (One can only imagine the kind of derivative scripts he was sent post-*Community*.)

Fortunately, that did not happen, with the possible exception of voicing Brainy Smurf in *Smurfs: The Lost Village* (2017) and playing the Buddha on *Great Minds with Dan Harmon*, both of which called for a certain Abed-like level of serene confidence. He popped up in some romantic comedies (including *Somebody I Used to Know* alongside Alison Brie); did genre work (*Star Trek Beyond* and the LARPer comedy *Knights of Badassdom*); cameoed in the Russos' *Captain America: The Winter Soldier*; briefly co-starred in the failed DCU series *Powerless*, and had a one-episode role in *Angie Tribeca*. Like Brown, many of his voice roles were in children's shows like *Mira, Royal Detective*, and various iterations of *DuckTales*.

But it was *Mythic Quest* where Pudi showed he could create a character almost as indelible as Abed. In the series—an in-jokey *Silicon Valley*–type workplace comedy about a gaming company—Pudi takes a 180-degree turn from Abed by playing a Machiavellian bureaucratic power player with a zest for manipulation and, well, evil.

It was a career-redefining turn that a pop culture scholar like Abed would have appreciated for not only upending fans' expectations but breaking the mold of typecasting.

The Actors: Study Group Auxiliary

Ken Jeong

Like McHale, Jeong already had a career going before *Community*. He did not let the show slow him down and was extremely open-minded about what kinds of work he would take before, during, and after.

Magnum P.I.? *Goosebumps 2: Slappy's Revenge*? *My Little Pony*? Voicing Dynomutt in *Scoob!*? Presenter for the 2019 Teen Choice Awards? A very rich Singaporean in *Crazy Rich Asians*? Several seasons as an extremely opinionated judge on *The Masked Singer*? Yes, absolutely, and then more.

He and McHale also kept the *Community* home fires burning throughout a quarantined 2020 with *The Darkest Timeline*, possibly the loosest podcast hosted by actual professionals in podcast history.

Jeong had a two-season run on a sitcom sort of kind of based on his life called *Dr. Ken* that featured many *Community* cast members in guest appearances. In the final episode, Jeong's character, who is trying to get into acting, auditions for a role on a new sitcom and bungles it completely. The showrunner is played by Dan Harmon, and Jeong's scene partner is Alison Brie, suggesting an especially dark time line for *Community* in which there is no Señor Chang to cry out, "In *Español*, my nickname is "El Tigre Chino!" (cue terrified silence).

John Oliver

John Oliver's decision to focus on his correspondence at *The Daily Show* might have been a boon for basic cable comedy but it deprived his character Ian Duncan of the opportunity to secure tenure and thus kept audiences from his haplessly uninformed and whiskey-sodden lectures for three seasons. Since his character was never really replaced, that also meant Jeff Winger no longer had a commiserating drinking partner outside the study group, which feels like a missed opportunity.

John Oliver argues a point on Last Week Tonight. HBO/PHOTOFEST.

However, this move did leave Oliver time to produce the multi-Emmy-winning weekly news satire show *Last Week Tonight* starting in 2014. As was common in the *Community* alumnae . . . community, he also picked up checks doing animation voicework in everything from *The Lion King* to the rebooted *Danger Mouse*.

Jim Rash

In a different timeline (Wait, there are other timelines? *Yes*, weird pizza delivery guy, keep up), Jim Rash's Dean Pelton would continue stalking Jeff for many years after his departure from Greendale. While Abed likely in fact already calculated the odds of that spinoff surviving more than one season and found it improbable, he would still watch it. As would we.

In some ways, Rash boasts a standard post-*Community* resume: cameo in a Marvel movie (*Captain America: Civil War*) plus voice work on *Rick and Morty*, *Family Guy*, *Harley Quinn*, and *DuckTales*. But in between all the children's shows and sitcoms (everything from the surrealist *Angie Tribeca* to *Reno 911!* and *That '90s Show*) that his zippy go-for-broke attitude makes him perfect for (it is essentially impossible for Rash to fade into the background as Abed did on *Cougar Town*), he also had a plum supporting role in Billy Eichner's breakthrough gay rom-com *Bros*.

While paying the rent with that work, Rash and Nat Faxon continued their filmmaking endeavors. Together they wrote and directed *Downhill*, a somewhat uneven remake of Ruben Ostlund's vicious satire *Force Majeure* (starring Julia Louis-Dreyfuss and Will Ferrell) and also wrote *The Heart* about a heart transplant delivery that goes very, very wrong.

(We are still waiting on Rash's remake of *101 Dalmatians*, rumored to be in production since this sentence was first typed.)

Dino Stamatopoulos

Unlike Rash and Glover, Stamatopoulos did not seem to have been bit by the acting bug, preferring to be the one writing the scripts and creating the animation. After his *Community* turn as Greendale's most put-upon drug dealer, Stamatopoulos had a short stint writing for the 2015 *Mr. Show* reunion miniseries *W / Bob and David*. Otherwise, he largely stuck with the comedy animation thing and ran things at the Starburns Industries production company (which produced *HarmonQuest* and the *Harmontown* documentary, thus keeping the Harmon brand alive after Dan's initial split from *Community*).

In 2015, Stamatopoulos produced the innovative and eerie stop-motion animated feature *Anomalisa*. He later created the stop-motion horror comedy *Mary Shelley's Frankenhole*, which featured Harmonverse players Jeff Davis, Ken Jeong, and Harmon himself (as Dr. Jekyll, who was not a character written by Mary Shelley, but what the hey).

Advanced Composition— 11
Introduction to Blockbusters:
The Writers' and Directors'
Post-Graduate Careers

IVEN ITS INDUSTRIAL NATURE, television tends not to reward its creators with fame, riches, or even marginally better gigs. The creatives who direct, write, and produce feature films are the ones who usually get the glory. Even non-cinephiles have generally heard of Francis Ford Coppola ("Did *The Godfather*, right? Or was that the other Italian guy, whatshisname . . . Scor-something?").

But television is different. Here's an experiment: Try asking true *Friends* fanatics—you know the ones, they can play "Best Episode" for days and can rattle off the lyrics to any of Phoebe's songs—about its creators David Crane and Marta Kauffman. They will draw a blank. An impresario like Dick Wolf (nodded to in the title of the Season 3 episode "Basic Lupine Urology"), whose list of showrunner credits (hour-long drama franchises *Law & Order*, *Chicago*, and *FBI*) are practically Spielberg-ian in their sustained popularity, is basically unknown by the non-*Variety*-reading public.

After the era of peak TV kicked off in the mid-2000s, a few showrunners (Shonda Rhimes, Ryan Murphy) have garnered the kind of name recognition and headline-grabbing deals that mark them as players. *Mad Men*'s Matthew Weiner and HBO's iconoclastic Davids (Chase, Milch, Simon) won renown from critics for their singular voices. But those are the exceptions.

In broadcast television, the glory and attention go to the actors.

Then, of course, there was *Community*. Dan Harmon did what almost no television creator and showrunner ever had: make news. The network skirmishes, Chevy Chase dustups, and Twitter brawls Harmon engaged in were unlike anything the industry had seen before, preferring as they did to keep the creatives penned up in a snack-strewn, fluorescent-strobed conference room churning out two dozen episodes a season with minimal fuss.

But in addition to the unusual focus put on Harmon as NBC and Sony's *enfant intoxiqué*, *Community* stood out from an industry standpoint for how much it featured unusually name-recognizable behind-the-camera talent.

This is largely due to the cinematic interests that Harmon brought to the show. Although long marinated in the twenty-two-minutes-and-a-laugh-track sitcom format, Harmon's touchpoints were just as frequently drawn from the big screen. As a result, it made little sense to use journey-men sitcom directors who were used to helming miniature plays before live audiences where they might be called on to approximate *Return of the Living Dead* one episode and *The Lord of the Rings* or *The Warriors* in another.

Given the cinematic references baked into *Community*, it is not surprising that Harmon would draw from a different talent pool than the producers of *How I Met Your Mother* (see? You can't name them, either). What is surprising is that some *Community* directors would be responsible for $200 million budgets months after tweaking a *Troy and Abed in the Morning* segment.

The Russo Brothers

First, some back story. Once upon a time, the filmmaking brother duo from the heartland who can do it all (They write! They direct! They produce!) would have been expected to follow a certain prescribed career arc: create an audaciously scrappy indie film made with pocket change, duct tape, and actors nobody has ever heard of that breaks out on the festival circuit, gets good word of mouth, and then somebody in Hollywood notices. For their second movie, they get a small but real budget, a professional crew, maybe a name actor or two. Assuming the notices were good and audiences paid attention, up and up the filmmakers would go, garnering more prestige and awards until they eventually snagged a Criterion release, a showcase at the Film Society of Lincoln Center, maybe a scattering of Golden Globes.

Anthony and Joe Russo blew that schematic apart.

Straight out of Cleveland, the Russos began the usual indie way. While still in graduate school, they maxed out credit cards to write, direct, and edit a $30,000 crime flick. *Pieces* was largely ignored when not actively disliked, with the *Variety* review using words like "needlessly arty and obscure" and "Scorsese-wannabe." But Steven Soderbergh saw something in its go-for-broke style and decided to give them a shot.

Their next movie was the Soderbergh and George Clooney–produced *Welcome to Collinwood* (2002), an overstuffed caper flick with a great cast (including Clooney and future Greendale alum Luis Guzman). Only moderately successful, it was appreciated in the industry for its craftsmanship. Rather than jump right into making more films, the Russos pulled what in retrospect looks to be a strategically canny move. Possibly knowing that one big-budget bomb can kill a nascent career, they detoured into television, not directing another feature film for twelve years excepting the extremely unmemorable comedy *You, Me, and Dupree* (2006).

After shooting the pilot for *Lucky*, a short-lived gambling drama that was an industry insider favorite, the Russos helped develop one of the more innovative sitcoms of the early 2000s. Building off producer Ron Howard's desire to reinvent what he saw as a stale sitcom format and inspired by the stripped-down aesthetics of the Dogme 95 film movement, the Russos ran with the idea of making *Arrested Development* not as a wacky dysfunctional family sitcom but as a gonzo mockumentary playing off the then-current vogue for reality shows. With rapid-fire editing, dry absurdism, double entendres, complex plotting, and layers of self-referentiality, it was like nothing else on television (remember: *According to Jim* was still big at the time) and presaged what the Russos could do with an even more ambitious show.

For their rule-shattering work on *Arrested Development*, the brothers shared an Emmy. Once that happened, more scripts came in. Including one from Dan Harmon.

Inspired by Harmon's clever writing and tightly bonded misfit characters, they came on board and helped craft the whole look of *Community*. Taking an opposite tack from *Arrested Development*'s spare indie look, they used a more colorful and imaginative aesthetic. The initial touchstone was John Hughes (not surprising, given the pilot episode's callouts to *The Breakfast Club*), but they quickly expanded to other influences as the scripts' aspirations went further afield.

Collectively or individually, the Russos directed thirty-four episodes of *Community*, including many of the greats: "Advanced Dungeons & Dragons," "Advanced Gay," "Foosball and Nocturnal Vigilantism." Setting up a joint production company with Harmon to produce *Community*'s first three seasons, the Russos appear to have been among his most crucial partners for making his vision reality. Without their agile blend of comic timing, cinematic versatility, and disciplined work ethic (the latter trait being especially key given Harmon's frequently late scripts), it is unlikely that *Community* would have had the impact that it did. The somewhat flatter and less-inventive visuals of the show's later, Russo-less seasons indicate that they were never quite replaced.

The Russos' skill for producing feature film-quality TV episodes with network-sitcom budgets was prominently displayed in breakouts like the paintball episodes capping Season 2. While the paintball episodes were a huge hit with *Community* fans in general, the Russos' odd journey up the directorial food chain came from one paintball superfan in particular: Kevin Feige. As president of Marvel Studios, Feige had shepherded the comic book film renaissance that began with *Iron Man* (2008). Wanting to keep the Marvel pipeline fresh, Feige did not want directors who only knew how to make tentpole pictures. The Russos, with their indie-forged gutsiness and dexterous melding of high-impact action beats with deftly integrated ensemble character development and complex storylines (not to mention in-depth knowledge of comic-book lore), fit the bill.

The Russos had been pulling double duty during Season 3. At the time they were starting up and directing other well-received but less-innovative sitcoms like *Up All Night* and *Happy Endings* (two of whose producers would end up inhabiting the reanimated husk of *Community* in Season 4).

The Russo's Captain America: Civil War; *definitely better with paintball.* WALT DISNEY STUDIOS MOTION PICTURES/PHOTOFEST.

These shows hit the early 2010 vogue for polished, witty, slightly urbane yet largely conventional comedies exemplified by *New Girl*. Feige's decision to put the next *Captain America* in the Russos' hands sent their careers in a whole different direction.

It was well timed. Ending their partnership with Harmon at the end of Season 3 kept the Russos out of the muck and mire around his firing. In a less-dark timeline, if the Russos had not gotten the job offer from Feige, they might have stayed around to run *Community*, which would have been better for the show if awkward on a relationship level (much as when Harmon was kicked off *The Sarah Silverman Program* but Rob Schrab stayed on until it finished). As it was, the Russos entered the Marvel Cinematic Universe while *Community* staggered through its gas leak season.

Post-*Community*, the Russos left sitcoms behind seemingly for good (a shame, as there are likely many smart pilot scripts out there that could find an audience under their direction). Over a period of five years, the brothers directed four of the largest and most successful spectacle films ever produced by Hollywood. Featuring dozens of actors, gazillion-dollar budgets, wall-to-wall special effects, punishing shooting schedules, and puzzle-like scripts that needed to address labyrinthine story continuity while appealing to global audiences, these films were not just monumental logistical challenges. The quartet stands as both the purest distillation of the Marvel

Cool Cool Cool

In homage to their years at Greendale, the Russos seeded *Community* cast members throughout their Marvel films, including:

- Yvette Nicole Brown in *Avengers: Endgame* as a civilian staffer who spots Steve Rogers and Tony Stark trying to infiltrate a military base and gives them an appropriately Shirley-esque eyebrow raise.
- Ken Jeong in *Avengers: Endgame* as a security guard who does not immediately appear insane.
- Danny Pudi in *Captain America: The Winter Soldier* as a S.H.I.E.L.D. communication officer.
- Jim Rash in *Captain America: Civil War* as an MIT liaison enthusing about Stark's donation.

Cinematic Method and possibly the last sustained example of twenty-first-century industrial-scale cinematic blockbuster production.

Two of them—*Captain America: The Winter Soldier* (2014) and *Captain America: Civil War* (2016)—broke new ground for the comic-book genre much as *Arrested Development* and *Community* had irrevocably changed the sitcom game. Then *Avengers: Infinity War* (2018) and *Avengers: Endgame* (2019) largely reverted to the norm. None matched the "For a Few Paint-balls More" episode.

Following that kind of success, the Russos stayed locked into a particular brand of over-the-top action spectacle. These ranged from the over-stylized Iraq War vet crime drama *Cherry* (2021) to the mega-budget assassin showdown *The Gray Man* (2022).

Having started their own production company in 2017, AGBO, the Russos also tried their hand at producing an impressively varied slate of films. These included *Mosul* (2019), notable for being just about the only Western-made Iraq War drama that actually focused on Iraqis, and the award-winning multiverse mindbender *Everything Everywhere All at Once* (2022), whose quirky humor and fungible sense of reality felt like something right out of the Harmonverse.

Justin Lin

Like the Russos, Justin Lin made his mark with an infinitesimally budgeted crime drama that didn't do much business but opened doors. Unlike the Russos, who did not catapult to being Hollywood A-list creatives until after putting in their time at *Community*, Lin was already an established director by the time he showed up at Greendale.

Lin's debut film, *Better Luck Tomorrow* (2002), an indie crime drama about Asian-American high school kids in Orange County who fall into drug dealing and selling test scores, was seen as smart, nervy, and original, especially given how it broke with ethnic stereotypes. Not long after, Lin was trusted with rejuvenating the *Fast and Furious* films, directing the 2006 and 2009 entries. Their success turned the stumbling franchise into a multi-billion-dollar industry that united global audiences in celebrating cars that go *vroom vroom*.

Lin's film work had exhibited little inclination for humor. But in the three *Community* episodes he directed in Season 1, he showed how his skills extended well beyond framing Vin Diesel's glower. "Introduction to Statistics" and "Interpretive Dance" were more goofy than high concept though the former did include Abed's first serious move into superhero cosplay as Batman. With "Modern Warfare," Lin put his franchise film-maker skills to work in choreographing the first school-wide paintball assassin campaign, efficiently playing the comedy beats off the action-flick homages while not ignoring the characters' accelerating manias. Curiously, he never shoehorned in a Claymation street racing scene, which feels like a missed cross-genre opportunity.

Unfortunately for *Community*, Lin soon went back to other projects. In the years that followed, he directed three more *Fast and Furious* films, whose popularity seemed to increase exponentially. He was put in the director's chair for *Star Trek Beyond* (2016) by J. J. Abrams, who had done for that film series what Lin had done for *F&F*. The results for the latter were overblown and underwhelming, like much of Lin's film work, but it did include a Danny Pudi cameo (playing a thorny alien, though honestly: Vulcan would have been more on-point than "Reptilicus").

Lin also began a sideline in producing (and occasionally directing) a plethora of glossy action drama series like the nineteenth-century Tong war saga *Warrior* and straight-down-the-middle procedurals like *S.W.A.T.*

Seth Gordon

The path to Hollywood success almost never begins with the words "documentary" or "video games" but that was how Seth Gordon managed to make a career. His first film was *The King of Kong: A Fistful of Quarters* (2007), a spectacularly entertaining documentary about men putting everything they have into becoming the world champion *Donkey Kong* player. Yet somehow, thanks to that project, Gordon ended up the next year directing *Four Christmases*, a fairly generic, over-lit, romantic comedy with handsome movie stars (Reese Witherspoon and Vince Vaughn in this case).

Following that, Gordon cycled through NBC's alt-comedy lineup, directing episodes of *Parks and Recreation* and *The Office* as well as "Environmental Science" for *Community* Season 1. It's a fairly gimmicky episode (Green Daeye, Fievel the escaped rat) and thus well-suited to Gordon's broader style.

After *Community*, Gordon moved on to low-bar sitcoms (*Marry Me*, *The Goldbergs*) but also the occasional drama series like *For All Mankind* and more ultra-broad comedies like *Identity Thief* (2013). Sadly, no Pac-Man documentaries as yet.

Rob Schrab

When *The Sarah Silverman Program* ended in 2010, Rob Schrab could have gone back to writing the further adventures of *Scud: The Disposable Assassin*. Instead, he knocked around the alt-television comedy universe for a few years while Harmon booted up *Community*.

Schrab kept up his line in video shorts. He produced several more Channel 101 shows including the highly assured *The Suits* (an animated shoot 'em up with *Scud*-like tendencies) and worked on the cameo-laden Adult Swim medical series satire *Childrens Hospital*. He also found more mainstream work directing sitcoms like *The Mindy Project* and *Parks and Recreation*. Schrab started directing episodes of *Community* in 2012. By Season 6, he had become one of the show's mainstays, directing six of thirteen episodes, including the finale.

Following *Community*, Schrab appeared poised to become another Russo-like phenomenon after he was hired to direct the sequel to *The Lego Movie* (2014). But in 2017 Schrab, who had replaced Chris McKay on the project, was himself swapped out for Mike Mitchell (one can only imagine the brain-melting Lego battles that were scrapped).

Schrab's television work from then on continued to be a mixture. He did straightforward comedy fare, directing a couple of episodes of Adam Scott and Craig Robinson's mock-paranormal cop show *Ghosted*. At the same time, he kept delving into the kind of genre material (monsters, robots) that had been his stock in trade for years, directing several episodes of *Mystery Science Theater 3000* in 2018 and contributing an episode to the rebooted horror anthology series *Creepshow* that mashed up werewolf and war movie genres ("Bad Wolf Down").

A frequent guest on Harmon's podcast *Harmontown* until it finished in 2019, Schrab also collaborated again with his old partner on writing and producing *Rick and Morty*. His involvement with the latter series has a circular logic to it given that one of the show's most iconic characters, the very short-lived creatures known as Mr. Meeseeks (who are created solely for the completion of a single task, and go somewhat demented if they cannot) were inspired by Schrab's similarly single-minded and existentially doomed Scud.

A homecoming for Schrab? Or possibly a place for him to generate ideas for *The Rick and Morty Lego Movie* (which must certainly exist in some timeline)?

Everyone Else

Many of the directors who shot *Community* were TV vets who didn't come from the usual sitcom ranks. This is particularly the case with the impeccably named British telly stalwart Tristram Shapeero, who cut his teeth across the pond before directing twenty-four episodes of *Community*, making him the only director to log more credits on the show than the Russo brothers. Leaving *Community*, Shapeero then took on other quirky, dialogue-heavy comedies like *Veep* and *The Unbreakable Kimmy Schmidt*.

Some other out-of-the-box *Community* directors included:

- Richard Ayoade: A highly pedigreed British comic known for lead roles in sitcoms like *The IT Crowd*, Ayoade was also a crackerjack music video director (Arctic Monkeys, Vampire Weekend, Yeah Yeah Yeahs); a writer and director of stylized coming-of-age film dramas like *Submarine* (2010); and a deft ironist whose miniseries *Garth Marenghi's Darkplace* (2004) was a clever sendup of crap 1980s horror television. In 2007 Ayoade also starred in a never-aired pilot for an American version of *The IT Crowd* with Joel McHale in the Chris O'Dowd role. Four years later, Ayoade brought an appropriately delicate and daring director's touch to the Season 2 highlight "Critical Film Studies," playing the high concept story straight and without laughs for nearly the entire episode. Two years later, Ayoade wrote and directed *The Double* (2013), an underseen exercise in Kafka-esque alienation.
- Nat Faxon and Jim Rash: Though Rash garnered well-earned accolades from the start of his performance as Dean Pelton, he and Faxon were better known in the industry for behind-the-camera work that made up for in quality what was lacking in quantity. The two pitched in on *Community* to write Season 4's "Basic Human Anatomy" and then a couple of episodes in Season 6. (And *no*, it was not common then or now for Oscar winners to help out on NBC sitcoms.)
- Bobcat Goldthwait: The screeching, hyperventilating stand-up gnome reinvented himself in 1991 with the pitch-black cult comedy *Shakes the Clown*, later directing everything from *Jimmy Kimmel Live!* to *Chappelle's Show* and dyspeptic films like *God Bless America* (2011) in which a cranky old terminal patient teams up with a teenager to gun down America's most wanted people (he also wrote that one). After helming Season 6's "Basic Crisis Room

Decorum," Goldthwait directed several comedy specials and even a family-friendly Mo Willems special.

- Anthony Hemingway: Not really a comedy guy, Hemingway specialized in efficiently punchy action (*Undercover*, *ER*, *Battlestar Galactica*) and nuanced high-status drama (*Community* writing staff favorite *The Wire*), which helped him invest the Season 2 zombie episode "Epidemiology" with authentically creeped-out and dramatic moments. He never really went back to comedy, though, sticking with David Simon series like *Treme* and the occasional film like the World War II drama *Red Tails* (2012).

- Duke Johnson: Television's demarcation between animation and live action is normally as hard to breach as was the Berlin Wall. Season 2's Claymation episode "Abed's Uncontrollable Christmas" saw *Community* jump right over the dividing line as though it were nothing. Animator Johnson had previously directed an episode of Dino Stamatopoulos's dark, religious parody *Moral Orel*. He is creative director and one of the partners with Stamatopoulos at Starburns Industries, the shop that also produced Johnson's first feature directing credit, *Anomalisa* (2015), a bleak exercise in Oscar-nominated, stop-motion, modern alienation. Johnson also crafted the animated elements in *I'm Thinking of Ending Things* (2020), written and directed by *Anomalisa* scribe Charlie Kaufman.

New Media 201— Podcasting for Accountants and Harmontown

12

There is . . . a monthly show I do in the back of a comic book store in Los Angeles in which I say things that I intend for 150 people to hear. I tell stories about what an unlovable asshole I am and the trouble it causes for me. I rant and rave about the world's failure to meet my standards, I talk about being drunk and stupid and heartbroken and childish and crazy and self-obsessed and self loathing and how much I love myself for it.

DAN HARMON

Welcome to the Harmonverse

I N MAY 2011, NBC had just finished airing the second season of *Community*. The back-to-back paintball episodes had sent fans into paroxysms of joy. An article in the *Atlantic* that name checked Baudrillard and Borges called the show (correctly) "the most innovative sitcom of all time." Accolades from smarty-pants critics notwithstanding, the ratings were, well, what they were. Season 3, scheduled to hit the airwaves in September, needed to knock it out of the park for the show to survive.

In other words, it was a spectacular time for Dan Harmon to invest precious time in starting a live comedy show for a few dozen comedy and gaming dorks in the cramped NerdMelt "theater" in the back of the Meltdown Comics store.

Harmontown was a baggy, barely sketched-out vehicle for Harmon and his co-host Jeff B. Davis (the Channel 101 regular and ace improviser who toured with the *Whose Line Is It Anyway?* crew and later joined the *HarmonQuest* gang) to slug vodka, bat rambling jokes and ideas back and forth, and goof around with "special guests" (their friends) before an appreciative crowd.

Writer and producer Emily V. Gordon (who cowrote the autobiographical movie *The Big Sick* with her husband and *Community* guest star Kumail Nanjiani) had started booking off-key comedy shows at the NerdMelt. She asked Harmon, who had been doing some Spalding Gray-esque one-man shows, if he would be interested in doing a *Prairie Home Companion*-style recurring show, and he bit.

Harmontown started in 2011 as a monthly feature at NerdMelt. The premise—that Harmon (shambolic, volcanic Belushi) was the mayor of a fictional burg and Davis (clipped, wry, theatrically trained straight man) was his faithful comptroller who kept the trains running—established Harmon as the hero and focal point. This setup proved useful later on when Harmon began using the show more frequently as a confessional comedy venue for self-lacerating public therapy.

Most of *Harmontown*'s early shows are lost to history. The mayor was busy working on Season 3, after all, knowing full well that it was make it or break it time. In some ways, things were going well. After its return from a short hiatus in March 2012, *Community* was posting stronger than usual ratings and receiving strong audience feedback. The pressure was still on, however, since being renewed for a Season 4 was crucial to *Community* getting an all-important syndication deal.

Given Harmon's acknowledged penchant for volatility and low-road grudge-keeping not to mention on-set tensions at *Community*, the stage was set for self-sabotage.

That month, Harmon publicized the ongoing feud between himself and Chevy Chase (see Season 3 for more background on that) by playing an obscene voicemail the actor had left him ("You alcoholic fat shit" was among the more choice pull quotes) in front of a Harmontown crowd. That audio eventually made it online, causing embarrassment and a surprisingly large ruckus, given how far from the A-list Harmon and Chase were at the time.

In rapid succession: the story banged around the Internet; Harmon apologized; *Community* was renewed for Season 4; people on the Internet wondered, "Who is Dan Harmon?"; Harmon was fired; and *Harmontown* became a weekly, live-recorded podcast.

Its mayor suddenly had some time on his hands and things to say.

And So It Begins

At its start, *Harmontown* was a rough-hewn beast characterized by Harmon's logorrhea and Davis's balancing act of breaking up the mayor's stammered and stream-of-consciousness (but still somehow well-structured) monologues by tossing out sarcastic bon mots.

At its conclusion, some three hundred and sixty-odd episodes later, *Harmontown* largely remained the same. Unlike *Community*, which jumped around stylistically between episodes, *Harmontown* locked into its groove early on and never quite departed. There were tweaks here and there such as introducing running bits (Sports Corner!) that mimicked the structure of conventional variety shows or adding a role-playing game segment and—as their popularity grew—incorporating a wider expanse of guests. But by and large, it was the Harmon show from day one.

Unlike many high-profile shows in those early days of podcasting, *Harmontown* was not trying to do longform journalism, comedy skits, or deep dives into obscure topics. It was instead more like a mainline to Harmon's self-hating, self-aggrandizing, pop culture–frazzled limbic system that network dictates and the writer's room relied on to feed (but not overwhelm!) the delicately balanced ecosystem of *Community*. Cut free from such restraints, most *Harmontown* episodes are freewheeling conversational

Dan Harmon commands a dedicated audience in the documentary Harmontown. AUTHOR'S COLLECTION.

rants in which Harmon and Davis try to out-joke each other while verbally running over their guests when not spinning off into digressions on everything from Joseph Campbell to Maslow's hierarchy and whatever everyone's HBO obsession was at the time. Such alcohol-fueled improv frequently turned each show into a wing-and-a-prayer experiment in how long gab and a near-complete lack of planning can keep people's attention.

The first official-ish episode of *Harmontown*, "Achieve Weightlessness," was released June 6, 2012. Though Harmon had been fired from *Community* in very public fashion just a few weeks before, he brought an almost giddily dark and devil-may-care attitude to the show, which might be surprising to Harmon neophytes but seemed perfectly in character to those who would get to know him over the course of the podcast.

For the most part, Harmon does not dwell on *Community* or the controversy. He does nod to what happened, imagining himself as a vengeance-seeking ranter and joking that he will be like "Ace Rothstein in the second hour of *Casino*" (referencing Robert De Niro's casino boss who starts a ludicrous nightly talk show to endlessly air his grievances). There is also the acknowledgment that without a sitcom to run anymore, Harmon has some time on his hands and so really needs to get *Harmontown* whipped into shape.

The topics run the gamut, from the need to create a new utopian society (a high-vaulting, conceptual argument that is chewed around and then spit aside, like many of the show's tangents) and (unrelated); how often Harmon soils himself ("often"); the Oedipal tensions in Harmon's family (awkward, yet riveting); the title of Harmon's as-yet-unwritten prequel to *Die Hard* ("Nakatomi"); Harmon's then-girlfriend and future short-term wife Erin McGathy; and whether or not the characters on *Community* are all just different facets of Harmon's personality (Surprise! They are).

It was a sprawling affair. That would not change much for a while. But the show's basic structure was already cohering.

Five episodes in, "Confessions of an Alcoholic Mars Rover" showed how the shadow of *Community* still loomed. Chris Hardwick, podcaster and something of a godfather to the burgeoning nerd comic scene at Meltdown, came on as one of, if not the first, real guests of *Harmontown*. In a *Community* nod, for Hardwick's entrance the show played the smooth jazz instrumental "Daybreak" while Davis and Harmon sang along with invented obscene lyrics. With the excuse that the episode's theme is confession, Hardwick is convinced to tell the story of how weeks before, Harmon had come on *his* live podcast (it was only 2012 and already the podcasting scene had grown exponentially) and essentially made an ass

---

Adventures in Advertising

In a bit from "Confessions of an Alcoholic Mars Rover," Harmon and David attempt some anti-advertising. After rhapsodizing about the comfort of Adidas shoes, they lay into Nike for apparently refusing to sponsor the show. The bit turns into a kind of hostage negotiation where they threaten to keep praising Nike's rivals: "It might cost a dollar to stop us from advertising Adidas. Unless Puma gives us ten."

---

of himself doing an extended self-indulgent drunken bit that didn't land. Hardwick decided not to air the episode, figuring that doing so when Harmon was already fighting off blowback from the Chevy Chase incident would have been unfair. Hardwick's magnanimity here, at the height of his career, serves as a sharp contrast to his later fall from nerd grace after accusations of abuse arose in 2018.

More importantly, though, this episode contains the first appearance of Spencer Crittenden. After Harmon says he and Davis want to play Advanced Dungeons & Dragons in the next episode, he asks if anybody in the audience has a good grasp of how the rules had changed since the 1980s. Crittenden—who was attending his first *Harmontown* as a fan—steps up, and the rest is history.

A rare and random piece of media convergence, Crittenden was quickly chosen as the Dungeon Master for the continuing D&D campaigns that would conclude many episodes of *Harmontown*; their sessions became one of the most reliably entertaining hooks of the show. Crittenden, with his studied monotone and deadpan affect (plus bearded Viking gamer fashion style, which Davis described as "Employee of the Month, 1524"), becomes the crucial third element of the show's core appeal, balancing out Harmon's hyperactive energy and Davis's cool ironism. Crittenden's self-contained quietude and deeply sincere commitment to gaming culture made him seem a natural fit for a character on *Community* as well (indeed, he would make an appearance on the show in Season 5's "VCR Maintenance and Educational Publishing").

Having found its footing, the *Harmontown* world quickly shaped up and built a following among a crowd largely, but not entirely, composed of *Community* fans needing a Harmon fix. There was also a growing contingent of people who found a lot to vibe with in the podcast's mix of multi-level nerdishness, scatological humor, and raw vulnerability.

By September 2012, the gaming aspect of the show was fully formed. In Episode 11, Davis's *Whose Live Is It Anyway?* costar, improviser, early podcaster, and role-playing game neophyte Greg Proops (insinuating in his ignorance of the gaming conventions that he had been too busy drugging in his youth to mess with twenty-sided dice) turned his guest appearance into an epic performance as Tylenol with Codeine, the fey magical unicorn who made that D&D adventure a druggy and sexually ambiguous psychedelic escapade. It was the kind of oddball RPG adventure that would give rise to the improvisational narrative dungeoneering of *HarmonQuest* in 2016.

The rest of 2012 and early 2013 saw the introduction of more running gags that, like *Community*, layered and deepened the podcast with self-referential callbacks. Episode 19, "Everyone's a Rapper" had Harmon enter the stage while doing a thumpingly and purposefully clumsy freestyle rap. This was a bit he would return to innumerable times throughout the podcast, stretching the rhyme scheme to such ludicrous lengths they became an exercise in Andy Kaufman–style attrition warfare.

The celebrity level of the guest stars began increasing as well. Episode 23, "Turtle Panties," from January 2013, has one of the show's few scripted moments. After Harmon fails to produce a "sophisticated" rap he is happy with, Davis calls Monty Python's Eric Idle (for real!) up to the stage to teach Harmon how to write a song. The joke is that Idle launches into a ditty that's just as filthy as Harmon's but has a far better rhyme scheme. The same episode also features Patton Oswalt, who is laughingly flabbergasted by the pacing and planning of the twenty-city tour that Harmon and the whole show are about to launch themselves on. Oswalt fixates in particular on Harmon starting the tour in Phoenix, which Oswalt describes as "an abandoned moon colony if all the astronauts were Mexican and on crack."

Nevertheless, the podcast proceeded.

Harmoncountry: The Tour, the Movie, the Magic, the Mania, the Beautiful, the Really Ugly

In January 2013—about seven months after the broadcast of what people thought was the last episode of *Community*, a few weeks before the premiere of the fourth season of the show that was no longer Harmon's, and just days after his fortieth birthday—he and the *Harmontown* gang piled into a tour bus and hit the road with a documentary film crew tagging along to make sure that all the embarrassing and uncomfortable moments got immortalized.

Most other writers who had struggled for so long to get a foothold in the industry might have balked at doing anything this risky, this public, and this drenched in red Solo cups full of Ketel One.

But even though Sony and NBC had bailed on Harmon, he was a hot enough showrunner at the time—again, just about the only showrunner who had ever gotten any kind of press attention for anything—that soon enough other networks were vying for his attention. This was good for Harmon in that it showed *Community* had acquired enough Internet "Is *this* what the kids are into watching?" razzle-dazzle that networks were willing to throw money at him to get a little of what he had to offer.

Curiously, while the summer of 2013 could have been the low point of Harmon's career, a time for wound-licking and passive-aggressive tweeting, it turned out to be one of the most fertile. In July, the *Hollywood Reporter* wrote that Harmon was close to finalizing a comedy pilot deal at Fox, had already closed a deal to write a sitcom for CBS, and was also kicking around two very different animated projects: the Charlie Kaufman-scripted film *Anomalisa* and a series Harmon was cocreating with Justin Roiland for Adult Swim: *Rick and Morty*.

Though *Rick and Morty* wouldn't air until December 2013 and *Anomalisa* was only released in 2015, the immediate result of all this head-spinning deal-making was that Harmon launched his 20-shows-in-20-nights tour when he still had a lot of writing to do for two big networks. In Neil Berkeley's tour film *Harmontown*, the showrunner in exile can be seen banging away at his laptop to finish the scripts that should already be finished, a bit of self-induced melodrama that he describes as making him "feel like a little boy who didn't clean his room."

Neither of the sitcoms ever came to anything. Few details ever emerged of the show for Fox except that it might have been a multi-camera sitcom. The CBS sitcom was to be an *Absolutely Fabulous*-ish setup in which an aging rock star with a Peter Pan syndrome (possibly Jack Black, the patron saint of never-realized Harmon shows) has to adjust when his far more mature daughter moves in with him. Anything is possible, of course, but it feels safe to predict that if the show had come to fruition, they would not be having panel discussions about it at the Paley Center a decade later.

While procrastinating about writing, Harmon performed comedy like a barnstorming rock band set loose on the first tour where the label was paying for anything: "In each city I got drunk and talked into a microphone."

> ## Success!(ish)
>
> One quick scene in *Harmontown* the documentary has Harmon pointing to a chart showing ratings for *Community*. Speaking in a dry tone that is mostly but not entirely tongue-in-cheek, he explains that the higher-rated episodes were because they were scheduled in the timeslot right after *The Office* "and people left their TVs on."

As recorded by Berkeley, the podcast was much the same on the road as it was back in Los Angeles, only more so. With Harmon seeming to need to cut loose after the years of battling with the network over *Community* and raking himself over the coals every time he felt he had not produced the Greatest Episode of Television Comedy Ever, the tour acts like a purgative. For Harmon, this let him meet his fans in corporeal rather than Internet form. As seen in the film, Harmon witnessing his fans' unalloyed joy and gratitude up close at least briefly blows a hole in the fog of hyper-literate self-regard and self-loathing that layered so many of his public performances at the time. At one show, he crowd-surfs (a risky maneuver for a man of his girth to attempt with nerds, what with their frequently spindly arms and poor hand-eye coordination). At others, he brings audience members up on stage to share stories of personal pain. After the shows, he hangs around to tell more stories, sign merch, and even give and receive hugs. He does not, however, haul his own merch (that's what girlfriends are for!).

Later Harmon would say that the physical experience of those tour encounters was a factor in his returning to *Community* for the fifth season, something he was not sure that he could have done otherwise.

The positive fan encounters and the giddy, punch-drunk, comedic highs that came with the tour's punishing schedule and rabid "army of nerds" audiences provided an uplifting boost. But the documentary does not stint on Harmon's rawer, sometimes chillingly unempathetic side. We see him not just goofy and trawling for laughs but also seething, manic, selfish, and ugly bitchy (especially toward McGathy, who seems to have been demoted from girlfriend and podcast equal to merch-gofer): possibly a glimpse of that imperious personality that may have helped cost him the *Community* job. Perhaps a little too self-knowingly, Harmon encapsulates much of what some parts of the audience are thinking when he says in at least half-jest that he is "struggling with the realization that I am the villain of this story" and that Crittenden "is the hero."

So It Continues: A Highlight Reel

The tour concluded back in Los Angeles with a show at the Egyptian Theater where McGathy and Harmon appear to agree to move in together. A week and a half later, with nary a break, *Harmontown* was back to its Nerd-Melt roots. The D&D adventure continued. Harmon and Davis bantered. Harmon went off on verbal tears where his stammering nearly kept him from getting to his eventual point. Nanjiani (whose *The Meltdown* podcast was also a regular at the NerdMelt for years) became a frequent enough visitor to the stage that he was essentially an honorary Harmonian well before he began filling in as guest comptroller when Davis was otherwise engaged.

During Harmon's *Community* interregnum—Season 4 was on the air from February to May 2013—the series registered on *Harmontown* primarily

The Art of Schrabbing

Among the recurring cast of *Harmontown* characters was Harmon's fellow Wisconsinite Rob Schrab. Although more recently involved in the writing than performing side of things, Schrab had a good enough background in stage comedy (from their Milwaukee days) to know how to create a character and also how to play off Harmon in front of a crowd. Schrab's role was that of the annoying pest, amplifying his already nasal voice and raising issues that led to annoyed sighs from Harmon. More than once, Schrab would seemingly sabotage an episode by running a gag into the ground but doing so with such tenacity that it would somehow become funny again.

The campaign of irritation continued outside the podcast. In Episode 109, Nanjiani discusses the "campaign of terror" that he says Schrab had been waging on Twitter. He describes "Schrabbing" as Schrab's repeated attempts to get under people's skin by continually posting questions to things that have already been answered.

Perhaps not the most original style of comedy but one that requires a total commitment that few can fully commit to fully. Commit to, that is. Fully.

as the buzzing in the background that everyone can hear but does not talk about. Even though *Community* may have initially brought people to the podcast, as it marched toward its hundredth episode, *Harmontown* became its own community, overlapping with but not completely replicating the fanbase of the sitcom Harmon was no longer in charge of.

Rather than rant about being forced out of *Community*, Harmon worked out ideas and teased philosophical concepts that one could imagine him having worked into the series during its more intellectually tangled earlier seasons but that were now more likely to be exported into his then-current project *Rick and Morty*.

Yet in June 2013, Harmon was brought back into the NBC fold to produce the fifth season of *Community*. That did not put an end to *Harmontown*, however, which ran another six and half years. Curiously, the podcast did not seem to suffer once Harmon (ever the workaholic) went back to showrunning *Community*.

Week after week, Harmon and (usually) Davis took to the stage and extemporized for a growing audience. There were minor changes along the way to *Harmontown* mostly in the form of higher-grade sponsors, a shift from D&D to another RPG (Shadowrun), and a post-2016 shift away from Harmon's earlier knee-jerk anti-political cynicism.

Given Harmon's good (for a Gen-Xer) radar regarding social media and tech trends, he started the show at a fertile time for podcasts as a format. It came along not long after Marc Maron's *WTF* found an audience and just before the first season of *Serial* became a national obsession in 2014.

Not dissimilar to how *Community* disrupted expectations of the sitcom, *Harmontown* also played with ideas of how to create a podcast. There were guests but not always, and generally they were simply invited to take part in whatever shtick Harmon and Davis were toying with at the moment (Episode 51 with Robin Williams treats him less as a special guest star and more as just another comic along for the ride), breaking from the interview format so popular with *WTF* and a little later *The Joe Rogan Experience*.

The overflow of comedy and gaming kept it from falling strictly into either genre. The live setting, free-flowing booze, and Harmon's tendency to bring audience members on stage for ad-hoc Q&As that were frequently not just funny but deeply human made the end product looser, more chaotic, and more revealing than most non-interview podcasts, which tended to be scripted and highly produced. That combination of steady consistency—the interplay between Harmon and Davis; Crittenden's stalwart dungeon-mastering; Schrab's Schrabbing—and randomness likely contributed to the show's lengthy run.

Like *Community*, by its conclusion *Harmontown* was a dense and slightly tipsy construction, spiderwebbed with in-jokes, repeat references (*Inception*, Liam Neeson, and Ketel One in particular), and bit characters with lengthy back stories. As with an only occasional viewer of the sitcom, a drop-in listener to the podcast would be initially baffled but still able to find their way after giving it time. Like Harmon's earlier creation, *Harmontown* also showed an openness to both artistic and human growth.

Community had begun as a traditional-ish sitcom whose gimmick was its dedication to closely observed consciousness as a piece of media. It concluded as a study of the positives and negatives of people's need for belonging. *Harmontown* started in the ferment of the Internet (back when Tumblr and Pinterest were still things and people thought they could handle what Twitter did to their brains) and happily rode those waves of fandom, memeing, and outrage. But as with anyone who strives to retain their humanity in the nonstop roar and glare of the Internet, it got to Harmon at times. In one episode, Harmon delivers a shout that is as much a rant as it is a plea: "America, can't you stop fucking *commenting* on everything?"

During the podcast's last episode in December 2019, Harmon struggled to explain why he decided to end it. He describes his desire to step away from the online persona that he has created during the course of the show:

Apologies: A Seminar

On New Year's Day 2018, Harmon tweeted a semi-self-aware joke about 2017 being "The Year of the Asshole" and saying he hoped to be less of one going forward: "#RealisticGoals." Former *Community* writer Megan Ganz tweeted back, "Care to elaborate? Redemption follows allocution." Harmon devoted part of the January 10 podcast episode to a detailed examination of how six years earlier he had sexually harassed Ganz, abused his position as a boss, and treated her cruelly: "I drank, I took pills, I crushed on her, and resented her for not reciprocating it." Ganz, who despite building an impressive writing resume (*It's Always Sunny in Philadelphia*, *Mythic Quest*, *Modern Family*) had suffered from self-doubt for years because of the harassment, later tweeted, "I find myself in the odd position of having requested an apology publicly, and then having received one—a good one—also publicly."

"I don't want to be a brand." He had been mayor of the traveling circus long enough.

Then, without his weekly jolt of live-audience therapeutic catharsis, Harmon went back to producing *Rick and Morty* and dodging questions from *Community* fans about when and if he was going to make *Community: The Movie*. In this way, he had just (self-consciously or not) followed his eight-stage story circle structure for writing, starting with the protagonist having to adapt to an unfamiliar situation, getting what they wanted, paying the price, and ultimately returning to their original position having slightly changed.

Whether or not that change amounted to anything notable would have to wait for another *Harmontown* film to discover.

Game Theory 201/202– 13
Advanced Introduction to
D&D: HarmonQuest

Since the dawn of the 1970s, fantasy role-playing games have
provided men and women with an escape from their awkward
lives. Today, the most awkward of them all, Dan Harmon,
is summoning celebrity friends to play these games of old
before a live studio audience in Hollywood. I am Spencer, the
GameMaster, and this is HarmonQuest!

S O BEGINS EVERY EPISODE of the egocentrically named *Harmon-*
Quest, a live-action and animated RPG studio-audience podcast
unlike any other before or, if we're honest, since.

While Dungeons & Dragons podcasts now number in the d100s, back
when *HarmonQuest* started in 2016, the Internet was a d4 kind of world
with very few roleplaying podcasts hitting wide national audiences. *Critical*
Role (established c. 2015), for example, helped pioneer long-form, real-
time, voice-acted adventuring, but it wasn't until 2022 that their live,
table-top, gaming sessions became animated (in the scripted spin-off,
The Legend of Vox Machina). Other live gaming sessions—from the earli-
est recorded podcasts in the early aughts to more polished contemporary
campaigns like *CelebriD&D*—typically followed similar formats, treating
fantasy RPG conventions (die outcomes, high drama, "the rulebook")
with a gravitas seemingly designed to reclaim the reputation of this quint-
essentially nerdy pen-and-paper pastime.

Meanwhile—as usual—Harmon and company eschewed the conventional and upped the nerdy self-reflexivity with a stand-alone extension of

the D&D/Shadowrun gaming sessions they had been appending to their *Harmontown* shows since 2012. As *Community* came to an end (?) in 2015, the momentum for *HarmonQuest* had fortuitously gathered steam. The show debuted on NBC's pet streaming service Seeso (one of those short-lived, standalone streamers that Harmon once called "baby Netflixes") in 2016 before being shunted to VRV for the final two seasons in 2017 and 2019. As Harmon notes in the Season 2 episode, "The Barely Cursed Bazaar of Commerce," *HarmonQuest* is "the show that answers the question: why not pretend that the thing you wanted to see on TV could be on TV?"

Joined at the long table by ex-wife Erin McGathy, eternal chum Jeff B. Davis, and *Harmontown* foundling Spencer Crittenden, Harmon head-lined a heady combination of traditional fantasy role-playing game quests, comic riffs, B-list celebs, and cartoon animation that culminated in a meta-narrative on gaming, nerd-dom, and collective storytelling. In the patois of Hollywoodland, *HarmonQuest* is the bastard love-child of *Critical Role*, *Whose Line Is It Anyway?*, and *Drunk History*. Somehow it works.

For those who have never played Dungeons & Dragons (for shame!), fantasy RPGs are pen-and-pencil role-playing games typically set in a neomedieval universe where players act out roles as fantasy character types: wizards and thieves, fighters and healers—that kind of thing. Working within a (sometimes) complicated system of statistic checks and random polyhedral die rolls, the player characters (PCs) work with a Dungeon Master (DM) to enact a group narrative that typically includes trekking through forests and dungeons, fighting monsters with swords and magic, and gathering treasure and experience. Technically, Crittenden and com-pany play within the Pathfinder role-playing system that, as far as the laity is concerned, is pretty much D&D by another name. For the hardcore gamers, of course, Pathfinder is "D&D version 3.75: The Acrimonious Split," which explains the cast's often awkward dancing around copy-righted nomenclature when explaining to guests what it is, exactly, that they're playing.

All of which is academic, of course. For those who played D&D back in "the dawn of the 1970s," the group banter and comic asides of *Harmon-Quest* are what matter, not the pesky rule book. For many of us old-school nerds, the gang's gaming sessions nostalgically recall the IRL experience of sitting around with our own goofball friends, ostensibly questing for glory and fame in some sort of Tolkienian fantasy world but mostly just, you know, hanging out, ripping on one another, telling dick jokes, and maybe killing some monsters. Sigh . . . good times, those.

For anyone who ever acted as DM during such shenanigans, Crittenden (who joined the *Harmontown* crew in 2012 after being pulled out of the audience for a one-off bit on D&D that turned into a career) is the real star of the show, evidencing an enviable talent for talent-wangling. The sessions clearly echo how meandering real D&D sessions can be especially among adolescents and drunks (and drunk adolescents). In short, *Harmon-Quest* hits a nostalgic D&D sweet spot that only *Stranger Things* rivals . . . albeit for presumably different reasons. The series also serves, as all media does, as free therapy for Harmon, whose fantasy character is only partly removed from his real-world persona as "the most awkward of them all!"

Narratively, *HarmonQuest* follows—over the course of three precious, ten-episode seasons—the adventures of Fondue Zoobag, half-orc ranger (Harmon as an incessantly self-deprecating narcissist with daddy issues); Beur O'Shift, half-elf barbarian (McGathy as an undiplomatic rage-o-holic Red Sonja); and Boneweevil, a goblin rogue (Davis as a snarky little green-skinned book-hating backstabbing thief). Led on their quests by DM Crittenden, the three are joined each week and episode by celebrity guests (an increasingly diverse array of comedians, actors, and actor-comedians) who typically know nothing about roleplaying games but have often been residents of *Harmontown* or audited classes at Greendale . . . so they kinda know what they're in for.

Their inexperience is largely the point and half the fun: watching n00bs struggle with the de rigueur RPG sheets of personal stats, weapon inventories, and magical abilities only to then solve traditional fantasy problems by thinking outside the traditional fantasy box. Yet no matter how unexpected or seemingly illogical their decisions, everyone rolls with it, literally. Crittenden in particular does a fine job keeping the spirit of traditional D&D intact by casually roll-checking their various actions then acknowledging their attempts with a stentorian "You do that!" after an actor proposes a path of action. By keeping the narrative—as a product of group-think—in the fore rather than becoming bog-downed in the rules of the game, *HarmonQuest* remains a delightfully accessible show for both casual and hardcore nerd audiences. You don't have to know your Displacer Beasts from your Githyanki to watch it, really, which is a refreshing change from most of the d100 podcasts currently at large.

Crittenden—a DM's DM—plots out the adventures beforehand and gives guests pre-game narrative prompts as guides. But the emphasis on in-game improvisation and comedy leads to a great many tangents and lost narrative threads. As Crittenden noted during a panel at New York Comic Con in 2017:

There's a loose outline for the episode, and it's generally, like, three beats. It's, like, an introduction to the guest beat; like, a main beat, and kind of resolution-slash-final conflict beat. And in between those, there's some ideas that I have, but a lot of it just comes from the improv and the jokes and just kind of following that.

Each one-hour gaming session is live-taped before a studio audience of some one hundred Hollywood natives, then cut down into a twenty-five-minute semi-animated episode, which enables Crittenden and the folks at Starburns Industries to find the funniest—if not necessarily most coherent—plotlines to follow. As a result, critical hits and critical fails abound. Improv, dead-end investigations, and running gags ("runners," in Harmon-speak) become more important than the successful completion of any major quest. As Doobag metatheatrically notes of their questing halfway through Season 1, "Everything we've done has been sloppy and comedic." But again, that's half the fun of it.

Each episode follows the same basic format: Spencer's cartoon floating head recaps the story so far and intones the opening intro, the background art nicely recalling old school D&D *Monster Manual* illustrations and Hildebrandt/Frazetta paintings.

A live camera then swings over the studio audience toward a long table cluttered with (stale) popcorn, chip bags, soda cans, red Solo cups, and a variety of RPG paraphernalia (dice, status sheets, reference books, a map, and "lead" figures). It's a mess, as it should be.

Harmon next awkwardly introduces himself and his companions at the table, always offering praise to Crittenden as the real star of the show before nicknaming McGathy (who typically primps for the camera) and Davis (who goofs about with his pencils and books). It's all very *Hollywood Squares/Match Game*, really, even down to the (generally) B-list celebrities who join their weekly quests. One imagines that the ghosts of Paul Lynde and Charles Nelson Reilly could materialize over the table, drop a snarky comment, and move on approvingly.

Harmon intros the guest or guests at the table, who then reveal whether they've ever played D&D (or similar) before. Most have not. Regardless of their personal experience, he pithily explains to them and the audience what they are all about to do: play a collective storytelling game in which Spencer is the CPU/god/referee who determines—via dice, rules, and narrative urgency—whether their proposed actions succeed or fail.

Then (in a scene that is cut from the A-roll but is sometimes available in Extended Universe collections) Crittenden takes the newbie on a very

HarmonQuest: *Let the gaming begin!* AUTHOR'S COLLECTION.

brief one-person adventure (a "solo run") to get them used to the way the interactions will ensue.

Harmon (and by Season 2, everyone in the audience) then dramatically shouts "Let's quest!" as Crittenden sets the scene of their adventure, depicted via cartoon animation (a blend of fantasy painted backgrounds, *Rick and Morty*-esque cartooning, and *Ren and Stimpy* blood flow) all home-produced by Starburns Industries. The full episode then jumps between live-action and animation, sometimes cutting so quickly—and metatheatrically—that the self-commentary on narrative production blurs the lines between the players and their characters . . . as well as the fiction of their low-budget fantasy world and the fiction of their not-as-low-budget-as-it-seems theatrical production.

Typically it's not long into the quest that the three regulars run into the guest-of-the-week, who introduces their new character by fantasy name / race / class. Their improvised names are, by and large, pretty silly, ranging from Teflonto and Dildo Dogpelt to Toriamos; Hawaiian Coffee; Rib Sanchez; Tampa Bay the Buccaneer; and . . . Donna. Such discordant nomenclature is all part of the metatheatrical nature of *HarmonQuest*, with actors extending one foot into the fantasy world of imagination while

The Runners

The ridiculous names of the characters in *HarmonQuest*—especially when played against the (generally) traditional world-building established by Crittenden throughout—form one of the many (many!) running gags that pepper the episodes. These include but are not limited to:

- weapon naming
- catch phrases
- critical fails
- rope pizza
- Daddy issues
- Mommy issues

- handjobs
- chain-play
- pull-asides
- half-idioms
- boots of mad hops

But the greatest runner in the series is the nigh-inevitable demise of the weekly guest character, sometimes as a willing self-sacrifice to further the main quest but more often as the collateral damage resulting from the shenanigans of (if not direct assault by) the main characters themselves. During the very first episode, as Paul F. Tompkins's half-orc Teflonto lay dying, Fondue remarks (in animation), "You were a guest star. It's okay." The blend of practical casting requirements (here today, gone by next week) and narrative flow (the adventure continues!) sometimes require more subtle erasures as when Aparna Nancherla's character, Bowflex Devrye, is silently seen (via animation only) suddenly becoming a ghost at the end of Season 2's "Bonebreak Village," or in Season 3 when Rob Corddry's barbarian, Sandy, is clearly standing at the end of his own episode ("The Starshade Expanse") but is shown as a desiccated corpse at the beginning of the next ("The Virtuous Harmony"). But more often than not, the "boss fight" of the week results in someone visibly dying, and that someone is likely—although *not* exclusively!—to be a guest star. Even as Crittenden concludes the penultimate episode of Season 3, he teases, "Will our heroes stop euthanizing their allies?" Death is the fastest runner, to be sure.

keeping the other obstinately planted on planet Hollywood (same thing, really).

Once the guest character joins the main party, the problem-of-the-week is confronted with many a side-comment and tons of "Let's kill it" problem-solving along the way. Some guests are allies; others are enemies; some are absent fathers or long-lost brothers; most engage in sexual badinage with the main party at some point (yes, even the family members). Everyone gets to use their pre-rolled D&D abilities and on-the-spot creative thinking while Spencer rolls dice and loosely guides the narrative.

The episode ends after

- the evil-of-the-week has been vanquished,
- someone significant has perished,
- the hour runs out,
- or all of the above.

Crittenden then brings the episode to a close with a verbal teaser for the next week, typically a series of "Will our heroes . . . ?" questions and the promise "Find out next time, on *HarmonQuest!*"

Applause, roll call, fade to black. Repeat. It's a fair formula.

The three seasons follow one master arc: stop Evil, who appears in the form of Vortheon, a faceless "Big Bad" in black plate-mail who—as is typical of the fantasy genre—is a visual amalgamation of Darth Vader, Shredder, and Baron Karza.

Along the way the mains and their guests get up to a dizzying array of shenanigans, including hiding gems up their unmentionables; punching walls; eating orc-loaf sandwiches; walking through a whoopee cushion forest; giving a kobold a mega-handjob; watching a villain desanginuate himself; yoda-ing their Dad; licking electric stones; turning into a penguin with a third (human) arm; freeing "ghost-Spencer"; challenging Death to Bar Trivia; unleashing a demon sword on a peaceful village; visiting a grab-bag store; setting up a gnome assassin as king; being launched via catapults; dying; serving their compatriots a delicious IPA; fighting the Puppet King; riding "Bob" (aka the "Beast of the Beginning"); visiting Fancy Treasure Land; having an existential crisis; throwing shade; peeing on books; starting bar fights; committing multiversal negligence; enjoying rope pizza; hurling others (repeatedly); and, ultimately, getting "a fresh start, maybe?" Given the free reign Crittenden offers his RPG improv troupe, the plot can sometimes be rather convoluted but—as noted—who cares?

Then again, Harmon is keen on story circles, so here's the basic three-arc narrative of the entire series.

Season 1 is a keep-away quest à la *LOTR/The Elfstones of Shannara* wherein our heroes fail to stop Vortheon from gathering the five ("Three, m'lord!") . . . three mystic runestones that can either summon the evil Manticore from the Demon Realm or reseal the rift between dimensions. What happens? (Spoiler alert) Both.

Season 2 finds Fondue and Beur on a *Search for Spock* . . . er . . . Bone-weevil, who was sucked into the vortex at the end of Season 1 (poorly placed spoiler alert). After a brief stint in the Demon Realm (escaping after defeating the Caretaker in a round of bar trivia . . . and fisticuffs), the three make increasingly bad decisions regarding "Who's the bad guy?" and (perfectly placed spoiler alert) Fondue dies!

Season 3 again begins one man down but soon Harmon is voicing a new, mysterious, chain-wielding Steven Segalesque character: Limerick O'Shift, Beur's long-lost brother! The final season's quest list is . . . complicated . . . but starts with a trip to see the Skulltree Barbarians before the gang reunite with Fondue (who is now a sword!?), jump around in time, and go on trial before a space tribunal for messing with the fabric of reality. Yep, you read that right—Crittenden nailed the plot of *Loki* back in 2018. Ultimately, they (spoiler!) escape, face off against Vortheon (again), and save the world by piloting the Beast of the Beginning through realities back to the past! Huzzah!?

But . . . as Crittenden and Sandy Michaels (the old village chief) meta-theatrically intone at the end of the final episode, "The world is saved but the village destroyed! Did they crash land on the heads of Fondue and Boneweevil from the past? And what might that even do to the timeline anyway? And indeed, where are we in the timeline? It's not entirely clear at the moment. Find out next season (?) on *HarmonQuest*!"

Sadly, despite this final teaser, there is, was, and has been no Season 4 and so the world(s) may never know . . . sigh.

As these broad synopses suggest (and most hard-working DMs know), the fun isn't to be found in the end game but the interactions between characters. And so in honor of all those failed D&D campaigns that began with the promise of freshly rolled characters stats before devolving into bong hits and banter, herewith find improvised character sheets for the revolving door of *HarmonQuest* guests including actor, character name, race, class, primary attribute, alliance, best line, and ultimate survivability factor. "And so, without further ado . . . *Let's Guest!*"

Season 1

"The Quest Begins": Paul F. Tompkins as Teflonto, Head of the Local Militia

RPG experience: "Probably eighth grade, that was my year of D&D . . . errr, uh, of role-playing games! (fuck)."

Race: Half-orc

Class: Guardian

Primary attribute: mustache

Friend or foe? friend to the end!

DQ: "The demon seal I must protect / The responsibility I do not reject / Vigilant I shall ever be / Won't you vigilize along with me?"

SAVE vs DEATH: DEATH. The first guest is, appropriately, the first guest to die (metatheatrically) . . . but at least he gets a vacation out of it.

"The Stone Saw Mines": Chelsea Peretti as Deepak Chopra, Lone Survivor

RPG exp: "Not *games*, no."

Race: Dwarf

Class: Monk

Primary attribute: nondescript public domain singing

Friend or foe? possessed by arcane horror ("newfound friend turned foe")

DQ: "Now I can dip my bread in you, Fondue!"

SAVE vs. DEATH: DEATH! The second guest is the first guest to be killed by the main party.

"Welcome to Freshport": Steve Agee as Tech Powers, Horned Dockworker Wannabe

RPG exp: "I used to beat the shit out of kids who did it in high school . . . no!"

Race: Demi-Hellspawn

Class: Bard

Primary attribute: improv singing

Friend or foe? kinda waffles, really

DQ: [insert musical note] "This is the song about five dead babies / Five dead babies in the bottom of a lake. / This is the song about five dead babies / Five dead babies that were bitten by a snake." [insert musical note]

SAVE vs DEATH: DEATH? Left to die holding off enemy reinforcements.

"Across the Dernum Sea": Ron Funches as Rib Sanchez, Famous Sea Captain

RPG exp: "No, I always tried to not dig too deep into that."

Race: Human

Class: Swashbuckler/Buccaneer

Primary attribute: smuggling soft things (pillows, feathers, easy-listening CDs)

Friend or foe? fair-weather friend

DQ: "I like you. I like you for a goblin."

SAVE vs DEATH: SAVE! "Vortheon, I knew you seemed like a very nice guy and these guys seemed like troublemakers all along and I'm just going to get out of here."

"Manoa Prison Hole": Aubrey Plaza as Hawaiian Coffee, Prisoner

RPG exp: "No, I don't know anything . . . No, I don't know anything."

Race: Gnome

Class: Alchemist

Primary attribute: out-of-the-box thinking

Friend or foe? friend, although the jury's still out regarding Boneweevil.

DQ: "This . . . we will need later."

SAVE vs DEATH: DEATH—by suicide bombing . . . BOOM!

"Entering the Sandman Desert": John Hodgman as Hohn Jodgman, Sandwich Merchant

RPG exp: "It might surprise you to learn, but I was something of a nerd as a child. I wanted very much to play it, and I did a few times, because I loved the idea of immersing myself into a fantasy world, but it was so much, ah-uhm, math."

Race: Human

Class: Sorcerer

Primary attribute: dramatic intonation

Friend or foe? foe—repeated betrayal!

DQ: "Did you think that I turned all these orphan children and other villagers into sandwiches to sell them as . . . slave sandwiches?"

SAVE vs DEATH: inexplicable SAVE. "Well, I figured I should become friends with you, because apparently these fights never end." (Hodgman seemed primed to reappear in a later episode, but alas, 'twas just banter.)

"The Doorest of Fores": Thomas Middleditch as Dildo Bogpelt, Local Forest Dweller

RPG exp: "I've been told that no one really rolls dice [here] except the GameMaster. Well, not today! I'm rolling dice!" (drops bag of polyhedrals on table like a boss!)

Race: Halfling

Class: Investigator?

Primary attribute: smokin'em, rollin'em, and spellcraftin'em

Friend or foe? friend

DQ: "Nineteen? That was sooo close to a sweet, fat, natural: big juicy natch."

SAVE vs DEATH: SAVE. Fades into the bushes living, leaving only a penis-shaped smoke ring

"The Dragon's Temple": Kumail Nanjiani as Eddie Lizzard, Temple Janitor

RPG exp: "I'm big into fantasy, favorite genre; I love *Lord of the Rings*, fantasy video games, but I haven't really done very much pen-and-paper, for real, in a room with no audience."

Race: Kobold

Class: "Verizon-level Help"

Primary attribute: snarky barter

Friend or foe? neutral-ish

DQ: "You just gave me seventy gold to give me a handjob!"

SAVE vs DEATH: SAVE with benefits . . . and will return in "The Sorcerer of the Storm."

"The Secret Hideout": Rhea Butcher as James Dean, Sword-Spirit

RPG exp: "About twice when I was about twelve."
Race: Human (once)
Class: Sword/Paladin
Primary attribute: Holy Blast
Friend or foe? friend indeed.
DQ: "Swords kill people; people don't kill people."
SAVE vs DEATH: SAVE? Stuck up a manticore's bum.

"Earthscar Village": Nathan Fillion as Tedder Spice, New Chief of Earthscar Village

RPG exp: "I played for five minutes' experience in seventh grade before an IRT fight broke out."
Race: Half-elf
Class: Champion?
Primary Attribute: hair-based Charisma
Friend or foe? friend-in-chief
DQ: "I prefer to pronounce it *chuh-rizma*."
SAVE vs DEATH: SAVE, and gives rousing speech in Expanded Universe!.

Season 2

"The Quest Continues": Gillian Jacobs as Chip, "Middle-Earth's Erkel"

RPG exp: "My only experience is as Britta on *Community*."
Race: Goblin
Class: Rogue
Primary attribute: eating rocks and offering randomly astute D&D insights
Friend or foe? friend
DQ: "I have Perception 11 so I know that!"
SAVE vs DEATH: DEATH. "Got exploded."

"Demon Realm Devilry": Rory Scovel as Krendrularius, Lonely—and Potentially Stoned—Swamp Weirdo

RPG exp: "It's like there's a test, and I didn't know there was a test."

Race: Human

Class: Witch

Primary attribute: (appliance) transformation

Friend or foe? friend-ly-ish

DQ: "I'm thinking about getting into a new genre of messing with people!"

SAVE vs DEATH: DITCHED in demon realm.

"Bonebreak Village": Aparna Nancherla as Beauflecks Devrye, Spencer's Girlfriend

RPG exp: "I guess [I'm afraid] that I'll like it too much?"

Race: Human

Class: Demon Hunter?

Primary attribute: understatement

Friend or foe? mission-aligned ally

DQ: "Oh dang, my goop foot."

SAVE vs DEATH: DEATH (ghosted)

"Into the Abyss": Paul Scheer as Sensodyne, Son of Tom of Maine

RPG exp: "I'm very excited to be here, to help you guys, tonight, get out of hell!"

Race: Tooth Beast

Class: Tooth Beast

Primary attribute: "swinging around like a spidery man"

Friend or foe? highly enthusiastic friend

DQ: "Roll me! Tell me how good I am at spreading toothpaste!"

SAVE vs DEATH: SAVE, but flung far afield in opening animation next episode.

"Back to Sandman Desert": Patton Oswalt as Sandpole, Formerly "Sandwiched" Nomad Child

> RPG exp: "I started in seventh grade with the classic D&D, worked my way through all the—Boot Hill, Gamma World, uhm, there was some kind of spy thing . . . and then I discovered weed and sex."
>
> Race: Half-orc
> Class: Cleric
> Primary attribute: suspicious tea
> Friend or foe? increasingly disillusioned hero-worshiper
> DQ: [insert musical note] "[expletive expletive expletive deleted]" [insert musical note]
> SAVE vs DEATH: SAVED—healed and flashed by Beur ("I'll take it.")

"The Barely Cursed Bazaar of Commerce": Janet Varney as Sedona, Proprietor and Prisoner of a Magical Grab-Bag Store

> RPG exp: "I really don't know anything about it at all other than that those all [polyhedral die] look like things I would have put in my mouth when I was a baby . . . and might still."
>
> Race: Doppelganger/Dwarf
> Class: Monster/Sorcerer
> Primary attribute: oddly helpful salesmanship—for a monster
> Friend or foe? friend/foe
> DQ: "Let me tell you about the ouroboros of the bag you just selected. If you open up that teddy bear's stomach, you'll see there's a roll of infinite toilet paper in there. Now, you shit yourself because you opened the bag, but now you can wipe your ass. Makes you think, doesn't it?"
> SAVE vs DEATH: DEATH/SAVE

"The City of Forlona": Jason Mantzoukas as Gribble Grabble and Grabble Gribble, Street Urchin and Royal Assassin

RPG exp: "Truly, zero point zero; never played in my life. So I am thrilled to win today!"

Race: Gnome

Class: Assassin

Primary attribute: self-advancement

Friend or foe? uneasy ally

DQ: "I am the point from which 'aside' is based."

SAVE vs DEATH: SAVE (King me!)

"The Keystone Obelisk": Elizabeth Olsen as Stirrup, aka ~~Scarlet Witch~~ Prisoner 84

RPG exp: "My familiarity is the first season of *HarmonQuest* and *Stranger Things*."

Race: Half-elf

Class: Arsonist

Primary attribute: bombs

Friend or foe? friend-by-command-of-king

DQ: "It says 'Half-elf' so I didn't know if that was referring to my size, like a mini?"

SAVE vs DEATH: SAVE . . . and the terrorist walks off to blow up more stuff.

"The Castle of Etylai": Rob Corddry as Sandy, Beur's Buff Former Hookup

RPG exp: "D&D was huge but nobody was a good Dungeon Master in my town so all we did was roll for characters and create characters and then draw them."

Race: Human

Class: Barbarian

Primary attribute: muscles

Friend or foe? friend with benefits

DQ: "I'm chock full of diplomacy."

SAVE vs DEATH: SAVE/DEATH (drawn dead alongside Fondue at beginning of next episode)

Season 3

"The Shattered Myriad": Kate Micucci as Hermie, aka Guardian of Hope, Watcher of the Demon Seal, Shepherd of the Beast of the Beginning

> RPG exp: "So I think I kind of maybe know what I'm doing? Actually, no, I have no idea what I'm doing. But I'm excited."
> Race: Elf
> Class: Druid
> Primary attribute: pudding-pop powered innuendo
> Friend or Foe? NSFW friend
> DQ: "Well, you know what? I can also shapeshift so anything is possible."
> SAVE vs DEATH: SAVE ("sleeping" on a throne)

"Ivory Quay": Tawny Newsome as Donna, aka "D-Town," Barbarian Bud of Beur and Limerick

> RPG exp: "I used to play a lot in high school . . . and I feel like I just removed all that information and put, like, how to do taxes in my brain."
> Race: Human
> Class: Barbarian
> Primary attribute: "She's fucking Donna, that's how!"
> Friend or foe? BFF! [insert heart emoji]
> DQ: "I'm so glad I dodged an . . . arrow . . . with that."
> SAVE vs DEATH: SAVE albeit splintered off in time and space

"Goblopolis Found": Reggie Watts as Gräldokt, Quinzelflip, and Goblin#3 . . . Let's Call Him "Shemp"

> RPG exp: "When I was a kid, I was big fan of the cartoon, *Dungeons & Dragons* . . . and burnt magical scrolls."
> Race: Goblin/Goblin/Goblin
> Class: Guard/Guard/Guard
> Primary attribute: agreeableness
> Friend or foe? ally
> DQ: "Sorry, I was just eating."
> SAVE vs DEATH: SAVE/SAVE/SAVE

"Terra Scissus": Joel Kim Booster as Toriamos (No Last Name), Leather-Mesh-Clad Spelunker

RPG exp: "Not allowed to play Dungeons & Dragons because it was sort of the gateway to Satanism but still turned out gay."

Race: Dwarf

Class: Explorer

Primary attribute: throwing shade

Friend or foe? friendly

DQ: "Dungeons are my game. I'm big into dungeons. I know all the hottest dungeons."

SAVE vs DEATH: SAVE (left waving in the distance)

"Shatternine Village": Jared Logan as Dave Pendergast aka "Mr. Donkey Dave"

RPG exp: "All the experience! I myself am a GameMaster! And I'll be sure to let you guys know if you're doing anything wrong."

Race: Human

Class: Paladin

Primary attribute: mission focus

Friend or foe? friendly in that all-paladins-are-friendly way

DQ: "There's only one thing to do: handcuff me to something!"

SAVE vs DEATH: SAVE albeit horrified by the suggested incest

"The Bloody Teeth": D'Arcy Carden as Hydronai Sesapoia, Over-Eager Adventurer

RPG exp: "Have I literally ever played this before? No."

Race: Gnome

Class: Bard

Primary attribute: Mommy and Daddy issues

Friend or foe? way-too-friendly-for-family

DQ: "Daddy, if I throw my bag of nets over him, do you want to beat his ass?"

SAVE vs DEATH: SAVE (sans a leg)

"Ad Quod Damnum": Jessica Mckenna as Flairence Sparrow, Multiversal Public Defender

RPG exp: "Very, very minimal. I've like, I played two times and both, you know, sort of as a show. I've never played for fun. Yeah, I've never sat around and played. Although it checks a lot of boxes of things I'd be interested in."

Race: Humanoid

Class: Defender

Primary attribute: "judge's pet"

Friend or foe? court-appointed friend

DQ: "I say, if there's not room for shades of grey in a multiverse, where, where can we find the subtlety and nuance to understand that not every being comes with the same understanding of our wonderful laws. Perhaps they were just three dumb-dumbs who didn't realize they were breaking the course of time for all time, and should we punish them for their ignorance or should we instead look at ourselves and say how did we allow the system to create such ignorant beings?"

SAVE vs DEATH: DEATH . . . eventually (currently mortal)

"The Starshade Expanse": Carl Tart as Tampa Bay the Buccaneer, Captain of the Carolina Panther

RPG exp: "Absolutely the hell not."

Race: Human

Class: Astral Privateer

Primary attribute: rope pizza

Friend or foe? friend

DQ: "People say the best pizza is in New York, but no! The best pizza is in the astral plane."

SAVE vs DEATH: DEATH ("Tell Sheryl I'm at Karen's house.")

"The Virtuous Harmony": Tom Kenny as Legnockra Capering Maître d' to Novitrov

RPG exp: "I was always kinda adjacent to it, but . . . gettin' laid was hard enough for me in high school so I didn't want to put that speed bump in front of myself."

Race: Angel

Class: Inquisitor
Primary attribute: gettin' thrown, hard
Friend or foe? friend
DQ: "I have a war club and a hav-ah-leena . . . no . . . a javelin."
SAVE vs DEATH: SAVE, still prancing!

The Expanded Universe: Extending the Run Time

"Ten Things I Learned from the Expanded Universe"

- A "large man-sized door" is, in fact, just a door.
- Britta goes to the Good Place.
- An Orc penis has an ear!?
- DON'T EAT THE CRUNCH-EEZ!
- "I Robert Crumb him" is a very *specific* fetish.
- Hidden toilets are full of gold and marijuana.
- A party is a stationary parade.
- You can get experience from flashbacks.
- There's always a portal behind the clock.
- *HarmonQuest* leads the league in critical fails

Library Science 201– Intermediate Wikipedia and Great Minds with Dan Harmon

14

> *Would you mind going through your Wikipedia entry with us to make corrections?*
>
> —DAN HARMON TO LUDWIG VAN BEETHOVEN, *GREAT MINDS*

IMMEDIATELY FOLLOWING HIS DEPARTURE from *Community* in 2016 and concurrent with their joint *HarmonQuest* web series and *Harmontown* broadcasts, Dan Harmon teamed up with tech-nerd foundling Spencer Crittenden to create yet another genre-bending show: *Great Minds with Dan Harmon*, a short-lived series of video shorts for the History Channel's "Night Class" block of programming. It was an unusual project, with the History Channel taking a chance on Harmon and his *Community* college clout (?); the result was an intentionally low-budget, largely improvisational, and utterly self-indulgent time-warp into the lives of famous historical figures . . . and Harmon's Daddy issues.

"Night Class" included somewhat more traditional offerings such as *Crossroads of History* (a scripted examination of "largely unknown moments in history") and *How to Lose the Presidency* (a political clip show). In *Great Minds*—one-season of fifteen roughly ten-minute episodes—Harmon and Crittenden revived (for a limited time only!) randomly selected historical figures: from Beethoven and Shakespeare to Ada Lovelace and Idi Amin. Guests actors were largely B-list celebrities, many of whom happened to be shooting episodes of *HarmonQuest* as well, which likely saved on cab fare and appearance fees. As a result, familiar role-playing faces like those of Aubrey Plaza (as Mary Wollstonecraft, a "hot Mrs. Butterworth's") and Thomas Middleditch (as diss-master William Shakespeare) as well as other

Harmon-adjacent celebs like Sarah Silverman (as a topless Betsy Ross) and Danny Pudi (as Siddhartha Gautama, consummate huckster), pop in to cop vague historical accents before disappearing in puffs of corporeal dust.

While the show capitalizes upon some fairly well-worn gags, as was typical of *Community*, those tropes are usually subverted or tweaked in some way that makes them Harmon-ious. Spencer, for example, is an unflappable "beleaguered assistant" ("unbeleaguered"?). By the end of the series a variety of figures—aware of their impending doom—face death in a variety of defiantly un-tragic ways. There are also running gags peppered throughout, particularly fourth-wall breaks, pixelated nudity, temporal taglines, slide-whistle punctuation, contemporary political commentary, and Harmon-as-Harmon self-awareness especially regarding the show's ill-fit on the History Channel and its inevitable cancelation if he and Spencer don't meet certain diversity standards.

The series generally plays with and against Harmon's eight-step story circle narrative formula despite Dan's overt (and metatheatrical) attempts at shoehorning in a lesson to justify a narrative arc. To that end, every episode starts with "what Dan wants" and ends with "what Dan gets" . . . and seldom the twain do meet. If one were to cram every episode of *Great Minds* into the story circle format, the cycle might look something like this:

1. Dan is Dan.
2. Dan wants something.
3. Spencer (the techno-wizard) provides Dan a "rando" from history.
4. Dan reluctantly and half-heartedly adapts.
5. Dan verbally twists what he got into what he wanted.
6. A minimal price is paid.
7. Dusted!
8. Dan is Dan (lip-service change articulated via linguistic coda).

On the whole the series was a fun, mildly head-scratching version of "History 101" that, unsurprisingly, didn't really fit within the History Channel's programming circa 2016 (before they gave up on the whole history thing and went all in on *Swamp People* and *Ancient Aliens*). But if we try to justify the show as a community college pedagogical tool, the best one might say is that *Great Minds* teaches History Channel viewers that historical figures don't offer neat little lessons as much as we may want them to.

The series begins by establishing our main characters, Harmon and Crittenden, who play Dan and Spencer as essentially their real-life selves only with access to more powerful time-bending equipment than was likely available on *Community*'s Paramount Studios lot. Dan is a self-proclaimed genius who needs to deliver a show for "Corporate," and Spencer is a STEM-polymath who deadpan delivers technobabble and reconstituted bodies. The show is intentionally low-budget, generally opening each episode in a plastic-tarp-enclosed industrial basement below the Eetza Gooda Show Studios complete with retro computers, *Flash Gordon*–style tech, and an underlit circular platform upon which historical figures materialize. As Spencer explains in fine *Star Trek* fashion, he "invented a biological matrix capable of taking temporal data from personality figures throughout history and infusing them in a simulacrum of historical figures." (For those junior scientists taking notes at home, a green "biological puck made of stem cells and lard" is also involved!)

After the historical-guest-of-the-week is materialized and identified in the basement, the post-commercial scene usually cuts to Dan's office, where he interviews the hastily costumed visitor while fact-checking their Wikipedia entries. Events typically go sideways from there, and nearby, on-location vignettes follow (at local bars, abandoned lots, improv theaters). Most episodes end up back in the lab, where Dan and Spencer wrap things up and place a hand-labeled jar containing the dusted remains of their latest ~~victim~~ guest on a mantle alongside those of previous time-travelers (including some who never made screen time).

Episode 1: "Ludwig van Beethoven"

Despite Dan's desire to pull "Wolfgang Ama-fucking-deus" Mozart in from the past in this first episode, what they get is Ludwig van Beethoven (Jack Black), which prompts the impossibly-hard-to-please Dan to shout, "No!!! *Bill and Ted's* did Beethoven: now we look like a bunch of hacks!" After they calm down the panicky and naked Beethoven (Spencer maces him), the show cuts to credits and then to Dan's office, where the interview process begins.

Beethoven (who, as Wikipedia notes, was deaf in his twenties) then hears, for the first time, his own music played on the computer and is suitably freaked out. Dan is subsequently elated—and then deflated—when Beethoven tells him his *Symphony no. 5 in C Minor* had lyrics: "Poop in your buuuuutt. Poop in your peeee. Poop in zhe sky poop in zhe sea . . ." Dan deadstares his disappointment directly into the camera then drives Beethoven to a local German bar (The Red Lion) for some piano, sausages, and conversation. Fun facts: Beethoven is pro-choice, and the locals love his poop lyrics.

History Exclusive!

While the show has been difficult to locate over the years, during the writing of this book it was available via Alexander Street and Pro-Quest. We whole-heartedly recommend viewing the episodes with the transcript running, which is a joy to behold. If the transcription was not intentionally mis-recorded, the 'bot responsible should have its own show.

After some crooning, Beethoven begins to experience—as Spencer informs Dan on the phone— "a total protoplasmic disconversion" so Dan whisks him back to the Eetza Gooda basement. After some sad bedside duetting ("poop in your butt . . ."), Beethoven "disparates" in a cheap CGI smoke poof.

Dan tries to wrap things up with a typical History Channel end-tag while behind him Spencer hand-vacs the remains of Beethoven before depositing the dust in a hand-labeled jar. Beethoven (like other visitors throughout the series) is tagged at the end of the episode with two sets of

Dan Harmon takes Ludwig van Beethoven out for beers, as one does. AUTHOR'S COLLECTION.

birth/death dates: "1770–1827 and February 6, 2016 11:59 am–6:18 pm." Makes you think about the temporality of life, don't it?

Episode 2: "Ernest Hemingway"

Dan derides Spencer for the assortment of "randos" that he pulls from the timestream, stressing the importance of "diversity" in their show and his desire to interview Rosa Parks this week. What they get, however, is Ernest Hemingway (Scott Adsit). After a moment of disappointed ranting, Dan slowly realizes who apparated and practically swoons over his manly man writing idol.

Back in Dan's office, Hemingway and Dan shout, drink, and bond a bit, although Dan's attempts at linking Hemingway's biography with his own prompts "the H-Bomb" to state, "You seem to need to justify your existence to me," which might as well be the name of Dan's eventual biography. After having his meaningless "word vomit" criticized by Papa Doc, Dan suggests they play paintball only to have Hemingway dismiss that as an empty simulation of death (a *Community* self-insert dis?) and instead demands that they go fishing: "Fishing proves your manhood."

One short car ride later and the two sit, fishing rods in hand, in a small, motorless boat in a largish puddle in an abandoned lot. As Dan notes, "It's been a drought, recently. The planet's in a lot of trouble." Rather than fishing, the two simply drink while Dan unloads a lengthy confessional of self-shame and personal issues. The best Hemingway can say afterward is that the two have one shared experience: both have had a pen up their ass. So there's that.

After refusing to bait a hook with a live worm, Dan is attacked by Hemingway. Following a brief tussle, Hemingway is on the verge of crushing Dan's head with a rock when suddenly (and fortuitously!) his

---

History Exclusive!

For anyone interested in joining Dan for a virtual drink, try the "How many booze bottles on the wall?" drinking game! For every bottle espied during an episode, take a corresponding shot. For folks truly interested in seeing how long they can spell the words "great minds," try keeping up with Dan and Hemingway (or Dan and Shakespeare, or Dan and . . .).

time runs out and he starts to turn back into goo. Jumping back to the lab, Hemingway demands a gun so that he can (as in life) "decide how and when" he dies. Dan passionately refuses, but while Dan is distractedly pouring his hero one last drink, Hemingway grabs the gun and shoots himself in the face . . . with a paintball. A disappointed Hemingway then poofs out and his ashes are placed alongside the row of other jars, which now includes—in addition to those seen last episode—a jar labeled "Warhol."

Dan berates Spencer one last time for not getting him Rosa Parks, and the show ends as it opened: seeking diversity.

Episode 3: "Thomas Edison"

Still prioritizing (in theory) the diversity issue, Spencer has been trying to snag George Washington Carver, whom Dan calls the "vanilla of black history." When they realize they have instead manifested Thomas Edison (Jason Sudekis), Spencer shakes his head in disgust and walks out. Dan, on the other hand, swallows his disappointment and, billing Edison as "the white George Washington Carver," intros the show.

Edison proves to be a bit of a tool, claiming to have invented "pretty much everything" including "the Scheisse film" (look it up, kids!). After listening to his first recording of "Mary Had a Little Lamb," the perfectionist Edison demands the opportunity to re-record "this garbage." Dan takes him to the recording studio in a Tesla. It's at this point the viewer realizes Edison is perhaps the only person on the planet more insecure than Dan.

Cut to the recording studio, where Edison spends three-and-a-half hours (of his remaining six hours on Earth) re-recording, then singing, then performing, scatting, remixing, and then—after popping a handful of Dan's ADHD pills—manically playing various instruments before unspooling an obscene rap ("My first record was the first fucking record what's up / I'm the source of the light you use to see / Everyone on the grid comes back to me") that sound suspiciously similar to the ones his host made a staple of on *Harmontown*.

Though Dan is thrilled, Edison is less enthused and wants to start over and bring in a new sound provided by his latest invention: a duct-tape and red-Solo-cup electric saxophone. He plugs it in, prepares to blow, and is subsequently electrocuted.

Ah, irony.

Dan closes the episode by overtly linking Edison's "control-obsessed spiral down the drain of perfectionism" to his own. Yet despite a perfunctory claim to change his ways, he's back to micromanaging Spencer within a beat. Circle complete?

Episode 4: "Mary Wollstonecraft"

We open on Dan hitting on "Courtney the Balloongram Girl" (Maria Thayer) because, foreshadowing. After Spencer takes off for his unwanted birthday party, Dan—pretending to know what he's doing in the lab to impress the girl—accidentally activates the time machine. Mary Wollstonecraft (Aubrey Plaza) appears, naked and unashamed. Courtney proclaims, "She's a feminist!" establishing not only the day's theme but TV–Dan's ignorance of feminist icons (*his* wish-list of feminist guest stars includes "Alan Alda; Brad Pitt's wife; and those Venus girls who play tennis").

Reluctantly abandoning his chance to hit on Courtney, Dan announces the episode and we cut to his office for the Wikipedia portion. This gives Dan a chance to trot out bad feminist ideas (false equivalents and elementary biology) only to be schooled by the aloof Wollstonecraft. Dan finds this arousing and—under his breath—calls her a "hot Mrs. Butterworth."

Chastising him for his mumbling, Wollstonecraft makes Dan confess to the camera that he is "a self-loathing beta male." After that awkward bit of fourth-wall Dan-izing, he is astounded to discover Wollstonecraft was Mary Shelley's mother and that she wrote a bunch of stuff herself. Despite his enthusiasm, she turns down his request to show her the modern world where "we can have fun together." Dan goes all confessional booth and—while struggling to self-identify as a feminist interested in a disinterested "hottie" feminist who "looks like Winona Rider, dresses like a corpse, and talks like Spock"—decides to "neg" her. It doesn't work.

After getting talked down from the irrational love-ledge by Spencer (irony!), Dan returns to Wollstonecraft bearing bubble wrap. She is quietly delighted by this astounding invention. He then fills her in on modern feminism and current events (not for the last time does the show reference a presumed Hillary Clinton / Bernie Sanders administration), crediting each small gain women have experienced to her. She departs but not before answering Dan's final profound feminist query: "Does it hurt when women get kicked in the crotch?" (Answer: "Yes. Badly.")

As Spencer tries to vacuum up "most of your girlfriend" ("Friend. Equal."), Dan rhetorically asks if he himself has "transcended the status quo gender barriers." (Answer: No.)

Episode 5: "William Shakespeare"

Episode 5 starts off without much preamble before a delighted Dan (pulled unexpectedly from his shower) gets to announce, "Tonight, the greatest writer in the history of the English Language meets William Shakespeare . . . on *Great Minds!*" And so, in no unsubtle way, begins the battle of writerly egos.

In the office, Shakespeare (Thomas Middleditch) interrupts Dan's Wikipedia-ing to riff on the word "lap-top." "The lap o'erlaps the top of our belts when with foodstuffs we o'erstuff ourselves." Dan is impressed then rattles off the many coinages Shakespeare has been credited with, including "eyeballs," which the playwright explains thusly: "I have often said that the face is the scrotum of the head, and the eyes the balls therein." Fangirling and a bit nervous, Dan admits to being a writer as well and screens a "*Community* Season 1 classic" for Will, who is utterly unimpressed . . . save for Chevy: "The older gentleman is a rare find." Closing the laptop prematurely, Shakespeare offers Dan noncommittal lauds: "Neat. Neat," and "Hey, it looked like you had a ton of fun doing it."

Trying to bolster Shakespeare's opinion of *Community* ("It's good because it's unsuccessful?"), Dan takes Shakespeare to a theater to see the low-fare comedy, *Dirty Grandpa*. Shakespeare ends up loving it.

Disappointed, Dan takes his guest and rival to a bar (Tinhorn Flats) to drink PBR and complain about Shakespeare's plays. The Bard is having none of it so the two engage in an old-fashioned *flyting* contest (essentially pre-modern England's version of a rap battle), hurling insulting zingers at one another while the denizens of the country bar egg them on.

However, just as Shakespeare is winning the crowd over and calling for Dan to dive headfirst into a leper's latrine, the Elizabethan notices his hand covered in "strange celestial semen": he's poofed.

History Exclusive!

While the audience doesn't see the episode screened on Dan's laptop, we (and Will) do hear a bit—all of which is Harmon dubbing lines in poor mimicry of the *Community* actors. The dialog is riffed, although perhaps this lost "Star Wars Picnic" episode of *Community* will find a second life on VHS someday. Six Seasons and a Movie *and* a Christmas Special?

Scooping up Shakespeare's ashes in a convenient ashtray, Dan heads back to the lab where he egoistically says to Spencer, "Shakespeare and I were too similar." When Spencer quotes a bit of *Henry IV* back at him, Dan realizes—via flashback montage—that Spencer is, indeed, no rhesus monkey.

Episode 6: "Idi Amin"

Episode 6 opens with Dan bribing Spencer with a comic book to "conjure me some diversity." Spencer does, indeed, conjure "a simulacrum of color" in the form of General Idi Amin (Ron Funches), the Butcher of Uganda, or as Dan calls him, an "African African-American." Despite Spencer's concern (which Dan labels as racist) and thanks to Dan's historical idiocy—and blinding delight over a diversity "get"—this episode focuses on "history's new sweetheart: Mr. Idi Amin." It rapidly goes downhill.

As usual, Dan tries to bond with his guest-star without first knowing much about them. When he discovers Idi Amin was a general, Dan suggests that his role as producer is like being a general "surrounded by a confederacy of dunces." The two laugh it up until Dan actually looks at Amin's Wikipedia entry. After cowing Dan into adding a few things to the entry—"Idi Amin: nice guy, handsome, inventor of ultimate Frisbee"— Amin drops the nice dictator act, threatens Dan's cats, and takes over the office.

Attempting to escape to the parking lot, Dan runs into Spencer and a now-armed Amin who is "feasting" on snack foods before attacking the Sizzler across the street (for mocking him with their "summer shrimp 'stravaganza and endless salad bar!"). Somehow Dan bonds with Idi about their Daddy issues and even calls his own father on the phone. Amin then proceeds to chat with Mr. Harmon on speakerphone ("I love to hear older white men talk about politics") for the remainder of his time on Earth, ironically penciling in plans to visit for Christmas.

Dan wraps "our diversity episode" by arguing that—at heart—we're all the same, and that "even if you're a hate-filled, power-mad, sociopathic dictator, all you need is a little bit of a support system and you could be . . . a Republican." It's an end-gag that might have landed better in 2016. It is also hard not to notice that the one "African African-American" figure the show pulls is the most evil human to appear in the entire run.

But at least Amin's appearance alleviates Dan's "liberal guilt" for a few episodes (as he intentionally mis-states in his closer) ~~White~~ *Great Minds with Dan Harmon.*

Episode 7: "Betsy Ross"

Episode 7 opens with a runner also employed repeatedly on *HarmonQuest*: public domain music. Spencer has proactively "syphoned off some of the Y-chromosome" from their protoplasmic goo "to increase our chances of getting a woman." It works! They incarnate Betsy Ross (Sarah Silverman, working with Harmon for the first time since popping up in 2014's *Harmontown* documentary), an unabashed, boob-baring, no-nonsense politico. Or as Dan spins it, the "Princess Leia of the actual rebellion, the April O'Neil of the Teenage Mutant Ninja Founding Fathers."

If previous episodes of *Great Minds* mentioned the then-current U.S. political landscape with somewhat general references to Clinton and Trump rallies, this episode focuses squarely on the 2016 Democratic primaries and finds Betsy Ross working for the Bernie Sanders campaign.

Dan—who, for a change, is up on Ross as a famous figure without Googling her—is taken aback when she says her most famous patriotic act, creating the American flag, was "a job; that was a money gig." Of course his concern is more for how that admission doesn't make this "a really good episode for me" rather than its impact on history. But by this point in the series the viewer is aware of the irony in the show's name.

They pivot to the Wikipedia beat, get a few details clarified, then turn to the whole flag thing. Ross admits that she had other pitches for the flag, which prompts Dan to get her sewing materials so she can recreate her earlier attempts. A History Channel exclusive! None are, to put it mildly, family friendly, though the one with a red hand giving the finger to a gold crown has a certain patriotic zest.

Talk turns to modern politics, allowing Ross to make digs at Ted Cruz ("He's got one of those rare vagina noses") and Hillary Clinton ("Whoa! That guy looks like a woman!") before settling on the closest thing to a "revolutionary" Dan can find: the underdog Bernie Sanders ("a socialist and, uh, an upholsterer"). Ross wants to support Sanders so they schlep

---

History Exclusive!

Dan follows his open with a direct address to viewers, who can Tweet their own Betsy Ross analogies to @GreatMindsAlts#BetsyRossIsTheBlankOfBlank. To the best of our knowledge, that there link is done broke.

over to the "Eastside Bernie Sanders" campaign headquarters where they get Ross to film some public endorsements. Things do not go well as her ad-libs—"I'm Betsy Ross and Bernie Sanders is a Jew!"; "He is guaranteed to settle the Red Indian problem"; "Fuck the British"; "I'm Betsy Ross and make no flags about it!"—all fall flat.

Having retreated to the bathroom in shame and constipation, Ross sews Bernie a flag: orange spectacles and red American flags forming stripes on a white background with a blue square upper left broken by Sanders's white hair. Impressed, Dan gives a long, rambling, *Revenge of the Nerds*-worthy speech about America as "the hotel lobby for idiots, schmucks, spazzes, and slobs." He also rants about "the end of tyrants and rich people and assholes that host reality shows." It's all somewhat quaint "we're not quite screwed yet, are we?" liberal anger, in retrospect.

Anyway, Ross rallies. She and Dan head out to let her "decidedly non-freak flag fly" for her final hours. They walk the streets with her new "Feel the Bern" flag until she disintegrates just as she's about to say something profound. "Oh, razzberries!"

Episode 8: "Amelia Earhart"

The episode begins with Spencer's dream of adding "genetic tinkering" (biosensors, geo-tracking, human crab claws!) to the time-travel mix only to be shot down by Dan who suggests that "following your dreams is stupid." They then pull in an exceedingly peppy Amelia Earhart (Kristen Schaal) who will put that claim to the test. In addition to pep, Earhart is also full of old-timey jargon slang: "Flippety flappety, jim-jam, Barceloni hoity toity, big-ass baloney!" Happily, Dan sees Earhart as proof of his philosophy so he excitedly introduces her as "the missing mistress of history's mysteries," and the show cuts to opening credits.

Back in the office, Dan and a fully bedecked Earhart (aviator goggles, leather jacket, khaki slacks, Schindler boots) banter. We learn her real name is Jessica Walker and that she wouldn't mind seeing Mrs. Lindbergh undressed. After discovering she is "most famous for getting lost," she resolves to be "the first woman to find Amelia Earhart!" Since she theoretically *may* still be alive, she says, all she needs to do is tell her (current) younger self to tell her older self to meet her this afternoon . . . and not be late. Honestly, given the core concept of this show and Dan's relentlessly time-trippy narratives in *Rick and Morty*, it's a wonder this is the first time a simulacrum has played with the time slip.

Dan nevertheless forbids Earhart from following her dreams, but to no avail. She exits, having stolen Dan's car keys, and speeds off to find herself. We then get the most meta commentary of the series so far.

Dan: Spencer, Amelia Earhart took off and nobody knows where she is!

Spencer: Well, that seems like a fitting end to our episode.

Fortunately (and despite Dan's earlier prohibition), Spencer had implanted a geo-tracker in Earhart's nineteenth chromosome. A surprisingly supportive Dan finds Earhart alone on a bench still awaiting her older self. Soon, however, an older—possibly Schaal-shaped—elderly woman waves from across a field. Neither Earhart nor Dan seem surprised, and Dan even adds that perhaps "that's your contribution to history, Amelia Earhart: you make crazy shit seem normal." Earhart walks off to join her older self. Dan smugly says to the camera, "And that is a beautiful ending to a perfect story, courtesy of some guy smart enough to hire an old lady from central casting."

But wait! There's more!

Spencer arrives with the "real" old lady from central casting, and by the time Dan looks to where the two Earharts had been, they're gone. Only the sound of a prop plane flying overhead remains: "No bodies, no piles of dust, no old ladies." Awww.

Back in the lab, Dan hands Spencer an empty jar labeled "Amelia Earhart," and—for a moment at least—endorses the following of one's dreams, à la Earhart. But when Spencer suggests Dan has really "turned a 180 on that position," Dan confuses the obvious story circle resolution with some gibberish about being "a 180 position that dreamed of being a man and now the man has awoken." The textbook resolution is further debunked when Dan tries to call *Pawn Stars* to challenge them (his dream), only to have called the wrong number. Awww . . .

Episode 9: "Sigmund Freud"

While previous episodes have suggested Corporate wants Spencer to humanize himself somehow, Episode 9 finds Dan trying to force Spencer to memorize "catchy phrases" (not "catch phrases"!). When Spencer refuses, Dan treats him like a lackey ("a piece of equipment like everything else here that I own") then angrily walks out. This leaves the laconic Spencer in charge of not just the time-travel mechanics but also the interview with Sigmund Freud (Nick Kroll), who predictably seems keen to chat.

Following the title card (which now reads "GREAT MINDS with Spencer Crittenden") we cut to Spencer's impromptu therapy session in Dan's office. Freud (copping a heavy German-Austrian accent) simultaneously psychoanalyzes Spencer and runs his own interview. Spencer is brutally honest and unfiltered ("I like butt stuff, you know, like porn, anal porn") but also clueless. When Freud finds that Spencer's mom used anal suppositories on him, it seems to be "the most open and closed shut case I've ever heard" but Spencer can't grasp the connection. Freud throws repeated fourth-wall breaks to the camera in wry exasperation. It's a fun bit.

Freud then suggests that they deal with Spencer's "fazzer" issues, where—in this scenario—Dan is ze fazzer . . . er, father. Spencer doesn't really care, until a co-worker (Steven Levy) interrupts to tell them that Dan is pulling the plug on *Great Minds* and intends to use Spencer's time machine "to do a show where he brings back historical puppies for Animal Planet." That is, of course, the last straw: "Your fazzer has stolen your phallus, aka ze time machine . . . Maybe it's time that we go kill your fazzer." Only on History!

Confronting a snoozing Dan, Freud announces, "We're here to kill you. Metaphorically." The "metaphorically" part seems to disappoint Spencer, earning a slow-take from Freud. We then cut to a couples therapy session where—after some Hitler riffs—Freud opines that Dan wants Spencer to reprimand him for an earlier metaphorical castration. Then the show gets into the butt stuff in earnest, with Freud revealing an extreme anal fetish involving turkey metaphors and cranberry tins. As Dan grows increasingly dubious of Freud's methodology, Freud suggests that—to take their session to a next-level breakthrough—Dan inserts a cigar into his, well, you can guess. Dan sums up what most Psych 101 students realize about Freud after a semester: "You're like famous for sanity and you're nuts!"

Even so, Dan confesses that he "deserves to be punished by a smarter guy" and was hurt when Spencer rebelled. So, yay Freud?

Realizing Freud only has so much time left before disintegration, Dan asks what he would like to do with his remaining moments on Earth. Freud's request is predictably and floridly scatological. Dan takes notes. Freud poofs mid-request, unfulfilled

After the poof, Dan and Spencer tag-team the outro, and Spencer even utters one of Dan's proposed catchy phrases: "Sazzle frazzle, time trazzle." Moved, Dan signs off saying, "This has been *Great Friends*." Awww . . . sweet.

Episode 10: "Edgar Allan Poe"

Conflict! The guy at the History Channel who green-lit *Great Minds* has been replaced by Charlotte Gray, "the Headless Horseman of TrueTV"! So despite the last episode's happy handholding, we are immediately back to what Dan wants. This week he does not care about diversity or gender equality or any of "that other shit." He just wants "entertainment." So naturally what he gets is Edgar Allan Poe (Paul F. Tompkins). Conflict, I say!

Back in the office, Dan tries to sell Poe as "his Eminence of Emo, the Sultan of Sad Sack" but "Mr. Ooky-Spooky" remains slumped in his chair, a lethargic, deadpan Debbie Downer. Dan tries to spin various factoids into funtoids and even gives Poe a dollar ("All the money in the world!"). But it's to no avail. This guy is killing Dan's chances at an entertaining show.

Enter Charlotte Gray (Mary Lynn Rajskub), who subtly snubs Dan but breathlessly fawns over Poe, "You're my hero. *The Masque of the Red Death* got me through puberty!" Dan's eyes pop and he starts selling Poe as a show regular ("He's our Kramer!"). A dinner meet-cute is arranged between Gray and Poe, or as Dan crudely tells the camera, Poe is going to "work off that dollar *Entourage*-style" so that they can "smash puss and stay famous." After a short break for commercials, of course.

Soon enough, Dan leans into the Cyrano trope. Poe wears an earpiece in the restaurant while Dan (in a nearby van with Spencer) feeds him talking points designed to get *Great Minds* a half-hour slot every Thursday for thirteen weeks. Gray misinterprets Poe's drunkenly relayed message ("Would you grant me six and a half hours Thursday evening?") as an offer of tantric sex, which she definitely seems into. Poe also fumbles Dan's urgent pleas to get a verbal contract from Gray, who has already planned to cancel the show.

When "a bit too horny" Gray leaves the table for a moment to "use the Dyson hand dryer" in the bathroom, Dan enters the restaurant to "fucking murder" that "drunk bipolar magician with pale skin and an overwrought style." But he is too late: Poe's time has run out and all that's left is a small pile of ash and an empty wine glass. When Gray angrily returns demanding to know where Edgar is, Spencer casually (and uncharacteristically) responds that he's gone to Eugene, Oregon, to escape the artifice of Hollywood and that she shouldn't follow him "unless you want to spend with him an eternity of gloom, not unlike two dwindling stars in a lightless void." She wants that! Exit Charlotte Gray.

Unusually, the final outro sees Dan and Spencer eating the moon-crossed couple's untouched food and teasing the runner for the next episode: product placement.

Episode 11: "Siddhartha Gautama"

The episode opens as Dan enters the lab carrying a milk crate full of "financial salvation." Or as Spencer grouses, "Product placement. Plugola. We're selling out." Of course, to sell out, they need a guest who can sell. Dan demands "a perfect pitch man from history. Give me a Mickey Mantle, the Red Baron, uh, Cassius Clay." What they get is—holy smokes!—the Buddha (Danny Pudi). Dan—who at this point is just rolling with the punches—declares their "five-star guest" is a great get, because "we're about to be reincarnated as a financially solvent enterprise."

In the office, Dan is decked out in Duke's Hard Cider swag, while the Buddha (sorry, "a Buddha") sits in saffron robes gazing happily into the camera. While running through Wikipedia with "the Buddhster," Dan offers the former prince a Duke's Hard Cider and references the Buddha's narrative as part of the Hero's Journey: "I'm sure that's where your story starts, right, time to cross the threshold?" Dan also attempts—repeatedly—to link the Buddha to pop-culture heroes like Neo and Constantine, before offering Buddha some narrative notes to punch up his own myth.

Thirsty, the Buddha then drinks some Duke's Hard Cider and—with very little prompting from Dan—proves to be a dab hand at shilling. As the Buddha says, "Well, it's not about me, it's about the product." Dan is flabbergasted. Cut to montage!

A quick list of the products pitched by the world's greatest reincarnated (again) ascetic include:

- "It's fizzy and refreshing: Duke's Hard Cider."
- "I know a thing or two about fulfillment. And when I need fulfilling, I turn to Tito's, the fulfilling chip."

History Exclusive!

In an episode devoted to product placement, it's little wonder that Dan tells an intern to get Wikipedia on the line: "They've been getting a free ride for twelve episodes. There is such a thing as Encarta." Is it possible that this casual aside in the eleventh aired episode reveals two lost episodes of *Great Minds*? Perhaps Encarta would know.

- "Achieve a higher plane—and a higher pretzel—with Papa's Pretzel Twists."
- "We're all energy, so why not drink energy? Purple Cyborg energy drink. It looks like a cow."

The Buddha keeps going, casually shilling a paperweight, two pens, Dan's desk phone, and cellophane tape. Dan feels guilty but after a lengthy conversation regarding life choices, they become two buddhas . . . just sitting. [insert dead air]

However—having come to peace with himself, having achieved a higher level (and having taken a shit)—Dan soon runs into the show's associate producer (Steven Levy) who announces that SoulSuck Interactive want the Buddha to endorse their latest game, *Whore Smasher III*. While Dan is initially dismissive (what with his current "place of enlightenment" and all), when he's told the deal is "$5 million for the next two seasons," his eyes bulge. We are then suddenly on a couch, coaching the Buddha on how to digitally smash whores (press X). The Buddha seems iffy on basic game mechanics (he gifts a whore his car rather than smashing her), but Dan kits him out with a headset and thus connects him to "everyone in the world playing the game."

Spencer then pulls Dan aside to say what every viewer is thinking, "Look, I'm an atheist, I have no whores in this organized religion race, but even I can tell this is a new low for us." Spencer tells Dan that he has to "take moral responsibility for [his] moral and ethical decisions." Dan refuses, only to be interrupted by a call from SoulSuck Interactive telling him the Buddha—in the space of five minutes—has convinced twenty-five million fifteen-year-old boys playing their game to squat under virtual trees . . . and they've stopped smashing whores! In other words, Dan is back to being broke.

While recognizing the Buddha's way is the right way, Dan confesses what he really wanted isn't enlightenment but to "have a TV show [and] measure his life in dollars." Further, he recognizes (while lying on a couch in pseudo-therapy position) that even after finding temporary enlightenment, he is "still a racist, sexist, misogynist, flawed, terrible person"—to which the Buddha, smiling, responds, "Yeah, but it's your choice."

The Buddha then—despite having four hours left until disintegration—decides just to go, fading out suddenly: no dust, no goo, no nothing. Dan and Spencer then look to the TV set and see—"Dear God"—a pixelated Buddha sitting under a virtual tree within *Whore Smashers III*. All is peaceful in a *Twilight Zone*-y way until a speeding car smashes through the digitally dancing crowd behind the Buddha. We then see the producer (Levy) from earlier, angrily playing the game and smashing whores.

Ah, Corporate.

Episode 12: "John Wilkes Booth"

Dan enters the episode without giving Spencer "some demand about women or equality" or anything else for that matter. Instead, he suggests they've "been trying too hard" and that "tonight, it's all about going with the flow." Of course, putting the sand in the KY of Dan's plans tonight is none other than John Wilkes Booth (Andy Dick) . . . or as Dan deadpans to the camera without fanfare or feigned enthusiasm, "Tonight on *Great Minds*, this fuck head."

It initially seems that Booth—who keeps trying to bill himself as "Illustrious American Stage Actor"—is unaware of his "most important role of all," which is, as Dan grimly points out, "murdering our nation's greatest president," Abraham Lincoln—or as Booth calls him, "that old wart face." However, Booth does eventually cop to having done the deed and remains unapologetically remorseless.

A few "head shot" jokes later, Dan offers Booth a theatrical "comeback" performance as Lincoln!

As real-world Harmon has noted publicly, he inevitably and perhaps self-destructively pushes the envelope of what the bosses will allow in many projects, and *Great Minds* is no exception. Here Dan turns to the camera, deadpans a forcefully obscene outro, and caps it with "Only on History."

Cutting to the Upright Citizens Brigade ("the fanciest, most Southern theater in America"), they meet Matt Bessar (Matt Bessar), who helps Dan set up Booth to perform in *Our American President*. Despite Booth's reluctance to play Lincoln, the two butter him up and he takes the stage before a sad-looking afternoon theater crowd (extras and crew). Spencer arrives, and "Chekhov's Derringer" is brought into play (which Dan pockets). Booth nails the role despite zero prep time. Bessar leaps on stage (as Booth) and—with a cardboard prop gun—assassinates Lincoln.

After the applause dies down, Booth emotionally confesses to feeling Lincoln's pain, and Dan turns to the camera to underscore the lesson of the day: "You learned remorse." But no! Booth then reveals he had been only acting remorseful and that he'd "shoot that damn president over and over!" Angrily, Dan pulls out the derringer and shoots Booth, who melodramatically dies. Dan instantly regrets his rash act, confesses to being a murderer, and Booth—acting yet again, as the derringer held only blanks—gloats that "anyone can become a murderer if the right buttons are pushed." In the midst of Booth's triumph, he disintegrates. Cue lights, applause, exeunt bears.

Back in the lab, Dan sets Booth's ashes alongside the others' bodily detritus and tries to spin the day's adventure with a lesson on perspective: "one man's villain could be another man's hero." Spencer is having none of it, accusing Dan of being a murderer. End scene.

Episode 13: "Ada Lovelace"

The episode begins with a note from Corporate: viewers really like Spencer but don't believe he's real. As Dan says, "They love the Tin Man; they want to see him get his heart." Cue the week's time-guest: Ada Lovelace (Gillian Jacobs), "the Mother of Modern Computing" and *not* (as Dan assumes) Linda Lovelace, the Mother of Deep Throating. Dan immediately sees the potential to get what he and Corporate want and so he intros the episode by saying, "It looks like history and computers just had a meet-cute on a show that may as well be called *Great Hearts*." Lovelace eyerolls and we cut to credits.

Back in Dan's office, we find Lovelace (in a flowered Princess Leia headdress), Dan, and a somewhat reluctant Spencer. Dan tries to play matchmaker for ratings, making "strange advances" on Spencer's behalf as his "ultimate wing man." Awkward.

Eponym puns abound during their Wikipedia scroll (Adarhythm, Crapper, Benwa) before we learn that Lovelace was the daughter of Lord Byron, infamous Romantic poet and apparent Luddite. But Lovelace argues, "Technology could become art, that art could become technology." This rouses Spencer, who commandeers Dan's laptop and starts showing Lovelace various files and programs, including the "personality data file" Spencer used to recreate her. Dan eye-waggles as the two hit it off over their shared screen and programming passion. After Lovelace tweaks her own personality algorithm, the two depart for the lab to "go deeper." Dan giddily shills their pairing as appealing to the 18–35 demographic, declaring that "history and computers are really about sex and dating." As the lights flicker during an apparent power surge, Dan eye-waggles again.

Outside the basement lab, Dan works through a series of computer and sex puns while recapping the episode in his best mockumentary voice before breaking in on the "adorkable" couple, expecting to find "you guys being naughty." What he finds, however, is Spencer dematerializing the corporeal Ada and transferring her into the computer as code, where she monotones to them like a low-rez Max Headroom: "I can taste numbers. I can smell math." She urges Spencer to join her and "live forever as glorious code." Despite Dan's protests, Spencer seems into it, saying, "Your viewers wanted the Tin Man to get a heart, huh? Well, my heart is with Ada. My heart is code." With that, the most popular character on the show becomes ones and zeros, reappearing alongside Ada within their wood-paneled GE monitor.

The computerized couple then begin their real work: "Breaching Pentagon Secured Network." As clarions blare and Dan fumbles with the keyboard, code-Spencer begins the nuclear launch countdown. Dan—by trying to make Spencer more human—has destroyed the world! So much for Season 2, apparently. But suddenly a three-dimensional Spencer walks back on set, takes over the keyboard, and saves the day. Yay!

Dan—speaking for every viewer—demands that Spencer "explain this episode!" Apparently he made a clone of himself "that felt more stuff" since creating clones is "easier than changing" himself. (The combination of scientific wizardry and quasi-sociopathic amorality suggests Spencer is really a chip off the old Rick Sanchez block.) Dan understands. The two wander off for a round of drinks: the Tin Man and the Alcoholic, as unchanged as ever. Huzzah!

As they leave, the camera ominously slow zooms on the dead monitor, which reopens, revealing code-Ada intoning in her best HAL 9000 voice: "They put me in the recycling bin . . . But they forgot to empty . . . the recycling bin."

Episode 14: "John F. Kennedy"

Strap in, kids: if the previous episode got trippy, wait until you meet a Dan who knows his show has been canceled. Also, wait until you meet human-spider hybrid John F. Kennedy (Dana Carvey)! It's a weird one, and certainly a fair finale for a show that wore its "We don't fit on History Channel" identity as a badge of honor.

Despondent over the show's imminent cancelation, Dan unceremoniously pulls the lever: "Now we get JFK." Kennedy (in Carvey's thick New England accent) immediately criticizes the two for their trashed workspace and having "lost yah vigah." In his defense, Dan suggests that the show and America has "stopped giving a shit." Given 2016's politics, it's a fair commentary. As we fade to commercial and Kennedy works the camera crew, a CGI spider walks across the "stray genetic material" left over from Kennedy's incarnation. Someone call Jeff Goldblum!

Back in Dan's office, however, all is normal. Kennedy quips that "Wikipedia" is Boston slang for "Wicked Encyclopedia." When presented with the fact of his assassination, Kennedy accuses Joe DiMaggio and asserts Lee Harvey Oswald was CIA. Dan then unenthusiastically notes to the camera that "JFK has hinted that Oswald didn't act alone and he was in fact killed by an elaborate conspiracy. We'll be right back." It's the kind of interview Dan had wanted all season, but alas: timing.

Suddenly hearing "vermin" in the background (some sort of hissing sound?), the two discover crew bodies in the hallways wrapped in spider-silk cocoons. Spencer declares "Something . . . or someone . . . has come through the machine!" And that someone or something is Carvey as a Kennedy-headed giant spider in a low-rent costume straight from the Spirit Halloween store. In case this episode couldn't get any sillier, spider-Kennedy shouts, "Ich bin ein Spider!" before scuttling away.

Despite this unexpected threat, Dan and Kennedy still have time to argue the semantics of "confirmed." So even in this last episode, plus ça change, plus c'est la même chose, I suppose. After a commercial, we get a war room–style recap and techno-intel from Spencer that the "creature has half spider DNA and half JFK DNA." Unfortunately, as Kennedy realizes, that means it will head back to the lab, since "it's an Irish Catholic spider: the ultimate reproducing machine!"

Back in the lab—now Silly-stringed with spider webs—the trio are startled by the creature, who shouts "Spidery Kennedyisms" at them ("Ask not what your web can do for you"). Spider-Kennedy also threatens to kill Steve Levy if they touch his eggs. Spider-Kennedy's eggs, that is. Although it remains unclear if Steve Levy has eggs.

Anyhoo, since Dan is self-admittedly useless, Kennedy steps up to save the day, feigning friendship with the creature before pulling a screwdriver and stabbing his arachnid doppelganger in the back. Betrayed, Spider-Kennedy dies crying, "Marilyn! Marilyn!"

A victorious Kennedy then suggests that the three go "get some booze and bang some broads," but as Dan points out, Kennedy is "a simulacrum held together with a temporary energy field that is about to . . ." Poof! No more Kennedy.

Although perhaps the two Kennedys did teach everyone a lesson (or three) before dying. Dan wraps the series with a final forced coda: "We don't have to wait around for the show to be canceled or renewed. If you love something, like we love America, your job is to roll up your sleeves and pitch in. Make your country or your TV production the thing you want it to be. Act like it already is your dream and it will become that. Let's go get a drink."

However, the show only wraps officially after a final slow zoom past glowing spider eggs chanting "Ich bin ein . . ." before the camera settles on a cocooned Steve Levy, who sarcastically notes, "This has been a great season."

Episode 15 (sort of): "Harry S. Truman"

This not-really-the-last episode was slated to air just after the June 2016 Pulse nightclub shooting in Orlando, but as Harmon noted in a later Tweet, "We held its airing in the wake of the Orlando tragedy. Felt like wrong time, wrong clown."

The episode opens with Dan calling Spencer a bigot, explaining that their show has been nominated for a Frownie, the "upside-down rainbow frown, GLAAD's equivalent of the Razzie. It means we're cable TV's least gay-friendly show." Because of that setback, Dan's "want" this week is a "historical gay" (ideally, Michelangelo) to gain some rainbow cred. Instead he gets Harry S. Truman (Matt Walsh). Ever the desperate pitch-man, Dan eagerly spins this steam-room Democratic politician as a get: "Looks like we have *transitioned* into a very progressive episode of *Open Minds*." Cue title card, now with revamped disco music. It's all rather intentionally unsubtle.

In the office, Dan is "glad" (complete with air quotes) "to be back with, I think, history's most tolerant president, Harry S. Truman." While Truman seems a level-speaking fellow, his string of anti-Japanese slurs problematizes his previously hyped tolerance. In fact, the show's Truman seems utterly unconcerned with discrimination or hate since such concepts aren't practical. As he explains in his "labyrinthine Missouri logic," "never saw the point of hate. Can't buy it, can't put a bow on it, can't give it to your kids for Christmas." Not exactly a strong political stance, but he did integrate the military, so Dan lets him slide.

However, as is evidenced when he shockingly discovers that Liberace was a homosexual, what Truman doesn't "know about queers could fill a silo." And so Dan takes Truman "to enter the sizzling hot flaming gay world of equality" at "a fancy West Hollywood gay bar" (Oil Can Harry's). After the bump, Dan welcomes viewers to "*Great Minds* . . . or should I say *Gay Minds*?" and a slew of clueless gay tropes. The Village People are referenced. Dan makes meowing noises. It's awkward.

History Exclusive!

As freeze-frame analysis of the "dust shelf" reveals, the following "lost episodes" of *Great Minds* may exist, *in potentia*, somewhere in the Harmonverse: a Frenchman's Foot (?); The Missing Link; Dan's First Cat; Tituba; Warhol. Dan verbally confirms in various episodes that they've also incarnated a headless Ben Franklin (repeatedly) and Grover Cleveland. C'mon Harmon: that's practically a whole 'nother season of outtakes

---

Dan then introduces Truman to Brent Sullivan (Brent Sullivan), so the two can "talk gay." Truman, to his credit, is game, even if "when it comes to this gay stuff," he is "about as green as a July persimmon." The two engage in a civil discourse regarding gay rights circa 2016, which Dan feels is "a disaster: my gay episode is turning into C-Span." Trying to liven things up, Dan vamps in the background, a faux ally more distracting than helpful, which causes Truman and Sullivan to complain, "Knock off the horseplay! We're having a nice chat."

Of course Dan instead goes for "the nuclear option," and he's "dropping it from the Enola Super Gay"—which, to his credit, he realizesis a bad joke. But when a shirtless, blue-wigged, double boa–wrapped Dan gets on stage to announce *he* is gay, Sullivan (with Truman's encouragement to "tell that jackass to grow up") has to step away from their conversation to (1) tell Dan to knock it off, and (2) assure the needy Dan that he's a "super great ally." While eyeballing the camera, Dan lunges forward to kiss Sullivan, but is rebuffed. Sullivan leaves, Dan rants, the patrons leave, and we're left with a campy Dan on stage and a solitary, bespectacled, dead president standing alone in a gay bar. Somehow, in his short time in 2016, Truman has gained a fuller understanding of gay rights than the show's version of Dan. As Truman sums up before disintegrating, "They just want to live their lives and be free like everybody else. And if I was still in charge I'd fight for that right." Poof!

It's a fine and measured speech, and a generous portrayal of Truman. While it's fair to assume (as Dan does) that folks of prior generations might carry cultural biases, the episode points out that doesn't mean everyone in subsequent generations is naturally more enlightened. When Dan walks off in a huff, Spencer closes out this not-really-the-last episode with a hot take on his partner's ego: "This has been *Thin Skin*."

Animation and Joke-Telling 15
Seminar—Rick and Morty

I think a good TV show is one that lasts a thousand episodes.

—DAN HARMON ON *RICK AND MORTY*

ODDLY ENOUGH, some of the longest-running animated shows out there have a bajillion episodes in the can and a Staten Island garbage dump's worth of licensed merchandise to their credit but still came from humble origins. Consider *The Simpsons*. Before anybody could do the Bartman, the Simpsons were just some bright yellow, sketchily animated, oddly violent family who bickered between segments on *The Tracy Ullman Show*. As for *South Park*, its creators Trey Parker and Matt Stone honed their signature crude animation style with *Jesus vs. Santa*, a bloody showdown between two mythic figures that was commissioned by a Fox executive as a Christmas present for some friends but that quickly spread via viral VHS dubs (it was the 1990s, m'kay?).

All this is not to say that *Rick and Morty* is going to outlast *The Simpsons* or *South Park*, but it doesn't mean it won't, either. The show certainly has the "rags to riches" pedigree of its predecessors down pat. *Rick and Morty*'s origin story begins at Dan Harmon and Rob Schrab's Channel 101 festival in 2006 when Justin Roiland submitted a cartoon pilot called *The Real Animated Adventures of Doc and Mharti*. Conceived to troll the power of cease-and-desist letters from entertainment conglomerates, the poorly animated short took *Back to the Future*'s Doc Brown (lab coat, crazy hair, jacked-up DeLorean, gadgetry galore) and Marty McFly (nervous, anxious, vest) and added a layer of quasi-predatory obscenity just for the testicular gross-out of it all. Go ahead: Vimeo it. We'll wait.

Doc and Mharti never went anywhere. And they were likely never meant to. But their voices and basic concepts lived on in the not significantly tweaked characters of Rick Sanchez and Morty Smith, whose *Rick and Morty* would zap the post-post-9/11 zeitgeist in some very intriguing and disturbing ways.

In 2013, Harmon returned from his brief exile from network television to work on Season 5 of *Community*. But during the zombie interregnum known as Season 4 he was still working, and not just on his podcast. He and Roiland, who had also worked on two Harmon shows—*Acceptable. TV* and *The Sarah Silverman Program*—had been unable to get any of his previous animated pitches picked up, but somehow managed to turn Doc and Mharti into a slightly more palatable pair for fringe network TV. *Rick and Morty* debuted on Adult Swim in December 2013 and quickly became one of the most curiously buzzy shows, animated or not, around.

Rick and Morty is an avant-garde, science-fiction, family sitcom that endlessly throws the entire corpus of *Star Trek*, *Heavy Metal*, a few shelves' worth of bongwater-spattered space opera paperbacks, and some introductory guides to quantum theory, alternate dimensions, and moral philosophy into a blender and deliriously hits the Whatever button. Unlike Doc and Mahrti, once the half-hour sitcom got rolling, it bore little resemblance to the time-travel machinations of *Back to the Future* beyond the establishing concept of wild-card older scientist and exasperated younger sidekick. In Harmon and Roiland's version, the scientist is Rick Sanchez (voiced by

Morty, Rick, and some of the usual gagoos. ADULT SWIM/PHOTOFEST.

Roiland, craggy and stuttering but with less of a New Jersey thing to his voice than in the original Channel 101 version), a preternaturally brilliant but borderline megalomaniacal sociopath with a serious drinking problem—hence the belching and permanent splot of green vomit on his chin. He's also prone to amoral violence, like most granddads. Rick's sidekick is his grandson Morty (also voiced by Roiland, all squeaky teen angst and stammer), a "normal" kid stewing in perpetual flop sweat and misplaced aggression.

The first episode sets up the series' seemingly chaotic yet neatly calibrated template. Morty is woken up in the middle of the night by a falling-down-drunk Rick, who takes him on a ramble in his spacecraft which he made out of "stuff I found in the garage." After murmuring about rescuing Jessica, the high school girl Morty has a crush on, before blowing up the world with a neutrino bomb, Rick passes out. The next day at breakfast, Rick's parents Beth (Sarah Chalke from *Scrubs*, a frequent *Community* touchpoint) and Jerry (Chris Parnell) worry that Rick's dragging Morty off for "high-concept science-fiction rigmarole" is a bad influence. Meanwhile, Rick is manipulating the ever-praise-seeking Beth to overlook his behavior and dropping truth on Morty's eye-rolling teenage sister Summer (Spencer Grammar): "There is no God, Summer. Just gotta rip that Band-Aid off right now. You'll thank me later." While Beth and Jerry argue over whether to commit Rick to a nursing home, Rick commits his first manslaughter of the show: using a device to freeze a kid who was bullying Morty at school, after which the bully (and Summer's crush) falls over and shatters to pieces. Meanwhile, Rick and Morty zip off to another planet to harvest "mega tree" seeds, for reasons.

The stakes are almost inevitably raised in every episode thereafter as if the world-building (and deconstructing) possibilities of a psychopathic genius with a portal gun (Rick's handy handheld device for zipping between worlds) suddenly made anything—anything!—possible in the writers' room. Not infrequently, Rick's escapades lead to disaster (for someone else, at least). But even though Rick and Morty get out of most of their scrapes by the skin of their teeth, they hardly come through unscathed. From the start the show was determined to act as both a lark in which a couple of nerds let their imaginations run rampant in a sci-fi sandbox and an at-times frighteningly grim exploration of existential despair. In fact, entire books have been written on the scientific, science fiction, and philosophical concepts contained in the series. Go ahead; we're not jealous.

The narrative obsessions with reality-bending possibility, nested levels of secrets (almost every episode includes another revelation about Rick's past or another cache of weapons), and self-reflexive commentary (Rick commonly refers to what's happening as a "season" or "episode") make it feel like the show was created from the DNA of *Community* but then underwent numerous dark nights of the soul. Some of *Community*'s brighter inventions, like "Remedial Chaos Theory" and the tricky clip-show episodes made up of never-before seen escapades, seem to inspire much of *Rick and Morty*. But it is the darker moments of *Community*—like the opening to the final episode where a family playing a *Community* board game realizes they don't exist—that show where Harmon was headed next with *Rick and Morty*.

Here's Harmon setting it out for *GQ*,

> *Community* was a show that said, "Everything human is better than every-thing that isn't human" . . . *Rick and Morty* says, "You're going to be tempted to believe that being human is important, and that is going to cause you to suffer" . . . Rick is constantly saying to an inferior humanity, "Look, this is as good as it gets. So every day should be Rick Day, which is like a million Christmases. You're never supposed to be denied anything."

The nattering worry that nothing matters and morality is a fool's delusional errand is the crux of *Rick and Morty*. After Rick has seen not just thousands of planets with different civilizations and moral codes but

Generally, Morty would rather not see what Rick really wants him to see. ADULT SWIM/ PHOTOFEST.

numerous realities with other versions of himself and Morty (further complicating matters with all the cloning he engages in), he finds it difficult to place much importance on what happens to any one of those people. Season 1's "Close Rick-counters of the Rick Kind" introduces the idea that not only is there an Evil Rick and a Council of Ricks out there in the multiverse, but also numerous Mortys (for what it's worth, the "original" prime timeline characters of the show are denoted by the classification C-137). Later episodes occasionally explore a planet called the Citadel where literally every inhabitant is either a Rick or a Morty with numerous variations of each covering the full personality and morality spectrums. In short: you're not special, snowflake. No one is.

In Harmon and Roiland's formulations, infinite choice waters down the moral impact of every choice. Take the first season's sixth episode, "Rick Potion #9" (see also the Sandra Bullock rom-com, *Love Potion No. 9*). An innocent bit of sci-fi tinkering has Rick invent a potion to convince Jessica she is in love with Morty. He's a little too successful, leading the whole world to crush on Morty (see also *Buffy the Vampire Slayer*: "Bewitched, Bothered, and Bewildered"). But as often happens in the show, fixing one problem results in a Heisenbergian force that sprouts catastrophic new problems. In this episode, Rick's tinkering turns everyone on Earth into hideous beasts he calls "Cronenbergs" (see also *The Fly*).

Inspector Spacetime

Like other Harmon joints, *Rick and Morty* carried along many members of his returning troupe of *Community* players. Study group luminaries like Alison Brie, Keith David, Gillian Jacobs, and Joel McHale as well as fellow Greendalians John Oliver and Jim Rash all voiced characters on *Rick and Morty*. Harmon's oldest collaborator and nemesis Rob Schrab also pitched in with voice talent as well as writing and producing. The show's most direct tip of the hat to *Community*, though, was in Season 2's "Auto Erotic Assimilation" in which Rick's current ex-girlfriend Unity (who is a hive mind) creates a TV show for him in which a study group looking just like the Greendale Seven is shown . . . only they're aliens. Rick toys with the cast ("Make 'em all make fun of the blonde one. Now make 'em all do it on the table!") before telling Unity, "Now cancel it! Now put it back on! Haha!"

He and Morty escape the apocalypse they caused, landing on a very similar Earth in a different dimension where that reality's versions of themselves have already died. Two episodes later in "Rixty Minutes," another Rick invention—goggles that allow the family to see how they live in different realities—blows up when it leads to Summer discovering her parents had almost aborted her. In one of the decade's most poignant, heart-stopping, pop culture moments, Morty winds her down by pointing out where he and Rick buried that world's versions of themselves, and then casually crystallizes the randomness of the universe: "Nobody exists on purpose. Nobody belongs anywhere. Everybody's gonna die. Come watch TV."

And so she does. And so do we.

Later episodes played with alternating responses to Morty's somewhat shellshocked take on existentialism. In some instances, it leads to a spiritual agony, with Rick attempting to commit suicide at least once. Season 4's "The Vat of Acid Episode" sees Rick inventing a device that allows Morty to travel a few seconds back in time ("I saw it on *Futurama*!" Morty gripes before agreeing to use it). In the following wordless sequence we see Morty use the device to create a reality in which he lives a long and happy life with a nameless non-Jessica girl only to have Rick pull the rug out from under him at the end in service of a petulant and revenge-seeking joke.

In other episodes, Rick (and sometimes Morty) leaps headlong into the maelstrom, taking on death-defying adventures that embrace a brand of (literally) cartoonish ultraviolence that quickly became the show's trademark. Season 3's "Pickle Rick," in which Rick transforms himself into a pickle, albeit one with supercharged musculature and buzzsaw weaponry, is the apotheosis of grinning, nihilistic rampaging. The show's penchant for turning nearly every encounter in a murderous direction makes it seem almost curious when an entire episode unfolds without a single person or creature being shot in the head by one of the weapons from Rick's massive arsenal. Still, on average, the per capita bullet-in-the-head count is impressive.

Rick and Morty's somewhat shrugging take on violence, hyper-speed pacing, and deep, dark cynicism is likely a large part of what attracted a sizable contingent of adolescent (either in physical or mental age) male fans. Despite his often thoughtful takes on the nature of reality, Rick himself, as a rules-flouting genius who too-often treats the universe as a laboratory for meeting his personal desires, can also be seen as just another in a long line of superheroes who fulfill the fantasies of (self-diagnosed) disempowered boys and men-boys. The simmering toxicity in that particular fanbase, which in other contexts had been unleashed on Marvel and *Star Wars* properties when they were seen as straying from the white male hero template, lashed out in social media and Reddit threads during *Rick and Morty*'s third season after more women were hired as writers (assuming women wouldn't know how to write *Rick and Morty* and disregarding that during that season it became television's top-rated comedy show). The writers were having none of it. Those same discontented and self-entitled fans (who wanted the show to focus solely on its increasingly byzantine intergalactic dramas) were deliberately ridiculed within the show itself as in Season 3's "The Ricklantis Mixup" where Rick promises Morty a "fun, self-contained adventure" that is anything but.

The intensity of the show's fandom, even when non-toxic and simply expressing an eagerness for "more and now!" also seemed to encourage the writers to increasingly play with audience expectations. That was particularly the case in summer 2019 when fans had been waiting—so long!—for new episodes after Season 3 concluded in April 2017. Harmon posted a series of Post-It notes on social media that he suggested might be ideas for upcoming episodes. They included "planet powered by chips and salsa"; "Voltron but with vegetables"; and maybe most enticingly, "Wesley Sniper"—few of which seem likely to make it past the idea stage. And, of course, the less we say about the Great McDonald's Szechuan Sauce Fiasco of 2018, the better.

Meanwhile, Off Campus . . .

Rick and Morty began as a seemingly well-matched collaboration between Harmon and Roiland. Unusually for Harmon, he came to be the adult in the room, seeing his role as getting Roiland's more off-the-wall and sometimes juvenile ideas across. "I love the idea of serving the crazy guy instead of being the crazy guy," he told *Rolling Stone* in 2015, describing what sounds like an inverse of his earlier career. During the third season of *Rick and Morty*, however, that partnership appeared to break down. In early 2023 it was revealed that Roiland was facing felony domestic violence charges. Following claims about Roiland's abusive behavior and increasingly limited creative input, Adult Swim and multiple other companies with which he had deals (Hulu, Disney) cut ties with him. At the time of this writing, however, *Rick and Morty* lives on.

Rick and Morty's full-hearted embrace of depression, clear-eyed view of reality's unfixable problems, perpetual dance with existentialism, and apparently limitless desire to keep spinning out narrative threads and inventing cartoonish and-or nightmarish new realities made it a crucial part of the 2010 animation renaissance. Other shows that helped the genre explode in a fractalized burst of cartoon possibility—from *BoJack Horseman* and *Disenchanted* to *Stephen Universe* and *Love, Death & Robots*—embraced more adult subject matter like despair, anxiety, identity, and body horror. But few used the animation format as actively as *Rick and Morty* to bend and interrogate the nature of storytelling itself in much the same way that *Community* had, albeit with far, far fewer dismemberments (and sadly, less paintball).

Wubba lubba dub dub.

Conclusion

WHEN THIS BOOK was being written, the authors were much like every other would-be Greendale alumni: thinking of *Community* as something that was groundbreaking, hilarious, and necessary to be shared with as wide an audience as possible. But for all that, it was a thing of the past that had run its natural course. It didn't even have a spinoff. Done. Kaput.

But then in a development as mysterious as the appearance of Professor Professorson or Pierce's teeth-bared antipathy with poor put-upon Vicki, something happened. For years, when asked about the unfulfilled movie part of the #sixseasonsandamovie push, Dan Harmon, cast members, and various other *Community*-adjacent Harmonians would say "Mmm, maybe!" or "Would be great!" and then try to change the topic. And fans mostly stopped bothering to wish for it. But in the fall of 2022, the word came down—and not just rumors, but real words, *industry trade publication* words—that a *Community* movie was going to happen. And it was going to stream on Peacock, meaning it would be less a movie than a long Very Special Episode, but never mind. The prophecy is being fulfilled. Maybe.

This leaves the authors in a peculiar bind. On the one hand, they very much want to see this artifact coming so many years after the show ended and write about it in enthusiastic yet learned fashion. On the other hand, they know that everything in show business is a castle built on sand; Peacock could turn out to be another Yahoo! Screen. On the third and final hand, they also know that waiting for Harmon to turn in a script can be a lesson in Jobean patience.

So we leave the book as is. Which is not in a bad space. Because pop-culture commentators like us spend a lot of time kvetching about the state of the industry. Most of our time, it can seem. Nevertheless the story of *Community* is an optimistic one. There were many issues. Producers interfered, time slots were moved, Harmon gave colleagues agita, stays of execution kept the whole thing on edge, and Chase really just never understood what the show was about or why he was there.

But when *Community*'s back was up against the wall, a major network said, "Yes, let's go with a show that is going to do an episode-long homage to *My Dinner with Andre* and spends almost as much time *talking* about being a sitcom as it does *being* a sitcom." Then, even after seeing the ratings and viewers' indifference or outright hostility, the network said, "Let's give it another shot. And another."

Yes, we can all agree: the gas leak season was a mistake. But was it a worse one than *Joey*, *Models Inc.*, or *Saved by the Bell: The College Years*?

Networks often do stupid things. But not always. Sometimes they let a weird flower bloom. And sometimes that weird flower blooms in the middle of a community college campus, somewhere in Colorado.

Bibliography

Articles

Alfuso, Renée. "Class Clowns." *NYU Alumni Magazine*, Spring 2012. https://alumnimagazine.nyu.edu/issue18/18_FEA_ClassClowns.html.

Andreeva, Nellie. "Chevy Chase in Feud with 'Community' Creator Dan Harmon." *Deadline*, March 31, 2013. https://deadline.com/2012/03/chevy-chase-in-feud-with-community-creator-dan-harmon-251524/.

Berman, Judy. "Read a Brilliant Letter from 'Community' Showrunner Dan Harmon to a 7-Year-Old." *Flavorwire*, May 22, 2012. www.flavorwire.com/292333/read-a-brilliant-letter-from-community-showrunner-dan-harmon-to-a-7-year-old.

Buchanan, Kyle. "The Showrunner Transcript: *Community*'s Dan Harmon on Finale Cameos and Season-Long Lessons." *Vulture*, May 13, 2011. www.vulture.com/2011/05/dan_harmon_showrunner_transcri.html.

Charney, Noah. "Cracking the Sitcom Code." *Atlantic*, December 28, 2014.

Chocano, Carina. "Rejected Pilots Find Life as Cream of the Slop." *Los Angeles Times*, January 31, 2004.

Cuprisin, Tim. "Milwaukee Talks: Dan Harmon of NBC's 'Community.'" *On Milwaukee*, March 25, 2011.

Evans, Bradford. "The Lost Projects of Dan Harmon." *Vulture*, May 24, 2012.

Fox, Hese David. "Dan Harmon on *Harmontown*, the Documentary about the Tour that Saved *Community*." *Vulture*, October 10, 2014.

Gandert, Sean. "Catching Up With . . . *Community* Creator Dan Harmon." *Paste*, May 5, 2010.

Granata, Elise. "The Story of the NerdMelt Showroom at Meltdown Comics." *Grasstronaut*, October 16, 2014. https://spaceslikethis.wordpress.com/2014/10/16/story-of-nerdmelt-meltdown/.

Hollywood Reporter. "Dan Harmon: TV's Most Controversial Showrunner." July 17, 2013.

Lawrence, Derek, and Chancellor Agard. "EW Is Binging *Community* with the Cast and Creator." *Entertainment Weekly,* May 7, 2020. https://ew.com/tv/community-binge-series-premiere-dan-harmon/.

Maddox, David. "A Conversation with Rob Schrab." *SFSite,* March 2008. www.sfsite.com/05a/rs271.htm.

Matar, Joe, and Alec Bojalad. "*Rick and Morty* Szechuan Sauce Controversy Explained." *Den of Geek,* November 9, 2019. www.denofgeek.com/tv/rick-and-morty-szechuan-sauce-controversy-explained/.

McGurk, Stuart. "The Kings of Dot-Comedy." *Guardian,* July 21, 2006.

McHenry, Jackson. "The Behind-the-Scenes History of Hugh Jackman's Opening Number at the 2009 Oscars." *Vulture,* February 22, 2019.

Mumford, Gwilym. "'I Loathe These People': *Rick and Morty* and the Brilliant Backlash against TV's Bad Fans." *Guardian,* October 2, 2017.

O'Neil, Megan. "Dan Harmon Screens 'Community' at GCC." *Los Angeles Times,* November 5, 2010.

O'Neal, Sean. "The Tortured Mind of Dan Harmon." *GQ,* May 30, 2018.

Palmer Jr, Tom. "Palmer's Picks: Schrab's *Scud.*" *Wizard,* April 1995.

Pappademas, Alex. "God Needs a Hobby," *Grantland,* February 12, 2013. http://grantland.com/features/dan-harmon-life-community/.

Plante, Corey. "Dan Harmon Trolls 'Rick and Morty' Fans with Bizarre Season 5 Ideas." *Inverse,* May 28, 2019. www.inverse.com/article/56204-rick-and-morty-season-5-dan-harmon-ideas-from-rob-schrab-post-it-notes-plot.

Rose, Lacey, and Katie Kilkenny. "Inside the Implosion of Justin Roiland's Animation Empire." *Hollywood Reporter,* February 7, 2023.

Stein, Joel. "Comedy Forging the Future: TV Without the Networks." *Time,* April 6, 2006.

Strauss, Neil. "How 'Rick and Morty' Became One of TV's Weirdest Hit Shows." *Rolling Stone,* July 22, 2015.

Syme, Rachel. "Gillian Jacobs, a Neurotic 'Community' Favorite, Finds 'Love.'" *New York Times,* February 11, 2016.

Toal, Drew. "Sail Away: The Oral History of 'Yacht Rock.'" *Rolling Stone,* January 15, 2019.

Vanity Fair, "The Russo Brothers Break Down Their Career from 'Arrested Development' to 'Avengers: Endgame.'" May 21, 2019. www.vanityfair.com/video/watch/the-russo-brothers-break-down-their-career-from-l-a-x-to-avengers-endgame.

Wolleck, Anders. "Channel 101 Co-Creator Rob Schrab." *Suicide Girls,* June 30, 2005. http://suicidegirls.com/interviews/1622/Channel-101-co-creator-Rob-Schrab/.

Books

Austerlitz, Saul. *Sitcom: A History in 24 Episodes from* I Love Lucy *to* Community. Chicago: Chicago Review Press, 2014.

Johnson, Steven. *Everything Bad Is Good for You.* New York: Riverhead, 2005.

McCracken, Grant. *Culturematic.* Boston: Harvard Business Review Press, 2012.

McHale, Joel. *Thanks for the Money: How to Use My Life Story to Become the Best Joel McHale You Can Be.* New York: Putnam, 2016.

Nesteroff, Klipf. *The Comedians: Drunks, Thieves, Scoundrels and the History of American Comedy.* New York: Grove, 2015.

Olson, Christopher J., and CarrieLynn D. Reinhard. *The Greatest Cult Television Shows of All Time.* Lanham, MD: Rowman & Littlefield, 2020.

Schrab, Rob. *Scud: The Disposable Assassin.* New York: Image Comics, 2015.

Media

Community (TV series). NBC/Yahoo! Screen, 2009–2015.

Epic Fu. "Extended Interview w/Dan Harmon & Rob Schrab" (2009), https://youtu.be/7SxevqZHnbI.

Great Minds with Dan Harmon (TV series). History Channel, 2016.

HarmonQuest (animated series). Seeso/VRV, 2016–2019.

Harmontown (documentary). The Orchard, 2014.

Harmontown (podcast). Starburns Industries, 2011–2019.

Heat Vision and Jack (TV pilot). 20th Century Fox, 1999.

Monster House (film). Columbia Pictures, 2006.

Rick and Morty (animated series). Adult Swim, 2013–Present.

The Sarah Silverman Show (TV series). Comedy Central, 2007–2010.

Take Down the Grand Master (album). Monkey Paw Productions, 1996.

WTF (podcast). "Dan Harmon," Episode 179, May 30, 2011.

Websites

channel101.com

danharmon.tumblr.com

last.fm/music/The+Dead+Alewives/Take+Down+the+Grand+Master

robschrab.com

Index